SAGE was founded in 1965 by Sara Miller McCune to support the dissemination of usable knowledge by publishing innovative and high-quality research and teaching content. Today, we publish over 900 journals, including those of more than 400 learned societies, more than 800 new books per year, and a growing range of library products including archives, data, case studies, reports, and video. SAGE remains majority-owned by our founder, and after Sara's lifetime will become owned by a charitable trust that secures our continued independence.

Los Angeles | London | New Delhi | Singapore | Washington DC | Melbourne

The Exceptional memoirs of an unlettered Dalit refugee who educated himself and went on to became and award-winning writer.

Writing incisively on modern India as he sees it, this Dalit writer offers a critique of Indian society. A refugee post-Partition, Manoranjan Byapari spent his early years in the refugee camps, lost his sister to starvation, a brother to tuberculosis, and later became a political criminal who narrowly missed getting murdered during the Naxal movement. He was taught to read and write while he was in jail by a fellow prisoner. After his release, he went on to become not only a published author but also a Sahitya Akademi award-winner.

PAPERBACK
9789381345139

For special offers on this book and more visit **stealadeal.sagepub.in** **Steal A Deal**
YOUR ONE-STOP-SHOP FOR LOWEST PRICE

www.sagepub.in

How I Became a Writer

How I Became a Writer
An Autobiography of a Dalit

Sequel to the award-winning book
Interrogating My Chandal Life

Manoranjan Byapari

Translated from the Bangla by

Anurima Chanda

Foreword by Sipra Mukherjee

Los Angeles | London | New Delhi
Singapore | Washington DC | Melbourne

Copyright this English translation © Anurima Chanda, 2022

Translated from the original Bangla book *Itibritte Chandal Jivan* (2016) by Manoranjan Byapari. Copyright of the original Bangla text with the author.

All rights reserved. No part of this book may be reproduced or utilized in any form or by any means, electronic or mechanical, including photocopying, recording, or by any information storage or retrieval system, without permission in writing from the publisher.

First published in 2022 by

SAGE Publications India Pvt Ltd
B1/I-1 Mohan Cooperative Industrial Area
Mathura Road, New Delhi 110 044, India
www.sagepub.in

Samya
16 Southern Avenue
Kolkata 700026
www.stree-samyabooks.com

SAGE Publications Inc
2455 Teller Road
Thousand Oaks, California 91320, USA

SAGE Publications Ltd
1 Oliver's Yard, 55 City Road
London EC1Y 1SP, United Kingdom

SAGE Publications Asia-Pacific Pte Ltd
18 Cross Street #10-10/11/12
China Square Central
Singapore 048423

Published by Vivek Mehra for SAGE Publications India Pvt Ltd. Typeset in 11/13pt Baskerville Old Face by Fidus Design Pvt. Ltd, Chandigarh.

Library of Congress Control Number: 2022935468

ISBN: 978-93-81345-77-1 (PB)

Samya SAGE Team: Aritra Paul, Amrita Dutta and Neena Ganjoo

To
The memory of Shankar Guha Neogi.

~

To
Ananta Acharya for his constant support.

—MB

To
JNU which taught me to listen, really listen,
to the voices from the margins.

—AC

Thank you for choosing a SAGE product!
If you have any comment, observation or feedback,
I would like to personally hear from you.

Please write to me at **contactceo@sagepub.in**

Vivek Mehra, Managing Director and CEO, SAGE India.

Bulk Sales

SAGE India offers special discounts
for purchase of books in bulk.
We also make available special imprints
and excerpts from our books on demand.

For orders and enquiries, write to us at

Marketing Department
SAGE Publications India Pvt Ltd
B1/I-1, Mohan Cooperative Industrial Area
Mathura Road, Post Bag 7
New Delhi 110044, India

E-mail us at **marketing@sagepub.in**

Subscribe to our mailing list
Write to **marketing@sagepub.in**

This book is also available as an e-book.

Contents

Foreword
by Sipra Mukherjee   xi

Acknowledgements   xix

A Note by the Translator
by Anurima Chanda   xxi

Part I School Shenanigans

1. My First Visit to the Helen Keller Institute for
   the Deaf and the Blind   3
2. The Warden and the Mother Killer   8
3. The Four Guards   18
4. More on the Warden and Introducing
   the Teacher-in-Charge   25
5. Tensions at Work   30
6. Tact or Free Flow like Pebbles?   36
7. Checkmate   40
8. Something Fishy   45
9. Arm Wrestling   52

10. The Unlettered Are Not Fools	58
11. Lessons in Morality	68
12. Embattling Superiors	81
13. Mother Killer	93
14. The Secretary of the Organization for Disabled People	99
15. Boro Sahib	107
16. How Duttada's Intentions Came to Nought	118
17. Mutating Viruses	131
18. More Pilferage and Persecution	140
19. To Eat or Not to Eat?	148

Part II The Right to Write

20. Jogenda, Ashokji and *Podokkhyep*	155
21. More Literary Expeditions	169
22. Ananta Acharya, Khokon Majumdar and Dalit Writings of Bengal	181
23. The Story of Jibon Das	195
24. A Tumultuous End to a Decade	203
25. The Publication of *Itibritte Chandal Jivan*	213
26. A Job Offer Gone Wrong and Returning to Chhattisgarh	223
27. The Patna Literature Festival	238
28. Literary Accolades	253

29. In Pursuit of *Parivartan*	273
30. Boro Sahib's Desire to Felicitate Me	278
31. The Bangla Akademi Award and Other Honours	288
32. An Interview with 24 Ghonta	302
33. My Writing Philosophy	317
34. The End of an Era	322
About the Author and the Translator	335
Index	336

Foreword

Sipra Mukherjee

It is an honour to be asked to write the 'Foreword' to the sequel of Manoranjan Byapari's autobiography, very well translated by Anurima Chanda. Its publication indicates the growing market for literature by writers from the so-called lowered castes, who have remained largely unknown and unread for decades. Beginning with Omprakash Valmiki's *Joothan* in 2003, the first English translation of a Dalit autobiography, Samya has played a pioneering role in initiating greater visibility to literature from the margins, and this collaboration with Sage offers wider sustained access.

When translating the first part of this autobiography, I had been struck by what I could only term the non-marginality of this text authored by Manoranjan Byapari. This non-marginality included the language used by the writer, the space it depicted and also the subject it dealt with. A significant discussion on Dalit literature and its translatability has centred on the very different language that is used by the writers; a language to which the readerly and the writerly public were, and still are, somewhat alien. The adjectives used for this language have been 'raw', 'vulgar', 'shocking', which were in accordance with what Raj Gauthaman in *Dalit Panpaadu* (1993) had said Dalit writing should do, 'outrage and even repel the guardians of caste and class' (Holmström: xii). In this book, though, the language was the standard written vernacular, with some exceptions as one could expect to come upon in any text. What was more striking was that the space dealt with was largely the city Calcutta/Kolkata, that has been written about ad nauseam. Even more striking was the fact that the subjects this Dalit writer documented were mainstream political movements like the Naxalite movement of the 1970s and Shankar Guha Niyogi's Chhattisgarh Mukti Morcha in the 1970s and 1980s.

There was also a largish section on the experience of the Bengal Partition. These two much-talked about subjects, the Naxalite political movement and the Bengal Partition expectedly had an impact upon the making of the subject through the pages of the book. It was not a marginal victim restricted to a marginal, ignorable, forgettable space. This was a subject placed entirely within the 'happening' context that was part of the political and academic discourse. This proximity to the supposedly 'mainstream' space and subjects added much interest to the narrative, because the perspective was very different from what the other narratives on these spaces and subjects had led us to expect. In many ways, this non-marginality of the Dalit text reflected the reality of late twentieth-century Bengal, after the shake-up of the Partition had displaced entire villages of people, and the need to hold body and soul together had brought thousands nearer the urban areas. In the wider context of India, too, the more recent Dalit narratives portray the cityscape as often as these do the rural context, writing of issues and spaces that have been considered 'mainstream' in the heterogeneous reality of India. Pigeonholing or dismissing Dalit writings as narratives that deal 'only with the margins' would now be entirely delusory.

With these divergent narratives finding their space within literature, the familiar histories now need re-telling. Partition history, as well as urban and political history, has since been required to re-think its milestones and crossroads. That events and spaces were experienced differently by different subjects have been fleshed out by these later texts. Re-telling of histories inevitably drags in questions of identity, and the other question that has been raised is that of our given notions of selfhood. Within the geographical space of Bengal, the identities of both the 'Dalit' and the 'Bengali' need to be situated within the wider and more diverse space laid bare by these narratives. That the nationalistic politics of mid-twentieth century and Partition realpolitik unsettled notions of Dalit Namashudra identity and consequently had an impact on

Bengali Dalit unity are subjects that have been repeatedly written upon by Sekhar Bandyopadhyay (2004, 2011). The identities of the Namashudra, Dalit, East Pakistani and Indian had needed to be negotiated and manipulated for the subjects, a process that was resolved as frequently through compulsion as through voluntary individual choice.

The history of Bengal as an enlightened and progressive space too has come increasingly into question with these accounts. West Bengal and Communism have enjoyed a long marriage, and the identity of the Bengali has on occasions been seen as inseparable from the ideology of Communism. But women communist writers like Manikuntala Sen and Sabitri Roy have raised questions about the Bengali bhadralok's communist image. That the secular and egalitarian perspective that is expected from a communist has been found to be wanting in many has been documented in their narratives. That traditional and patriarchal mindsets created an uneven field within the party despite the camaraderie and allegiance to the greater cause have been documented. Since the early 1990s, after the tragic suicide by the university student Chuni Kotal, a tribal girl from the Lodha community, Dalit writers have questioned the alleged casteless-ness of the Bengali. The belief among Bengal's communists that class identity subsumed caste identity and that moving towards a classless society would enable an eventual erasure of its caste divisions have not found takers among either the scheduled castes or the scheduled tribes of Bengal. It is this statement about the subterranean but strong presence of caste discrimination within West Bengal that this second part of Byapari's autobiography articulates. The seemingly narrow, petty viciousness that is part of the narrative is the lived reality of the subject who finds that caste does still hold its ground in the 'class-ed' society.

While much has changed since the publication of the first book, much has also remained the same. Byapari's story is representative of so many lives in our poverty-stricken and unequal society that the relevance of the book is unquestionable. Most of these other lives end midway through their stories, without fulfilling the potential. Byapari has been lucky and so has lived to tell his story and achieve as his merit deserved. Would the term 'testimonio', used for many Dalit first-person narratives, be a correct description of Byapari's autobiographies? The testimonio, a term borrowed from Latin American cultures, is a narrative that speaks not of the individual, but of the collective. The first part had traced the exploited, raped, abused boy's journey to adulthood through the world of politics and through the violence of living on the edges of society, to the moment where a chance encounter with the writer Mahasweta Devi ushers in the possibility of his entering the world of literature.

This sequel depicts Byapari securing an ordinary job through a friend connected to the Communist Party then in power. He refuses, though, to be engulfed by the job, and struggles to keep his identity as a writer alive. As his dedication and determination begin to bring him fame as a writer, the narrative veers towards the story more of an individual rather than of a community. Remarkably few among the Dalits achieve fame and recognition as writers, and consequently Byapari's is a story that is very different from many of his community. What is striking, though, is that Byapari is not free of the identity of the untouchable Dalit despite his fame. In fact, his success stokes the envy of those who believe the untouchable Byapari to be aspiring beyond his ken. The book details the endless harassment and the meanness he faces in his workplace by colleagues who find it difficult to acknowledge a cook's literary skills. These passages that narrate the petty and inconsequential details of spiteful and insignificant human beings, clawing at each other within a miserable cramped space, with no access to greater dreams or nobler visions are difficult reading in places. It seems to wear down the spirit of the reader. What comes as a greater shock is that these people are all members of, or friends of the members of, the Communist Party with its ideology of equality and justice. The first time Byapari is grilled about his caste identity in the school, he is shocked at the narrowness and caste-ridden minds of those who have pledged themselves to communist ideology. There is much consternation among the school authorities on learning that a person belonging to a once untouchable caste was to cook the food for students, many of whom belonged to the upper castes. The long-drawn out altercations that ensue with this disclosure leaves Byapari shocked and disgusted:

> My ears and head started buzzing. Where had I landed? I knew that people from the Left did not believe in caste. They were atheists. They believed that everybody was equal and equally respectable. Then *what* was this that I was hearing? And, *why* was I hearing whatever was being said? (p.14)

In these accounts, Byapari's narrative reveals an experience similar to that which the women of the Communist Party had faced. Deluded into believing that an ideology could raise human beings above the senseless differences imposed by society, both Dalits and women have found themselves betrayed.

The crippling patriarchy and casteism of human beings, however, does not weaken the power of the ideology itself and we find the Chandal cook arguing feistily with the Teacher-in-Charge (Bordi) on the rules that govern an employee's working hours. Refusing to work after his day's shift is done, Byapari faces her wrath. He enlightens her on the history of the workers' movement in Chicago, where 'a group of workers fought for the right to work for eight hours'. Upon being told his job has no time limits since it 'falls under the emergency category', Byapari retorts,

> Healthcare facilities, fire service, police, army, these are all emergency departments. They are available for twenty-four hours. But remember this; their departments might be that under the emergency category but this does not extend to the staff. All the staff has eight-hour long shifts. If due to some urgent matter someone has to stay for more than eight hours, he is paid an overtime amount for his additional services. (p. 89)

His reply and demeanour indicate how the politics of the possible work through literature, mingling the canvas of fiction with the possibilities within our everyday lives:

> I did what a representative of the working class would do had it been within the world of one of my own stories. The way Bordi, like one of the overlords, had called me forth to show off her positional power in front of her people, I too, was eager to show her that I was a knowledgeable and brave representative of my class of people. (p. 88)

Notwithstanding the churlish perversity of society, Byapari is awarded the Suprabha Majumdar award by the Paschimbanga Bangla Akademi in 2014. As he himself seems to believe towards the end of this narrative, he has achieved success. Invited by universities all over India, feted at conferences and now, after the recent elections, as an MLA of the Trinamool Congress Party, Byapari's life does, indeed, sound unreal and fantastic.

A testimonio brings to light injustice or oppression done to a community. The speaker bears witness to the injustice, speaking not for herself or himself alone, but for many. Byapari repeatedly faces humiliation and discrimination because of his caste, and suffers from the poverty that cripples the lives of the majority of the Dalits. Yet the trajectory of the life of this once perpetually hungry boy has been quite unique and unusual. As Byapari himself writes when he is making the acquaintance of fellow-Dalit writers in his city, his 'relationship with these Dalit poets and intellectuals was fairly new':

> Actually, I had never worked in this field. That which I had so far been involved with was a dark continent for them. They hardly had any knowledge of it. Their world was surrounded by Ambedkar, Jyotiba Phule, and Periyar down to Kanshi Ram and Mayawati. They only knew of me as a poor rickshaw-puller who also wrote a bit on the side... A word here might not be irrelevant that just as there is class within caste, there is also caste within class. If I was hated by one section for being a Chandal or a Namashudra, another section hated and ignored me for being an uneducated poor rickshaw-puller. Hence, I was equally an outcaste for both sections...' (p. 192)

Despite being repeatedly invited to the nation's most prominent literary festivals, it is doubtful that Byapari would consider himself mainstream. I remember an incident at a workshop where a fellow translator had introduced Byapari with an emphasis on his name, 'Manoranjan', which means entertainment, amusement. While Byapari had rejected the meaning of his name, saying he was there more to speak harsh truths than to entertain, at the end of the day he confided that he did feel that this was expected of him. If people invited him, he said, they expected fireworks, and he did need to perform accordingly. The cynicism in his voice about society had been unmistakable.

References

Bandyopadhyay, Sekhar. *Caste, Culture and Hegemony: Social Domination in Colonial Bengal.* New Delhi: Sage. 2004.

——, *Caste, Protest and Identity in Colonial India: The Namashudras of Bengal, 1872-1947.* New Delhi: Oxford University Press, 2011.

Gauthaman, Raj. *Dalit Panpaadu* (Dalit Culture). Puducherry, 1993; 2nd ed., Chennai: NCBH. 2019.

Holmstrom, Lakshmi.. 'Introduction', Bama, *Sangati*. New Delhi: Oxford University Press, 2005.

Roy, Sabitri. *Swaralipi*. Kolkata: Bengal Publishers, 1952.

Sen, Manikuntala. *Sediner Katha*. Kolkata: Nabapatra Prakashan. 1982.

Valmiki, Omprakash. *Joothan: A Dalit's Life*, trans by Arun Prabha Mukherjee. Kolkata: Samya, 2003.

Acknowledgements

The first person I must acknowledge my gratitude to is my mastermashai at the Presidency Jail who taught me the alphabet. As I mentioned in *Interrogating My Chandal Life*, he started me on a journey that has changed my life forever. Without his loving care and generous wisdom, I would have remained in the unlettered darkness, as millions like me have remained.

I owe a great debt to my family that cannot be ever repaid. My wife, Anu, who is proud of her husband the writer—I have tried not to let her down in this respect—and my two children, Mahasweta and Manik. They have always stood by me, despite the immense hardship our family has repeatedly faced.

My gratitude to my old friend and supporter Ananta Acharya who has always remained by my side and who has kindly sorted out the many questions raised in this translation.

My gratitude to my translator of the sequel, Anurima Chanda, who has worked with dedication. She has worked closely with me throughout. I do know from the experience of the translation of the earlier book that translations cannot be rushed and she has worked as fast as she could without compromising on quality. As in the previous volume, I thank all my friends at Samya for their steady faith in my work and their commitment to this translation project.

I am grateful to Sipra Mukherjee, the erudite translator of the previous book, for writing the Foreword to this volume.

My gratitude, as always, to my numerous readers and my many friends, without whom my identity would still have been a jail-returned rickshaw-wallah.

A Note by the Translator

Anurima Chanda

In a watershed moment, the first publication of Manoranjan Byapari's autobiography, *Interrogating My Chandal Life*, beat almost 200 books of different genres to win the first ever prize for non-fiction for the year 2018 at the Hindu Lit for Life fest held on 13 January 2019, at the Sir Mutha Venkatasubba Rao Concert Hall in Chennai. Reading out the citation on behalf of the 5-member jury, Kamini Mahadevan mentioned:

> Numerous books have portrayed the everyday life of marginalized communities, in particular Dalits, challenging the dominant narratives of nation building. Published originally in Indian languages, some of these are now available to us in English translations.... Among the emergent narratives of Dalit lives and struggles available in English ... *Interrogating My Chandal Life* stands out both for its literary merits as well as for countering the view that class and caste discrimination do not afflict modern Bengal. The jury felt that this book was exceptional in its searing honesty and sheer depth as a personal narrative and for its keen sense of victory. Byapari unflinchingly portrays the harshness of poverty, hunger, homelessless, physical abuse and humiliation. His telling is matter-of-fact, devoid of sentimentality, self-pity or victimhood, something rarely found in narratives of deprivation. But far from beating him down, his prison days helped to pave the way for his becoming a writer and reignite his hope and struggle for a better life. [In] the activism of his mentor, Shankar Guha Neogi, who was in fact assassinated in Chhattisgarh, ... he

finds an exemplar of a new life. Through the narration of his predicament, Byapari illuminates the complexities of contemporary Bengal, be it the refugee crisis, the roots of Naxalism, the betrayals of Left parties and organization. The translator, Dr. Sipra Mukherjee, needs to be thanked for making Byapari's powerful work accessible to a wider readership. This is a book that will endure, foresee each of us to engage with ourselves and the issues that the book raises. (*The Hindu* 07:08:51)

In that emotionally charged moment, Byapari broke down into his gamchha while receiving the award from Rajmohan Gandhi. He could barely speak. People who are aware of his oratorical skill would know how rare such an instance is. And why not: History was made.

Today, it is no longer unusual to look upon Dalit autobiographies as pieces of counter-historical narrative that can topple the base of the canon. The history that was made that day on the stage in Chennai was of such a kind. It was an 'unexpected' win (*The Hindu* 07:04:55), a word that Mahadevan almost used in describing the jury's judging process. It was a win for all those voices from the margin, carrying with them 'the other half of the story that [we] had not known existed' (Mukherjee, 2018: xvi). But, more importantly, it was a win that helped officially seal the centre's acknowledgement of its own criticism. It paved the road for a new journey with renewed vigour for the 'perpetually hungry boy' (ibid.), not 'entirely unfamiliar' to us (Byapari, 2018: ix), yet so unfamiliar. The sequel of the autobiography, *How I Became a Writer,* begins exactly at this point.

The first book of the memoir ends with Byapari's return to Calcutta from Dandakaranya with the job of a cook at a residential school. Byapari's worries are far from over. The fact that he takes up a job with no salary for the time being; a job which six others before him had been forced to quit in a week's time, is an indication. The sequel ends with a glimpse into Byapari's gradual entry into the literary world: another thorny path flanked with the obstacles of workplace politics and shelved manuscripts.

This account grows out of these seeds of struggle. It exposes the corrupt world of misplaced ideologies, the experiences of caste discrimination in a school populated by CPI(M) workers, the greed of publishers, the betrayals by one's own and the neglect of so-called intellectuals. It also documents the beginnings of unexpected friendships, of many memorable firsts and the power of persistence. The circle which the 'perpetually hungry boy' had dared to unleash with his rejection of death, seems to reach its final turn in this part of the autobiography. As Byapari says:

> My life which started as an illiterate child born to illiterate parents completed one turn as soon as I became a man of letters. To guide this in the right direction is, in my belief, taking it to the next level, to the final turn of the circle. (p. 159)

Identifying these two primary strands, I decided to split up the narrative into his work-life and his literary life in my translation with the support of Samya. In terms of the language, as mentioned by Sipra Mukherjee, Byapari writes in an urban and modern version. The major problem was in restructuring: the account in the first book, starting with his birth to his return to Bengal, develops quite organically, but the second part is more episodic. This is, perhaps, because of how the text came to be composed, where the story of his pre-employment days was written in retrospect and the rest as and when it happened. In the sequel, the narrative reads like a compilation of vignettes from his life—similar to journal entries. The narration was also interspersed with excerpts of newspaper coverage on him along with Byapari's own creative/non-creative works published/used elsewhere, including personal letters, his short stories and even a poem. A dual sense of meaning-making emerges from such techniques of documentation. On the one hand, there is the Byapari who is offering us a recreated version of his remembered self. On the other hand, we find another Byapari who is recreating his past and present for the sake of his own remembrance of his self as well.

Byapari's migratory life has cost him a number of things, including his citizenship papers. As he mentions in this book:

> My father was an illiterate person who had no idea about the seriousness with which certain documents needed to be prepared and preserved carefully to be able to prove oneself as a citizen of India. We came to this country in the year 1952 or 1953. The government did distribute the papers at the camp in Bankura named Shiromoni where we were put up, but everything was destroyed as we moved from place to place after the dole stopped. We did not have any house or any trunk to safely store these papers. Tied up in a cloth bundle and tucked away in the straw shed, nobody knew when these papers decomposed. Since then, we became citizens of this country but without any name or identity. As for ration cards, our names in the electoral list or land deeds—we have nothing. A single scratch of diplomacy on a piece of paper snatched away everything from us. (pp. 291-92)

Nobody would know the value of documentation as intimately as he who has lost everything, even his identity, because of misplaced records. Seen through these lenses, Byapari's attempt at meaning-making through intensive record keeping, both for the act of showcasing as well as preserving for himself begins to make more sense. What it also does, unfortunately, is to obstruct the flow of narration. My struggle as a translator was to straddle both these ends to reach a comfortable balance that retained the original while not compromising on its readability. My frequent interactions with Byapari meant that I wasn't unaware of the author's own compunctions regarding the editing of his text. I had to, therefore, practise extra caution. The author, the publisher and I took out the short stories and the poem, since these have been published elsewhere while most of the media coverage, which would be of considerable interest, was retained. My approach was to give more leverage to the larger entity of Byapari the individual than simply fixating on Byapari the author, which was already being covered extensively.

Language, as I have already mentioned, was not a major concern as a challenge in terms of its actual linguistic transference. I retained some of the very obvious vernacular phrases when the English equivalent sounded too forced. Usage of Hindi, a language that Byapari is quite fluent in and frequently uses in the text, has been directly pointed out in the translation itself to bring out the nuances of multilingual interactions. Names of vernacular journals have been retained in the original. Byapari also uses a lot of popular and spiritual sayings (from Kabir to Ramakrishna), oft-quoted verse couplets (from Kamini Roy to Rabindranath Tagore), and regional metaphors and idioms. Most of them have been rendered into English, sometimes literally in a format that makes sense (like a doha from Kabir) and sometimes by replacing them with equivalents in the target language. The regional metaphors and idioms proved trickier and needed more playful interventions. Another aspect of the text that posed a challenge for me was the underlying sarcasm, something that Byapari has a penchant for using. The cutting humour of the original seemed flattened out in the translation, which I tried to balance out by making the passages more descriptive. Although this led to the loosening of the source language, it managed to replicate the humour through a visual vocabulary. An interesting aspect of Byapari's work lies in his frequent allusions to popular urban legends circulated via word of mouth. No attempt was made to correct them or point them out separately, as these organically inhabit Byapari's social and cultural milieu, adding a rich subtext to his narrative.

Where did I falter as a translator? Sipra Mukherjee has spoken in her translator's note of the first book about going the Benjaminian way of choosing intention over word in her translation. On my part, every time I attempted to transcend the word, I found myself fixating on this particular episode from Byapari's life:

> With a twig I drew my letters on to this soft earth, *Ka Kha Ga Gha*. When inside the ward, I wet my finger to trace on the hard cement floor. When eating, I drew my letters on my curry-smeared plate. When I had nothing at hand, I wrote in my mind. I saw nothing but letters all around me. In people's faces, their smiles, their movements, their gestures of the hand, I could see the letters of the alphabet ... I seemed to be immersed in a

world of dreams. And one night I dreamt of this bright angel-like figure who told me, 'What you write on the prison floor are not the letters, but your life.' (Byapari, book 1: 208)

It seemed too much of a responsibility in being entrusted with his words—his life—and I ended up complicating my own task by putting the original on a pedestal being well aware how translation theory has long outgrown the notion of the high-status original (Bassnett and Trivedi, 1999: 2). Such intense faithfulness as a translator, I soon discovered, was highly limiting. At the initial stages, I found it difficult to even change the S-O-V form in the original Bangla to the standard S-V-O English format, gravely compromising the quality of the translation. It was only after distancing myself from the text after the first round of translation that I was able to look upon it more objectively. This, along with multiple revisitations, valuable editorial inputs, and critical introspection gave shape to the final text as it stands.

Such texts of alternate historiography are not just mediums of articulation but carry within themselves the baggage of trauma, pain and oppression. As a translator, and a non-Dalit one at that, the greater challenge lies in translating the collective suffering that lies embedded within the language of the text. As G. J. V. Prasad rightly points out:

> The major challenge ... is the inherent seemingly untranslatable resistance of the language of this literature. The linguistic nuances of this literature are of paramount importance and translation can erase the locational differentiations, cultural oppressions, and the resistance. This is made insidious by the fact of one's own non-Dalit identity. One must always be alive to the political charge of both the original writing and one's translational activity. The original writing is resistant to the very ideology that the Dalits would identify with such a translator and thus the non-Dalit translator has to learn to write that resistance into the translation or give up the task. (Prasad, 2011: 24)

I hope I have been able to do justice to that intent. My heartfelt thanks to Manoranjanda for his trust in me, Arunava Sinha and Sipra Mukherjee for their encouragement, and to Mandira Sen and Aritra Paul of Samya for their patience and support. May the sequel continue stirring up ripples and unsettling the centre as had been initiated by the first book.

REFERENCES

Bassnett, Susan, and Harish Trivedi, eds. 'Introduction: Of Colonies, Cannibals and Vernaculars'. In *Post-Colonial Translation: Theory and Practice*, Oxford: Routledge, 1999.
Byapari, Manoranjan, 'Preface'. In *Interrogating My Chandal Life: An Autobiography of a Dalit*, translated by Sipra Mukherjee. New Delhi: Sage and Samya, 2018.
The Hindu, 'Live from The Hindu Lit For Life 2019 - Day 2'. YouTube video, 09:07:38. 2019. https://www.youtube.com/watch?v=s VUNm9lewXA.
Mukherjee, Sipra, 'A Note by the Translator'. In *Interrogating My Chandal Life: An Autobiography of a Dalit*, translated by Sipra Mukherjee. New Delhi: Sage and Samya, 2018.
Prasad, G.J.V, 'Translating Dalit Tamil Literature into English'. In *Writing India, Writing English: Literature, Language, Location*. New Delhi: Routledge, 2011.

PART I

School Shenanigans

CHAPTER 1

My First Visit to the Helen Keller Institute for the Deaf and the Blind

I got the job at the school known popularly as for the deaf and the mute.

At that time, Anu, my wife, was teaching at a school under the Integrated Child Development Scheme (ICDS) Project in an Adivasi village by the name of Pittepuria. She had started on the salary of two hundred and fifty rupees which had now increased to four hundred and seventy-five. The Adivasis from the village adored her and showered her with their love, reserving the first harvest from their fields, the eggs laid by their chicken, the vegetables from their fields for Anu and even delivered wood at her doorstep to serve all her fuel requirements. With their help, I believed, she would somehow be able to manage life with our two kids on her own. I could use the opportunity to test my fate with a game of dice. If I succeeded I would be able to bring them back closer to our own roots again. With this intention, I decided to take up the job.

***

Standing on the Bypass, as far as the eyes could see in the direction of the eastward sky, lay a huge area which was almost entirely covered in wetlands. Fish used to be harvested here. The overlord of these lands was Bihari Mondal of the Khagen Naskar family. Ever since the Indira Gandhi government demarcated the upper limit of these lands, most of them had been transformed into land that could be used as wished by the owner. Later on, those lands were illegally seized by the CPI (M) Party (henceforth CPM) workers or been handed over to them. Even though the people seized the land, its legal ownership stayed with the government. With time, the government—or should I say the CPM Party—seized back these lands from the farmers and fishermen, handing them over to others. They built hospitals, banks, supermarkets, hotels, lodges, and various other business establishments around the area, resulting in its rapid development.

On my first day, following the instructions given to me, I got down at the last bus stop on that stretch, trying to figure out the way to the school for the deaf and mute. At last, I boarded a rickshaw as a passenger for the very first time. All my life I had ferried countless people on my rickshaw. I knew very well how it felt to pull the vehicle. What I did not know was how it feels to be driven around in one while one sat like a babu on its cushioned seat! I was finally able to experience that. It was not nice at all! A man with a walking stick was limping with difficulty on the side, another man was sweating under the weight of two heavy bags, two kids were waiting for their school bus. There was someone who looked ill, not able to board crowded buses. These sights made me uncomfortable. The 'cosy' seat started seeming unbearable.

The rickshaw-puller asked, 'Where do you want to go?'

'To the school for the deaf and mute,' I replied.

At this, strangely enough, the man's face contorted with hatred. He looked at me as if I were an outcaste. I was familiar with this anger, this hatred. I was able to sense in it an aversion towards the other class. But how could this be so? Why would the eyes of a toiling person from the working-class blaze with so much contempt for a school that had been established by a minister from the Left and was run by Leftist workers?

'The fare will be five rupees,' he said.

I replied, 'All right, let's go.'

'I hope you have change? I don't have any.'

'I will give you a ten-rupee note. Won't you be able to give me back a change of five?'

'No!'

His 'no' seemed to reverberate all around. This *no* was not just directed towards me, it was against an entire establishment. It carried in it a small but strong spark of rebellion.

I searched my pocket and managed to find five rupees in change. I told him that and said we could get going. He ground his teeth and knew I had it but didn't want to be cooperative. Pedalling away the rickshaw, he asked, 'Do you have somebody at the school?'

'No. I am visiting just like that.'

'Nobody visits just like that!'

We had gone some distance, when he said, 'My heart burns whenever I go near that school. But what can be done! I cannot refuse passengers once they board my vehicle.'

'Why does your heart burn?'

'Previously, the land belonged to us. We used to farm over there. The school has come up on *our* land by throwing *us* out. It is a joke in the name of a school! Just an assemblage of some deaf and mute children. We have not even been compensated till date.'

Finally, I understood the reason behind his anger. Once a farmer, now he had been reduced to a beast of burden, pulling a carriage. His anger was justified. I probed further, 'How are the people at the school?'

'Don't you know how they are?' he retorted back.

I told him I didn't.

'They are from your political party and you say you don't know!'

'I am not involved with the party.'

'Then why are you headed towards the CPM Party lair?'

'I am going for some work.'

'What work?'

'For the cook's position. That's why I am interested to know about these people who will soon become my fellow workers.'

'What do I say,' the rickshaw-puller replied, 'just like any other CPM Party member.'

The residential school was situated a little further up the alley. Its iron gates could be seen from afar. The rickshaw halted at the gate. I paid my fare and went up ahead, my heart pounding in my chest. I had not been this scared even while going to jail. It is true that some of the people in the jail might have been wicked, but the majority of them were good at heart. Their fate had landed them in prison, but kindness had not been completely wiped off their soul. Here the situation was completely different. My prior experiences with these people made me sceptical. Seeing me approach, one man came ahead and blocked my way. 'Where do you want to go?' he asked in Hindi.

He seemed like a guard. At the height of four and a half feet, this frail and thin Bihari man was bound to evoke sympathy in anybody's heart. Such was the pitiable condition of the school for the deaf and mute! Their relentless search had yielded this man from Bihar, but he was nowhere close to those typical Biharis known for their dexterity in stick-fighting, ones who would have been an obvious choice for such a job. Such a Bihari would come with a huge moustache set on a wide-chest, well-exercised muscular body, who would evoke fear in others just by standing with a stick in his hand. If this guy was put on a night watch, any thief would die laughing just at the mere sight of him.

I was a *Bangal* from Bastar.[1] I knew my Hindi well. I had learnt it because I needed to, just as I had once picked up the Bangla alphabet. Presently, I could speak and read both the languages fluently.

I answered back in Hindi, 'I have to meet the Super Sahib.'

'The school is closed today. If you need to get your child admitted, come tomorrow.'

'Not my child, *I* have come here to be admitted.'

The Bihari was shocked at this revelation. 'You want to get admitted?'

'I have come here for a job—the job of a cook.'

'Oh!' Saying this, he pointed his finger to the second floor of the building. 'The 'Sweeper' Sahib isn't here at the moment. Warden Sahib is here. Go and meet him, he will guide you.'

The residential school looked very different then. It was a tall two-storey building. The lowest floor had rooms that had been assigned for the school's official purposes. It had the office, the teacher's room, and Boro Sahib's sitting room (which could also be used as a bedroom when needed). There was also the office of the Teacher-in-Charge and a big empty room to be used as required in the future.

The first floor had eight rooms which were used as classrooms. The longish hall where the children were hosted was on the second floor. A loft on the roof was kept aside as the kitchen. Student dinners was served on the roof, while the stairs were used for the morning meals.

I slowly climbed up to the second floor. Ordinarily, the children would have finished their meals and left for their classes at this hour. For some reason I forget now, it was a holiday that day because of which the teachers hadn't come and the students hadn't gone to their classes. As soon as I reached the room and stood near the door, I heard a deep roar. Somebody was shouting—'I will beat you to death'. This was followed by the sound of vigorous hitting. It fell on the back of a ten- or twelve-year-old kid, bending him over almost like a bow. He cried out in agony.

NOTE

[1] A person from old East Bengal in pre-Partition India.

CHAPTER 2

The Warden and the Mother Killer

There was a man—it might be more apt to call him a black sumo wrestler. With his huge body, he was jumping from one bed to another—beds laid out for the kids to sleep in—and mercilessly beating them up. I looked at him with fear. His eyes were bloodshot. His hair was cut short. His skin was extremely dark. His height, almost six feet. Everything put together, he looked like a living terror.

He was really a terror. Every man in his neighbourhood unanimously acknowledged this fact within the confines of their homes. And it was not him alone. All his six siblings were terror personified. Many years ago, their worldly wise father had impressed upon them the importance of solidarity using a story from *Nitimala*.[1] Simply put, the story contended that it was easy to break one stick, but very difficult to break a bundle. Having taken the moral of the story very much to heart, the siblings had chosen to cohabit for life. If one day the six siblings decided to take to the roads rallying with flags with no other followers, there would still be no one to stop them from winning.

His eldest brother was a childhood friend of Boro Sahib, who was the overall head of the school, and also a big regional leader of the CPM Party. Given the fact that he was the brother of his childhood friend, Boro Sahib treated him with a lot of affection. He had personally offered this man the job. Otherwise, he didn't really need a job. The five brothers had amassed so much wealth with their land promoting business that five subsequent generations could have survived on that without having to move an inch. He had still taken up the job to appease Boro Sahib. He would come around ten o'clock in the morning, stay for an hour and then leave for home. Having spent the afternoon eating lunch, napping and relaxing at his home, he would return later at night for his second round of duties.

His post was that of the Warden. During his free time, he hung out with a bunch of people who had nothing better to do. Needless to say, they were all members of the CPM's youth organization who would sometimes even carry out the 'pious' job of beating up people from the opponent's party. In those days, the Warden would spend every waking hour devising new ways to torture people. His friends had given him the nickname of Runu Guha Niyogi.

Some people might still remember that Runu Guha Niyogi was an infamous police officer in the seventies. He took great pleasure in inserting hot boiled eggs into the private parts of Naxal women. His favourite pastime was stamping people with the tip of his cigar. Any Naxal prisoner found with burnt marks on their foreheads, would doubtlessly attest to this. During 1977, when the Left Front came into power, everybody expected that this officer would be tried in court and punished. In actuality, he got a promotion. This was because the Jyoti Basu government, just like the government before them, utilized him in a similar way. Even after Niyogi's retirement, he was offered quarters in Lal Bazar's protected enclave.[2]

The Warden's innermost desire had been to work at the police department, that is, if he were required to work at all. He wanted to garner a reputation like Runu Guha Niyogi's. When that did not materialize, he was forced to live out his fantasy vicariously as a Warden by beating up anyone in his immediate vicinity.

The Warden had reached the other end of the hall, jumping all the way. While retracing his path, he suddenly noticed me, a stranger, standing at the doorway. He looked startled. Who was this man? Was he the guardian of any kid? These guardians were deeply nefarious. They created ruckus for any untoward incident that happened; threatening to take it to the Supreme Court. According to a warrant issued by the Supreme Court, children could not be subjected to any sort of physical or mental abuse. Did they know that children were like lumps of clay? First the clay had to be sifted, then prepared, then crafted into the mould, then dried under the sun, and finally burnt in the fire. Only then could it be turned into a usable pot. If kindness came in the way of pummelling these kids, how would they ever become humans? And if one did not want to make good humans out of them, why even bring them here? They should go back home.

Coming towards me, the Warden asked, 'Who are you?'

'I have come here for the cook's job,' I answered.

He finally drew a sigh of relief. I was definitely not somebody who could create trouble for him. Panting heavily, he threw his giant body on a bed and said, 'Please sit. The Super has gone to the market. You can talk to him after he returns.'

I sat down in a corner of one of the children's beds. The deaf and mute kids kept watching me intently and I them. From the age of six to twenty-six, there were 'children' of various age-groups. I had never before seen so many deaf and mute kids in my life. Lacking the gift of language, used by people to express their thoughts, I was unable to understand what these children were thinking about me.

Around this time, a sexagenarian woman entered with a kettle of tea. Her other hand held two cups. Some of the staff at the school addressed her by the name of Mother Killer. I would get to know the reason behind this name in a couple of weeks—when she would beat up the kids mercilessly and I would plead with her to let them go for fear of their deaths.

She was alone in the world, having lost her husband at a very young age. Many people suspected it to be a case of suicide. She had not remarried. Eventually, she left her small village in Bardhhaman and managed to reach Buddhadeb Bhattacharjee's brother's household, where she took charge of his kitchen.[3] In her role, she also found the opportunity to boss over the other household helps. This was long back, when the CPM leaders had not yet become rulers. Their pride was still lying dormant in the foetal stage and had not yet been exposed. As a result, the party leaders who frequented the house did not see it as beneath them to interact with her. She grew especially close to one person who had been an accused in the Sainbari murder case but had eventually changed his name and become the registrar of a university.[4]

With time, following the course of nature, she grew old. Her body was no longer as strong as before. The cow who is unable to work the plough or give milk anymore has no value for her master and is driven out of the cowshed. But in her case, instead of handing her over to the butcher, this brother of Buddhadeb handed her over to Boro Sahib who then found her shelter in this residential school with a prior warning to all, 'Respect her like your own mother. Obey her word. One word of complain from her, you are done for!'

There is a saying that even when the tiger gets old, it does not forget its tricks. The same was true for Mother. She moved to the new place, but carried on with the same fierceness. She wouldn't hesitate from hitting the deaf and mute children for the slightest offence. The other employees were spared the physical abuse, but Mother made sure to make up for it by targeting the choicest of slurs at them.

Before Mother could pour the tea in the cup, the hostel Super arrived. She knew he would come. So she had brought two cups, one for the Warden and the other for the Super. For herself, she had brought a glass.

Every small or big employee of this school was a CPM Party worker or supporter. Such was the case either from the very beginning or had happened later due to some compulsion. There is a joke that if a Hindu converts to Islam, they declare a death sentence on cows. Since they don't know Arabic and can't read the Quran, they aren't accustomed to offering namaz, and they can't keep a fast for Roza for being unable to withstand the pain of starvation; the only way they can prove themselves to be a true Muslim is by consuming huge quantities of beef. The newbies of the CPM Party were somewhat similar. They were reluctant to attend the Party classes. They didn't desire to mull their heads over the tenets of dialectical materialism. Reading journals or newspapers was not of any interest to them. The significance of Marxism? What was that? Their only job was to make noise for the CPM Party and create greater noise against the opponent party. This is how they wanted to prove that their allegiance to the CPM was greater than that of the older folks.

In this crowd, the only exception was that of the Hostel Super, Gayen Babu. Although he was with the CPM and in the service of CPM, when it came to discussing his political identity, he would introduce himself as a Congressman's son. 'In my blood there is the blood of the Congress Party,' he would claim. It was true that the Hostel Super was the son of an ex-MLA from South Bengal. At that time, MLAs weren't as shrewd and diplomatic as today. In fact, a few of them were completely illiterate. They couldn't even sign their own names, and had to use thumb impressions to withdraw their MLA allowances. Therefore, of course, they had no idea how to extract oil from sand.

A long time ago, I had come across a comic strip in a torn-page from *Nobokollol* of a fat man in dhoti and vest frying snacks. The billboard hanging from the side announced, 'Ex-MLA's Snacks—as Hot and Spicy as His Speeches'. Despite the unabashed lampooning, the scene had some hidden truth in it. In all honesty, these former MLAs weren't as sly and cunning as the ministers today. So, when they lost their MLA position, they were forced to spend their lives in dire financial straits. Currently, however, the MLA position was a big one. Merely by becoming a panchayat member, one could buy a small-scale zamindari.

This MLA was such a person who did not know how to safeguard his future. The Congress nominee, who had contested from the same seat after him, ended up defeating Boro Sahib twice in a row. The upcoming elections were close. The Congress was a party known for its internal fissures. Keeping all his grounds covered, Boro Sahib had started preying on these fissures to win the next round of the elections. He knew that the present Congress MLA was not on good terms with the former Congress MLA. This aside, having lost his former seat, he was leading his life in abject poverty.

Taking advantage of the situation, Boro Sahib approached him one day. 'Congress hasn't given you a ticket. This is a complete betrayal. It's time to avenge yourself. Defeat Congress from this seat. Make me win. Just like a watermelon,[5] stay with them but work for me. I will pay you handsomely.'

This seemed profitable to the former Congress MLA. But one could hardly have faith in people like Boro Sahib, born a Bengali, belonging to the caste of Brahmins, and politically affiliated to the CPM. Therefore, even though the former MLA agreed, he laid down his conditions: payment first and then the job. 'It's your government now. If you so wish, you can do it. Get my son a job. After that, I promise that I will openly campaign for you.' It was because of this reason that the former Congress MLA's son had been offered the job of the hostel Super in this school. Just like Ramakrishna Paramahansa, who spent his life blaming his fate and the gods for forcing him to earn his living under Rani Rashmoni, who belonged to the lower castes, this son too used to blame his father and the Congress.

It is true that the MLA cleverly coerced Boro Sahib to give his son a job, but Boro Sahib was not a fool either. He had not immediately handed over the joining contract to the son, but waited patiently till the election chapter was over and the former MLA's contribution had been effectively assessed. But that is another story. Presently, after pouring out the tea for the Warden and the Super in the two cups she was carrying, Mother realized that there was another man in the room. 'Who is he? I haven't seen him here before.'

The Warden replied, 'Boro Sahib's recruit. He is the cook.'

'What is your name?'

The question was directed at me and I obliged, 'Manoranjan Byapari.'

'Byapari? You mean from *vyapaar*— business? What business do you own? I haven't heard of such a surname before.'

I answered, 'Previously our surname used to be Mandal. It was changed during my grandfather's time, I don't know why.'

'Not a Brahmin?'

'No, I am a Namashudra.'

'What caste is that? I have heard of Brahmins, Kshatriyas and Vaishyas. I have also heard of Pods, Kaoras and Bagdis. I have heard of Chanrals. But Namashudra—this I have never heard of!'

I didn't like Mother's tone. It felt obnoxious to be interrogated about caste in an organization run by Leftists. Once, I had been subjected to extreme humiliation over the caste question as a cook for a child's rice-eating ceremony.[6] I had never been able to forget that. Today, I was no longer so weak. I charged my cannonball at my opponent—'We used to be referred to as Chandalas and Chanrals previously. Now we are known as Namashudras.'

My caste identity caused Mother's face to distort. Within the precincts of Hinduism, I was an untouchable. The upper castes had to take a bath to cleanse themselves if they happened to touch us. Unable to keep her anger to herself, Mother blurted out, 'Did my brother find no other person as a cook except a Chanral? Not everybody here is from the lower castes, you know. There are Brahmins and Baidyas among the children. How will they have food cooked by you?'

My ears and head started buzzing. Where had I landed? I knew that people from the Left did not believe in caste. They were atheists. They believed that everybody was equal and equally respectable. Then *what* was this that I was hearing? And, *why* was I hearing whatever was being said?

Smiling, the Warden asked, 'What will happen if they do eat?'

'It will be a sin,' replied Mother.

'Nobody believes in this nowadays.'

'People believe what they have to believe. I know that my brother is in the party, but does that mean that he will not pay heed to the Chanrals and the Doms? Lower caste or no caste, he does not care who is cooking. But what about his wife? My brother does not wear the sacred thread around his body, he does not pray. My sister-in-law, on the other hand, does everything. They even have a big Kali idol at their place.'

Here, she was referring to Boro Sahib as her brother. Bhai Phonta had just gone by—the festival where the sister puts a mark on her brother's forehead, praying for his long life. Mother had adorned Boro Sahib's forehead with a mark this time. Ever since that day, she only referred to him as 'my brother', earning some added importance from others.

Mother's surname was Saha. It was not a high-caste surname. However, she had spent a large part of her life in the house of a pious Brahmin of the Bhattacharjee surname. The ancestors of these Kulin Brahmins were pioneers who inculcated such false pride in their profession.[7] It is true that somebody from this Bhattacharjee family had written plays in keeping with the Leftist tradition, but that was strictly for the consumption of the outside world. Within their household, every ritual was religiously followed. Like a piece of iron turns magnetic in the vicinity of a magnet, Mother had turned a superstitious Brahmin with her long association with this family. However, her superstitions were solely restricted to rituals, not food. On the subject of food, she did not distinguish between vegetarian and non-vegetarian. She eyed both eagerly and paid them equal respect.

Mother's attitude intensified the smile on the Warden's face. He asked, 'Mashima, what will you do now? He is Boro Sahib's recruit, which means he's come to stay. There is no other way but to eat what he cooks.'

Mother replied, 'I have enough good sense to know what is to be done.'

'What will you do?'

'Should I tell you?'

'Of course! Tell me what's on your mind.'

'Fire is a universal cleanser. I will boil the rice and the vegetables on fire. That will do the trick!'

'You will do this every day?'

'Twice a day.'

'It will cause you unnecessary trouble.'

'So be it. I can deal with that.'

'Rather than that why don't you eat the same way as the others. Forget this touchable and untouchable thing!'

'Never! I am not going to do anything impious in the last few years of my life.'

Nonetheless, Mother was in a fix. I was right there in front of them. Everybody was having tea; propriety demanded that I, too, be served some. There was a lot of tea but no cups. The cups were up in the loft, where the kitchen was. Who would take the trouble of going up all these steps to get there! She looked around her. Suddenly, her eyes went towards a window. There, on the window sill was a broken cup without its handle, almost faded in colour. A teacher from Midnapore used this cup as his shaving bowl. He had gone home for the holidays, leaving the cup behind.

Right after landing from Midnapore, this teacher had engaged himself with the task of shopping and cooking at Boro Sahib's house. He was an enterprising fellow who continued his educational pursuits while doing such odd jobs. Nowadays there are many such institutions that guarantee a pass certificate on the simple condition that you get enrolled there. They don't require one to attend classes every day; once or twice in a month or a week is enough. This was how he became literate. An amiable man, Boro Sahib was extremely fond of him. This landed him a job at this school as a sports teacher.

Sports count as extracurricular activity. It does not require one to have any contact with education. Leave alone the post of a teacher, around the beginning of this government's term the man who became the Sports Minister was only an eighth pass-out. That he had any links with sports was an insult even his staunchest critics would not make. He was a true bully. If he could become a minister, why couldn't this man be a sports teacher? There was just one difference. To become a minister, one did not require a certificate. Dictatorial skills were enough. This man, however, had to make his own arrangements. In today's world, such arrangements were not a problem at all. Just a few days back, five to six lawyers, who used to practise at the court, were intercepted by the police for their fake LLB certificates. Similarly, many doctors have been exposed for their fake MBBS certificates. And a certain professor of a university is said to have nonchalantly carried on with his teaching for several years with a fake Ph.D. degree. If not for some Left-opposing police in their attempt to defame the government, such news would have forever stayed in the dark. Nobody would have had a whiff of these things.

The shabby cup that had been left behind was now picked up by Mother to serve me my tea. This wouldn't cause a dent on any high-caste Hindu's conscience. This is because it has been clearly stated in the great Hindu scriptures that if one has to serve food to a lower caste person, the utensil used should be an abandoned one and the food, leftovers. Pouring a little tea in the cup, Mother twirled it twice and threw it out the window in order to clean it. Then she extended the tea-filled cup towards me. 'Here, have tea.' I had just arrived and hence had no idea about the cup's history. I got to know that in two days. But at that point it was the lack of respect and love with which the tea was offered that embittered me.

I explained to myself, don't be upset, you crazy head. Try to be like the blue-throated Shiva who drinks venom. The same venom will turn into nectar once it enters your gut. There are so many like you who have to scavenge through dustbins just to stay alive. If you want to live, learn to eat everything. Otherwise, hunger will eat you instead.

NOTES

[1] A collection of moral tales for children.
[2] Lal Bazar is the police headquarters of Kolkata.
[3] Buddhadeb Bhattacharjee was the CPM Chief Minister of the Left Front government, 2000-2011
[4] The Sain brothers of Bardhhaman were strong supporters of the Congress and were brutally murdered by CPM members on 17 March 1970. The victims had refused to switch allegiance to the CPI(M).
[5] That is, green on the outside: Congress's colour; red on the inside, the CPM's colour.
[6] Narrated in the first book.
[7] Of special higher ritual status among the Brahmins, which gave rise to polygamy of unbelievable numbers where Kulin grooms were sought of by ordinary Brahmins.

CHAPTER 3

The Four Guards

The school had four guards. One of them was the Bihari fellow I met the first day. He spent twenty-four hours of his day at the school being unable to secure his own lodgings elsewhere. He ate in the hostel and slept in the office. Another person was Palda. His house was south of the Jadavpur station. He was a simple man who stayed out of other people's businesses. He came to work, completed his work-hours and retired for the day. Having contracted polio as a child, had left one side of his body crippled for life.

The third person was Saha. In the year 1984, he had immigrated to India illegally with a middleman's help. Initially, he put up at a rented place and worked as a labourer but somehow managed to find a way into Boro Sahib's palatial mansion one day, where he procured the job of a gardener. He was a clever man and did not take long to realize that this association would protect him from troubles that can cause headaches to anybody on foreign soil. He had no passport or visa, his name was not on the country's voting list, he did not even have a ration card for food. But he knew that everything could be attained, as long as he managed to remain in Boro Sahib's good books.

History attests that Hazrat Muhammad, Badshah Akbar, Brave Shivaji and Ramahansa Paramahansa were not properly educated. Yet, one could not call them to be fools. Their wisdom surpassed others. Similarly, even though our Bangladeshi Saha had never shown any interest in attending the classes held under the literacy mission, one could not call him a fool. Life had taught him the best lessons. He had learnt that nothing was as wonderful as having enough clout for climbing up the societal ladder. If that was not possible, it was best to take refuge under an influential person and lose all worries instantly. The cunning Saha had done exactly that. This had resulted in him acquiring a certificate from a rural school from the other side of Bengal testifying that he had passed Class Eight and a job in this school. At present, he would come to school at ten in the night, make his bed, turn on the fan and go off to sleep. First thing in the morning, he would go to Boro Sahib's place, stay there for a while carrying out small orders and then head back to his place. He was living a happy life in this country.

Dasda was the fourth person. Previously, he used to work in a fish shop and even before that, he used to go to the same school as Boro Sahib, a fellow classmate. Later, they got involved in politics together and fled from their respective neighbourhoods in 1972. Unfortunately, even today, Dasda was still stuck at the exact same place from where he had started—as an ordinary Party member—while Boro Sahib had climbed up the ladder real quick, making it to the top. For this reason, Dasda harboured a secret grudge against the party. So many years dedicated to the party, but for what! To serve as a mere guard! How shameful!

It is heard that when Siraj ud-Daulah became the nawab, the first thing he did was to summon the teacher who had taught him as a child. The old man was very happy to hear from the nawab. It was the happiest day in Siraj's life and the teacher expected that he was being beckoned for some reward or honour. But wonder of wonders! The moment the teacher arrived, Siraj landed a fat slap across his face. Why? To avenge the slap he had once received from the teacher. For reasons unknown, Boro Sahib seemed to have a lot of pent-up anger towards his childhood friend Das. Something must have happened in their childhood, the price for which was being exacted in this fashion now. Therefore, he sometimes made Dasda stand holding his ears.

This was around the time that I had begun work at the school as a cook. It had only been a month. Almost forty kids had taken admission, with a higher cap being set at fifty. My responsibility was to feed them. The search was on for a helper. A person had come in for the job—an Oriya cook who was acquainted with Boro Sahib—but after closely scrutinizng the working environment and the workers' behaviour for an hour—he left never to return. I was literally holding the fort alone. The kitchen was on the terrace of the two-storey building and the bathrooms on the first floor. Two of them were for everybody's use, while one had been reserved for Boro Sahib. It was kept securely locked, only to be opened when Boro Sahib visited. Since he was at the school that day, the door had been unlocked and the bathroom occupied.

I had to use the bathroom too. When I climbed down from the terrace, I saw a lot of people assembled near his door. All of them had come to see Boro Sahib. In a corner stood our middle-aged guard Dasda, holding his ears. This man had long crossed the age of sixty, even though the certificate which he had acquired from some school for the purpose of this job put him somewhere around thirty or thirty-two. I found it extremely amusing to find the same old man holding his ears like a child playing truant in school. I asked him, 'What happened, Dasda?'

'Nothing,' he replied, visibly embarrassed.

'Then why are you standing here this way?'

'He asked me to, so I am.'

I later came to know that Dasda wasn't the only victim. Boro Sahib inflicted this punishment on many. He even made them do sit-ups. This was one of his favourite pastimes. Every powerful person has one such pet game, which gives them pleasure and makes them feel good about themselves. I don't know if it were true, but a similar story was told about nawab Siraj ud-Daulah. Apparently, he loved to watch the sight of passengers of capsized boats drowning in the nearby river from the window of the Hazarduari Palace. To entertain him, his soldiers would follow his orders and make numerous innocent people undergo this fate. Dasda seemed to me like one of those helpless people: his self-respect shorn off and his body drowning into the abyss of contempt.

I joined the school with the assumption that nobody would know me there, given I was back in Bengal after so long and the school was located so far away from Jadavpur. My assumption was proven wrong as it turned out that Dasda knew me quite well. When I was a rickshaw-puller, he worked at a fish shop in a market nearby. Those who deal in fish, have a favourite trick known as *dandimara*. The word has been in circulation since the time that the wooden weighing scales (from where the word *dandi* came) have been in use. It meant giving less than the amount asked for. Just like Sakuni had mastered the art of gambling,[1] these fish merchants were so good at this that they could easily make seven-fifty grams of fish look like one kilogram. Nobody could detect it. Evenually, the *dari-palla* was replaced by the *kanta-palla*. The fish merchants found a way with this machine too. But the word *dandimara* remained unchanged.

One day, a lot of fish was being weighed out at that shop for some event. Dasda was carrying out his tricks quite wholeheartedly. I was there. Suddenly my eyes fell on the small magnet at the bottom of one of the weighing plates. It must have weighed around a hundred. I brought this to the buyer's notice. As can be expected, there was no end to Dasda's disgrace that day. It was after this incident that he had memorized my face. I used to drive the rickshaw; he must have seen me on the roads many a time. He had carved out my face on his heart. So, it was no wonder that he was immediately able to recognize me on the very first day. From the time of bumping into me at around four in the evening during his night shift, he must have been restless to disclose my real identity to everybody. 'Manoranjan! His actual name is Madan. The rascal used to be a rickshaw-puller. Extremely notorious. Our boys also gave him a piece of their minds one day.'

Every night at eight, a lively gathering assembled at the school. It was attended by the Hostel Super, the sports teacher, the Warden and another teacher. This fourth person was also

Boro Sahib's right-hand man. In fact, Boro Sahib had a number of these aides, each of them in charge of a particular area. This man was responsible for all things related to the school. He was to oversee the purchase of bricks, sand, cement and rods for a number of construction projects aimed at erecting tall buildings. Apart from this, his job was to be at Boro Sahib's beck and call whenever he visited.

The sports teacher was missing from today's *adda*. The Warden had reached a while ago—he usually could not make it before eight-thirty. Their family owned a lot of business ventures which included promoting, catering, dealing in Cadbury and mobile phones. Though his brothers were mostly in charge, he too had a fair share of responsibilities. This is why he often got delayed.

But it's true that he came twice a day. One was around ten o'clock in the morning. He stayed for an hour and left only once the children had eaten and left for their classes. Thereafter, he came again at eight in the evening and stayed for around an hour and a half till the children went off to sleep after dinner and the door was securely locked. Both times, he would diligently count the number of children present to ensure that nobody was missing. It is heard that a king had a minister whose main task was to count the number of waves in the river. Here too, at this school, there were two employees tasked with the job of head-count. If the former situation seems so improbable, it was difficult to believe that the school had a warden and an ayah, whose primary job was to keep track of the number of children.

On this particular night, there was a full moon in the sky. It was not the kind that reminded starved people of burnt rotis. This was a moon that was enchanting in its magical light. This was a moon similar to the one that had once been painted in deep anguish by the young poet Sukanta Bhattacharya. This poem had once been on the lips of every member of the Communist Party, which had now been sent to its grave and buried after a lot of deliberations. Today this moon had become a symbol of shiny silver coins. This moon had, therefore, emerged as the ultimate goal for every ambitious person: the invisible representative of the Party.

Under this beautiful moonlit night, a newspaper had been spread out on a bench in order to prepare a mix of parched rice and chanachur. During the day, this same newspaper had been the cause of irritation for all the CPM cadres by publishing a terrible lie on its first page itself. Apparently, people in Amlasol were dying out of hunger. What utter untruth! Ever since independence, nobody in this country had died of hunger. If at all, people were dying for eating rotten food. Who in their right mind eats that? And West Bengal? It was under the Left Front's able administration. Leave aside hunger people here in fact were putting on weight from excessive eating. As a matter of fact, this extra weight was the cause for all their serious ailments.

Tagore had once said I see, therefore the moon exists. If I don't see it, it won't exist anymore; it is my consciousness that turns emeralds green. Our religious texts too agreed to the poet's wise words. For, whatever did not exist in our possession did not exist in the universe. Simply put, whatever the self knows, is right, everything else is false. Then what about those numerous people I knew who readily agreed to live as beggars like me before the Left Front government came into power, but today had refrigerators stocked up with food that was rotting in excess? Knowing that, how could I accept the claim that people died out of dearth of food. It was all a big fat lie!

The evening snacks had by now spilled over and completely covered the news report so unfairly accusing the Left government. Around it sat a few satiated gentlemen, eating and gossiping. Dasda, saddened at his discovery about my identity, arrived there and directly launched into his tirade.

'Whom did Boro Sahib bring amongst us! Previously, we were all of the same wavelength. This guy is trouble! What was the need to get him here?'

'Whom are you talking about?' the Warden was interested to know.

'That man who joined as a cook.'
'You know him?'
'I've known him for thirty years now!'

Tea followed the snacks. There was a momentary pause to the conversation as soon as I entered and stood before them with a kettle filled with tea.

'I will tell you everything later,' assured Dasda to the others.

NOTE

[1] Shakuni was the maternal uncle of the Kauravas in the *Mahabharata*. His long-term aim was to destroy the Kauravas. The eldest Pandava prince, Yudhisthira, was defeated while gambling with him because of loaded dice, losing his siblings, himself and their wife, Draupadi, to him. This lead to the Kurukshetra War.

CHAPTER 4

More on the Warden and Introducing the Teacher-in-Charge

There were still many people in the country who believed that blessings could be earned by serving the disabled and the dispossessed. One such believer would send six litres of milk for the deaf and mute children at the school every day. But it was nearly impossible for six packets of milk to provide for so many children! As a solution, Mother would borrow some of it to make curd at her place. The rest was used for the innumerable cups of tea required through the day. The last remaining bit was mixed with water and fed to one or two sickly kids.

I left soon after serving them tea; Dasda took the opportunity to disclose the truth about me to the others. This was followed by a discussion among them as to what was to be done. In 1977 when the Left government came into power, the Warden—whose idol was Runu Guha Niyogi—was in his later teens. Right from that age itself, he was aware of the kind of power his two elder brothers, affiliated with the LCM (Local Committee Member), exuded in their area. Not only the ones with the all-powerful Boro Sahib's hand over their heads, but even the other party members, everybody had grown in arrogance with the party's consecutive wins, be it by whatever means possible. They had reached a point where they were confident that they could make anyone win the elections on their party ticket. The more they started relying on money and brawn, the more they desired to rule the masses and subdue them. By the end, it felt like common man was a prisoner waiting in his lockup cell for mercy, while all the party members, big or small, were like the prison commanders.

The Warden had grown up in such an ambience. He knew if he beat up people, they would bear it in silence. If a person was shouted upon, he would cry noiselessly. If somebody was approached for a beedi, the person would treat him with tea and a cigarette instead. If he boarded a rickshaw, the rickshaw-puller would prefer some goodwill instead of his due fare. Humans have both light and darkness, God and Satan within them. The path one followed, depended on the person: his personality, education, culture, family, the company he kept, his blood group and many other such factors. Therefore, a dip in the Chambal River was not enough to turn a person into a dacoit just like a person born into a priestly family had equal chances of ending up as a heartless 'harmad'.[1] Everything depended on the time, the situation and the person. Say, if Runu Guha Niyogi had not been given a free run by the government, if he had had to lead his life by running a grocery shop in his area, would he still have been able to exercise his perverted mentality in this unbridled fashion? Perhaps not. The opportunity came to him through his job and the times he was living in. He merely exploited it to its fullest.

There was a strange happiness in killing and torturing people. This was known by people like Nadir Shah, Taimur Lang, Hitler and Runu Guha Niyogi. The Warden was also aware of it. This was the reason his friends had given him the nickname of Runu. He carried this name with as much pride as Subhas Bose carried 'Netaji', Mohandas Karamchand Gandhi carried 'Bapuji', Sir Ashutosh carried 'Bengal Tiger',[2] Ishwarchandra carried 'Vidyasagar' and Rabindranath Tagore carried 'Gurudev'. However, the joy of beating one's opponent without any restrictions, as prevailed from the seventies to the nineties, was no longer the case. Times had changed. Not many were left to oppose. Everybody had joined hands with the CPM. Be it the master, the slave, the farm overlord, the sharecropper, the landlord, the tenant, the rich, the poor, the oppressor, the oppressed, the ruler or the ruled, everybody had forgotten their internal factions, and keeping their struggles suspended had joined hands under the same flag with the same song on their lips.

The Warden had not been able to find a job in the police department. Not only had he crossed the upper age limit, he had also not been able to acquire the necessary degrees on time. He was left with this job, which he took up by bottling the unhappiness in his heart. At times, he would therefore drown his grief in a glass of Scotch. Whatever be his post, he considered himself well above the others.

Everybody in this school was directly or indirectly associated with the CPM Party in some way or the other. Some were party members themselves, others had close relatives in the Party and some others had joined through the reference of somebody in the Party. This was the reason that many people felt that Boro Sahib had envisioned the school so that his own people would not die of hunger. Serving the disabled community was merely an excuse.

* * *

The school's Teacher-in-Charge was also here under the recommendation of another influential politician from South Bengal. It was her firm belief, mainly because of her position and the politician's influence, that she alone possessed the whip which could tame the tiger. Little did she know, though, that everybody possessed such a whip. Her current position previously belonged to another individual. During her predecessor's time, the school building was not yet complete, and the school was run from a temporary building. When the school shifted, for no apparent reason, the former person quietly resigned without a word. Rumour has it that he was a truthful, hardworking individual. Every monetary transaction would be meticulously checked by him before a voucher was signed. As a result, a faction gradually rose against him. He would be frequently manhandled and harassed. An individual pitted against an entire group, unable to take it any further, he was forced to resign. Presently, it is heard that he lives in poverty, but with the same integrity and without compromising on his principles!

Within a few months of my joining, the present Teacher-in-Charge arrived in this town from a village nearby. Her situation was similar to a tiny pond fish suddenly finding itself in a huge ocean! Her attitude was thus: I am the Bordi of the school. I demand everybody's attention and respect. I am the kind that can make everybody stand up in respect wherever I go. Smokers hurriedly hide their beedis at my sight and attendants arrive promptly at my ring. People tremble when I scold!' Back then, she used to threaten random people with a 'show-cause notice' almost every day.

Up until then she was the living terror threatening others, never having experienced the good fortune of being threatened herself. Having made countless people cry, she was yet to shed tears herself. It would all happen in good time! In a few years, when the Principal's own candidate would be appointed as a teacher, Bordi would find herself in her victims' shoes.

As the story goes, this new teacher, backed by her degree, became a threat to Bordi's position as the Teacher-in-Charge of this school. Desperate to retain her job, Bordi joined an organization to obtain a degree. She was caught cheating during the exams and word soon reached the Headmaster. The Headmaster eventually called her to the office and gave her an earful, causing the Teacher-in-Charge to break down in tears in front of the very same lowly employees she had terrorised for years. That day her tears flowed incessantly and her head remained bowed down. In the years to follow, this became the subject of her frequent rants.

NOTES

[1] Corruption of the word 'armada', brought to Bengal by the early Portuguese traders, associated with pirates by the people; used for the lawless political cadre of the CPM.

[2] Sir Ashutosh Mukherjee was the second Vice Chancellor of Calcutta University 1906-11, 1921-26, who built up the university to high standards with brilliant faculty like C.V. Raman (won the Nobel prize in physics) and Sarvepalli Radhakrishnan (philosopher and later President of India).

CHAPTER 5

Tensions at Work

My workplace had put me in touch with many such Leftists who were hungry for power, but none of them was as heartless and cruel as the Warden. Having gathered information about me from Dasda, he had taken upon himself to break me from within, piece by piece. It had been a few days since I had started work. He came to mark his attendance as usual at around 9am. His presence always created a sense of commotion on campus because nobody knew who his next target would be. As the Warden, he barely needed reasons to mess with somebody since he was perfectly capable of manufacturing reasons of his own.

He entered the school premises and found the light in the latrine to be on. A deafening roar ensued. Who was the guard on duty? Perhaps it was Bihari. All the anger was channelled towards him. 'Can't you see the light is on? Who will pay for all the wasted electricity? You?' Bihari replied timidly in broken Bengali, 'I switched off the light a while back. Somebody must have switched it on again while I was busy turning on the pump.' His explanation fell upon deaf ears. The Warden went on a rant that it was the same story every day. That all the guards were useless. 'Switch it off now,' he bellowed. 'I will say just this once. Make sure that this is not repeated.'

The moment he walked into the school, I would be summoned for a cup of tea. The expectation was that I put everything else on hold to serve him. Ten minutes to whip up a cup of tea and then deliver it to him wherever he might be. Complaints would follow, about things like the amount of sugar in the tea. Next in line would be to fetch him a cigarette from the nearby shop and then a matchbox. That his orders made a person climb up and down the stairs in the heat, greatly tickled him. It was his way of flexing his position and power. If Boro Sahib could make everybody behave like his pets, so could he.

On my second or third day here, I first found myself in this situation that would become a regular occurrence. The Warden had arrived, demanding his cup of tea. At that time, the day's dal was underway on the stove. I thought of finishing the job at hand, before preparing the tea. This caused a slight delay. He took it as a sign of my latent arrogance. He was known for using the choicest of abuses. I got a taste of it that day.

'What happened? Where is my tea?' he shouted.

I said, 'The food would have got delayed—the kids have classes....'

'Hang your dal!' he roared. 'Hang your kids! If I ask for tea, make that first. Keep aside your food. If anybody says anything, tell them it was my order.'

Naturally, I had to keep aside the dal and prioritize his tea, which greatly appeased his ego.

On another day, once I had already fed the kids and sent them off to school, I thought of writing a letter to my wife in Pittepuria. But everything had to be paused, when the Warden suddenly appeared out of nowhere. His eyes seemed to be burning with repressed violence.

'Are you done with all work?' he asked.

'Yes, I was just about to go for a bath,' I replied.

'You can take a bath later. Come downstairs this moment.'

'Why?' I asked.

'You will see.'

On reaching downstairs, I saw that a spade, a chopper, a hammer and a few nails had been kept aside. He said, 'Pick them up.' I did. He walked ahead, asking me to follow him. I followed him and reached a clear area where bamboo poles were strewn across the ground.

'Cut up the poles and plant them on the four sides of the ground to make a fence,' he commanded. 'We will turn this into a vegetable ground. Make sure to build a strong fence so that no cattle can enter.'

We had two gardeners. One of them came in the morning at six, sat at that very spot to smoke a packet of beedis and then left. Not much for him to do! He was around forty, weighing about thirty kilos, with a height of around three feet and was severely asthmatic. The other one, however, was well-built. He was around six feet tall, weighed around seventy-eight kilos, and was around twenty-two years at that time in 1972. He was initially put to use by the Congress Party and was now being used by Boro Sahib. His actual work was to put his brawn to good use, while the job as a gardener was merely for him to be able to draw a regular salary. He came whenever he wanted and stayed for as long as he felt like.

I told the Warden, 'My job is to cook. What is all this?'

'Boro Sahib's orders demand everybody to pitch in with everything here without any restrictions on time,' he replied, his eyes on the sky above my head.

'Was the order only for me? I guess not. Does everybody else do everything else here?'

'What are you trying to say? Does that mean that the Teacher-in-Charge should help you with cooking?'

'Did I say that?'

'Then what?'

'Ah, let it be,' I said.

'Not at all. Pray tell me what is it that you are trying to say? If you don't want to help with the fencing, no problem. I will inform Boro Sahib. Rest is up to you.' In South Bengal, Boro Sahib had earned the reputation of the dreaded fictional dacoit Gabbar Singh, whose mere name could make children sober up. He was no longer just a person but dread personified.

I reacted similarly. All my courage went for a toss. I remembered a piece of advice once given to me by a well-meaning friend.

When I had once said that 'I am ready to break but not to bend. That's my life's philosophy', my friend had countered this with, 'That is nothing but foolhardiness. Stubbornness does not work well everywhere. A branch that breaks off is reduced to fuel. But the flexible one bends, only to straighten itself again at the appropriate time. Don't you remember—One Step Forward, Two Steps Back! Who said this? Lenin! Was he a fool? Moving back two steps might look like giving up, but no. It is just like a bull which goes back a few steps only to charge at you with its head. Men do the same before punching someone. This is the way to be.'

This episode made me reflect on why men behaved civilly with each other? Mainly because, they expected a similar treatment in return and help when in need. He who was above these needs and had enough power himself had no requirement for such courtesy. This man was not just an individual. He was a representative of the ruling party and his behaviour bore stamp of this awareness. As long as the party remained in power, his attitude would remain unchanged. Ramakrishna had said that those who bore in silence lived, others were destroyed. The same was preached by my own poor father. Tolerance was the key here. There were so many other apparently reputable educational institutions which were known to torture their new employees. The fashionable name for this was ragging. I knew I had to wait patiently and soon all this would end.

Without further argument, I went to the field. The huge land had previously been a pond, filled up with the soil that had been dug out for the underground metro line. It was to be turned into a vegetable garden. The harsh afternoon sun breathing fire over my head, drenched my body in sweat and made my stomach burn with hunger. I got down to planting the poles to build the fence. It was not a day's work, but would need at least four or five more. I would have to make time for this every day after lunch. On hearing a noise, I looked up. There, on the first-floor balcony was the Warden with his cup of tea, watching me toil under the sun. Was that a sense of glee on his face?

* * *

I got into a heated argument with Mother Killer one day. The memory of my first day here, when she offered me tea in a dirty cup, had remained as a festered wound in my mind. I also clearly remembered the distasteful comment she had made about my caste.

I have already mentioned the kind man who used to send six litres of milk every day for the children, many of whom were extremely malnourished. Mother used to shamelessly cut a share from this amount, taking away as much as she wanted to make curd or other desserts. Some of it was reserved for her, while the rest distributed among the Warden, the Super, the Sports Teacher or other people she favoured.

There is a limit to everything, except for human greed. The quantity of borrowed milk kept on increasing with time as Mother's favourites started growing in numbers. Eventually the milk remained milk no more but mere water. One cup milk every day, for forty kids. That was a lot of milk. But owing to Mother, the consistency of milk started decreasing, as the children's anger towards me started increasing. How would they know the secret behind the missing milk!

All this usually happened in the first half of the day, around nine. That is when she came to claim her share of the milk. The kids came later, so they were spared the truth. On that particular day, something inside me snapped. Those who err and those who silently let others err, were both equally guilty. I don't know what came over me I went and clutched her hands. I said, 'Don't take so much milk. This is not right.'

Her sense of entitlement came from the fact that the school belonged to her rakhi-brother. She snapped back, 'Now you will tell me what is right and what is not?'

I was reeling with anger. I answered back in the same tone, 'Who else can you learn from? To learn something good, you need to be with someone who can differentiate between good and bad. Do you know anyone like that?'

The woman was extremely stubborn. She tried to take back the milk I had poured back from her bowl. Boro Sahib's tea was also made from this milk. Whenever he came, twenty more accompanied. They too were served tea made from this milk. Mother found her logic and strength from this fact.

She said, 'I refuse to be ordered by the likes of you. I will only stop if the Super or the Warden asks me to.'

'Why would they say anything? They are equal participants in this. Let the kids say—because the milk is for them. If they allow, I won't say a word even if you take the whole amount. But the fact that I am at the receiving end of the kid's anger while you all are responsible for this mess, is not at all acceptable to me.'

Mother poured back the milk into the main container and began climbing down the stairs hurling abuses at me. I was certain that a storm would soon arise. She would never allow this insult to pass. And why would she when she had the right support!

CHAPTER 6

Tact or Free Flow like Pebbles?

I had read the revolutionary Ananta Singh's autobiography, *Keu Bale Dakat, Keu Bale Biplabi* (Some Call Me a Robber, Some Call me a Revolutionary). I had met him only once in my life, when he was going back to his ward from the main gate of the Presidency Jail. He was on a wheelchair, being pedalled around by another person. My heart ached at the sight of him. It felt like I was witnessing the ruins of a heritage tree. At one time, the mere mention of this wheelchair-bound person would make the British Empire break into a sweat. As powerful as time was, it was also unpredictable. It had reduced an iron-willed personality to scrap metal. And it had pushed him into this country's jail, the same country for whose freedom he had put his entire life on stake. The country had attained freedom, but the people had been reduced to slaves.

I had not yet read Runu Guha Niyogi's *Sada Ami, Kalo Ami* (I Am White, I Am Black); I would read that much later. Everybody's life choices are driven by some rationale. I wouldn't have realized this had I not read Nathuram Godse's brother Gopal Godse's book *Gandhi Wadh Kyon?* (Why I Assassinated Mahatma Gandhi). The book explains the reasons which had compelled a man to aim his shot at one of the most influential leaders of the country. What was the origin of his anger? I might not agree with their reasoning, but that did not make it not reason enough for them.

I keenly believed that even though a life might be trivial, inferior or disgusting, there was something to learn from it which could come handy later. The same was true for our Warden. There was much to learn from him, too. People who scavenged through dustbins would know that sometimes one might also find delicacies in the garbage.

Salaried people knew it was more profitable to keep one's boss happy; how much work they did was irrelevant. I had learnt from various sources that for a promotion at work, men would gladly send their wives to entertain their bosses in all possible ways. I knew not what technique was used by the Warden to keep his higher-ups satisfied, but they were so happy that this man was allowed to hold his position despite doing nothing, sometimes not even showing up for work. My case, however, was a complete reversal of this. My boss, the Warden, could not stand me. It was as if he had pledged to use every opportunity available to torture and humiliate me.

There were days, when he would stand over me as I ate, glaring at my plate intently. His snide comments would make the food refuse to go down my throat. He would comment on the size of the fish on my plate, gesturing that I should have given it to the kids and taken the smallest piece myself. After the completion of my work, I would sometimes go out in the afternoon for my personal work. He would make the guard at the gate check my bag on the off chance that I had picked up something that wasn't mine. There was this one time that he checked my bag himself. Each time, they hid the real intent in humour. 'Looks like there is something in the bag. C'mon Dada, show us!' they would laugh and say.

The guard who was most excited about this was the Bangladeshi Saha. He too had managed to manipulate Boro Sahib quite well. He would come at ten in the night, make his bed and promptly go off to sleep. As soon as morning arrived, he would leave. One night, the tape recorder and other expensive accessories from two of Boro Sahib's newly bought cars were stolen. Despite that, there was no break to his nightly sleep schedule.

Saha was illiterate. He had never moved around in good company. He was as simple as could be. But Boro Sahib's indulgent behaviour had made him swell up like a turkey cock. Sometimes he would say things, whose effect he himself did not understand. He was least bothered about the consequences of his actions. That the regular bag-check was a way of insulting me was something he did not realize. I was sure that the Warden might have incited him. He must have said, 'Sahada, it's your duty now. If any expensive stuff is secretly removed under your watch, the responsibility will be on your head. Do you know what is in a bag? Checking them is part of your work.'

For this reason, my body would burn in rage whenever I came across the Warden. But what could I have done with that rage? If a flying crow shat on somebody's head, what could that person do! My position was like that of Naxal leader Azizul Haque who used to be beaten up by a guard while in jail. The school was a similar jail for me and I did not have any other option but to tolerate what happened. There was an amusing incident mentioned in Runu Guha Niyogi's autobiography. One of Runu's friends had the reputation of being an able officer in his department within the police force. A number of major cases had been cracked under his supervision. Even then, his boss mistreated him. He would find faults with his work and heckle him for that. The friend's situation used to hurt Runu. Finally, one day, he was able to find the real reason behind this behaviour with his sharp observation skills.

He came to know that his friend would sometimes play table tennis with his boss. Being an able player, he would win most of the matches. This was his only mistake. Losing to a subordinate made the boss angry which further resulted in his bossing around Runu's friend. Runu advised his friend to let his boss win more matches. His loss at the tennis court would bring him gains elsewhere. He would lead a happier professional life.

I was not as tactful. I had never been. In fact, anybody who led his or her life in a calculated fashion was not worthy of my devotion. My life had been free-flowing like the pebbles rolling down the mountain tops. Had I known how to be tactful, I would have easily avoided many dangers. But no, in these matters I was as blockheaded as Saha. On top of that, I could not tolerate the arrogantly toplofty Warden in the least. It was people like them who exploited the fruits of the labour of the CPM cadres who had joined the party to uplift the poor, resisting great pain and suffering. I hated such opportunistic people and hoped for their downfall.

CHAPTER 7

Checkmate

Another person joined us at the school. He would live on the school premises because he had nowhere else to go. Until recently he was staying at his wife's maternal place, till his wife and daughter drove him out. However, this was not the version he shared with others. Referring to Boro Sahib by his nickname, he always said in his thick Bangal accent, 'Keshto is my childhood friend. He requested me to stay at the hostel and look after the school and so I came. I could not turn down my friend's request. Why else would I come here!'

This Childhood Friend previously used to work at a pharmaceutical company. From whatever I could gather of his history, he belonged to an influential family. His family had left their footprints in both the areas of literature and politics. How could such a disgrace of a man be born into this family was a mystery in itself. Maybe this was in his nature, just as Shibram Chakraborty had so appropriately noted, 'That which is born out of bamboo is not bamboo itself but mere twigs.'[1]

It is my misfortune that I have nothing positive to write about the member of such an illustrious family. It might seem that I write only about scandals, but I have no other choice. Save for me keeping an account, how would others know of what I had to undergo in the journey of becoming me and how I was taken advantage of. A government-sanctioned residential school, run by a group of so-called Leftists—if I did not expose what grave brutes they were, I would be accused of withholding facts from the story of my own life.

This world is full of two kinds of people: one, who eats to live, and the other, who lives to eat. They only eat and do nothing else. Their stomachs churn ceaselessly with gluttony; their only thought all day is what to eat and where to find what to eat. It reminded me of a story where, upon his return from pilgrimage, a man was hounded by people keen on hearing about his travel experiences and the connections he had made. Yet all he could recount to these eager listeners was the food he had eaten at these places. Brothers, he would say, if you go to Amarnath, you will see that the Marwaris have set up shops on the road. Bread and sweets fried in ghee! Oh, how tasty it was! The Childhood Friend was of a similar temperament. All his stories ended with items of consumption like pabda fish, king prawns, hilsa paturi, and so forth.

After his wife threw him out, he spent a couple of days in a hotel. He must have thought that his wife and daughter would take him back once their anger dissolved, but that had not materialized. Having exhausted all his savings in this way, he was compelled to make a call to Boro Sahib. That was how he was directed to the school. Clearly, how difficult could it be to sustain a few more people out of the reserves for the forty deaf and mute children!

With two bags full of clothes and other things of daily use, he thus landed up here. The very first piece of information he shared with us was the fact that he was Boro Sahib's childhood friend. 'I was sent here to look after the school', he noted, further adding for everyone, 'Boro Sahib has ordered me to let him know if anybody disregards or disobeys me. That person will be kicked out.' Such was this persona he had created that even the Teacher-in-Charge would tremble at his arrival.

* * *

One Sunday, I was waiting for the kids to finish their baths and come to eat. At the allotted time, I was surprised with a no-show. Venturing out, I found them in their hostel room, with around eight chess boards laid out in front and all of them sitting in pairs. This was in preparation for some upcoming chess competition for the deaf and the mute.

The Warden was also among them, eager to play but nobody wanted to play against him. He was inviting his opponents only to beat them at the game. The victory shout after each of these games was enough to make anybody feel that he had defeated the chess grandmaster Dibyendu Barua himself. It was like he had won the Battle of Plassey[2] or taken over the White House.

I learnt how to play chess during my time in the jail. I remember my instructor telling me that it was a great game. An hour's practice every day was enough to exercise the brain muscles and increase one's reasoning capabilities. With a cook's job, it was difficult to find time to exercise my brain. I saw the Warden in the middle of a game. His opponent was a weak player, giving him ample scope to play casually. He was playing defensive without much care about guarding his own pieces. The game moved to a point where losing a rook would put the Warden's king and queen in such a precarious position that his defeat would be inevitable in the next move itself. On behalf of his opponent, I pushed ahead the rook and said, 'Let's play this.'

'What a foolish move! You will unnecessarily make him lose the rook. This is chess, not Ludo!'

I laughed and answered, 'I know this is chess. If you can take on the rook.'

The moment he played his move and put forth his queen, he fell into my trap. After that, who could save him from losing the game!

He asked, 'Do you know how to play?'

'A little bit, yes. Nothing much.'

The loss had made the Warden furious. He wanted to defeat me at a game and take his revenge. He said, 'Then let's play a game.'

I said, 'I have to go and serve food to the children.'

'It won't take much time. Sit.'

I sat down at the board with the black pieces. It seemed like Kurukshetra's battlefield for me. My opponent was the arrogant commander, Duryodhan, rushing ahead to crush my skull with his mace. I could see his proud brows. Just one small opportunity and I would make him fall on his face.

I had not yet read his idol Runu's autobiography. Even if I had, I don't know if I would have been influenced by his life. I had read the holy texts but could not fully agree or draw strength from the fact that this life was the karma of my previous life. It was difficult to have faith in assurances that suggested that whatever had happened, was happening and would happen, was for the general good. They all sounded bogus to me!

All my mothers, sisters and daughters who had been subjected to the violence of rape at the Marichjhapi incident, all my fathers, brothers and sons who had lost their lives to tigers and crocodiles—how could I see the goodness in whatever had happened to them? All the goodness seemed to have been sucked dry by my opponents, the army led by the Dushasans and the Duryodhans of the world. They had used us like pawns and pawned us over once we had served our purpose.

I deliberately lost one of my pawns to keep my bishop's line of movement free. The moment I saw the opportunity, I took my bishop to sit in front of the king and the queen. I kept the Warden occupied with random moves and stayed on the lookout for the appropriate opportunity. He had already killed one of my knights, one bishop, four pawns and one rook. I had killed one of his knights, one bishop and two pawns. As far as the score went, he was ahead of me.

At this juncture, I casually put a knight at a spot that the opponent would have no other way but to take it. If not, I could 'check' him and win a rook. He saw the first move, not the ensuing one, whereupon he attacked with his knight, leaving the board open for me. My queen went and directly challenged his king, just by the mere grace of my bishop. And triumph was mine!

His defeat felt like sweet revenge for all the torture he had heaped on me so far! He laughed and arranged the pieces again, but this time, the man was seething with anger. This made him make the wrong moves. He lost again. That day he lost four games to me, one after the other. His face grew dark like gathered clouds.

He said, 'Let's save it for another day. Will surely beat you next time.'

I replied, 'Even if I lose, I promise to give a good fight.'

NOTES

[1] Shibram Chakraborty (1903-1980) was a popular writer, known especially for his humorous stories, famous for their unique use of pun, alliteration, play of words and ironic humour. He also wrote poems, plays, non-fiction and novels.

[2] The battle where the East India Company defeated the nawab of Bengal, Siraj ud-Daulah and obtained the Diwani of Bengali from the Mughal emperor, which meant the right to collect the revenue of Bengal; the beginning of their conquest of India.

CHAPTER 8

Something Fishy

A twenty-day sign language learning workshop was organized at the school. The teachers were taught how to use their hands to effectively communicate different subjects to the deaf and mute students. It was jointly organized by our school as well as Ramakrishna Mission, Narendrapur. Around thirty-five experts from all over the country turned up to train our teachers, who could then use it to train the students.

The outstation resource people were accommodated at our school. My work now was to first prepare food for the kids and then cook a special menu for the experts: once in the afternoon, once in the night. Not in excess but in a measured quantity. The Super bought katla fish for the guests one day and cut it up into big juicy pieces. Anybody's mouth would start watering at the sight, but all temptation had to be curbed as it was reserved only for the guests. Even though the Hostel Super and many others stayed and ate at the hostel, they too weren't allowed any share from this. A total of thirty-five pieces had been purchased. The menu consisted of fine rice, finely chopped potato fries, moong dal with fish bones, spicy katla fish curry and papaya chutney.

It must have been around one or two in the afternoon. Lunch would take another one and half hours. Meanwhile, I thought of freshening up. The kids were still at school and no cats or dogs had access to the roof. Believing that the food would be safe, I covered them properly and went for my bath at the pond I usually went to, a little way off from the school. Soaping the oil off my body took some time.

I was only in charge of cooking. Somebody else was in charge of serving it. The guests couldn't be asked to climb up to the roof and eat in the open, so arrangements were made downstairs where they could sit on chairs and eat comfortably. That day, when the servers started serving, much to their chagrin they found seven pieces of fish missing—vanished into thin air!

Usually, Mother and the Childhood Friend did not share a cordial relationship with both of them vying for the same position of power. It was like putting two bulls together in one enclosure. Yet interestingly, despite their vast differences be it in terms of gender, educational qualification or place of origin, they shared certain uncanny similarities. They were both Ramakrishna devotees, in the sense that both of them practised his teaching: 'One should not have shame, hatred and fear'. They were also greedy about food and would steal at any opportunity available. Even though Mother was a widow, she had not turned vegetarian as was the common tradition and treated every food item with equal love. On Sundays, mutton days, the entire portion of the liver would be reserved for her. She would spice it up with garlic and onions and distribute it among the Super, the Warden and the Sports Teacher. The rest would go down her gullet.

Their general pattern was to try and acquire as much as possible through legitimate means, after which they resorted to stealing. They had already been caught red-handed a few times before. Once I caught Mother trying to steal fish but refrained from calling her out in respect for her age. Yet everyday thievery was a different deal because even if food fell short, one could always manage through other means. On this occasion, however, there were guests involved who were eagerly waiting to try out some special Bengal fish. How could this be handled? I knew for certain that it had been stolen by one of those two, but there was no proof.

Fish was missing? Hearing this, the Super came running. Both fear and anger were apparent on his face. These were Boro Sahib's guests. What would he say? What if he punished the Super?

Or worse still, suspend him? Finding me in front, he burst out in anger. 'What happened to the fish? Seven pieces! I counted them when I bought them.' I said, 'I have no idea. I cooked whatever you brought into the kitchen after which I went to take a bath. This is what I hear on my return.'

'I don't care whether you had gone for a bath or to take a stroll in the open air. Where have you hidden the fish? Get them out, now. If these people don't get to eat fish, they will inform Boro Sahib. I will have no other option but to take your name! You will land into trouble, I tell you!'

I was accused of a theft without any fault of mine and nobody supported me. I did not know what to do. Then I remembered, when I was going for my bath, the Childhood Friend and a boy named Raju were coming upstairs to have their food. Raju was an orphan. He had lost his parents to some accident, after which he was brought here on the recommendation of a political leader despite the fact that he was neither deaf nor mute. He was quite new here and not yet learnt the ways of the shrewd. The Childhood Friend had literally taken him over as his responsibility. He would take the boy with him wherever he went. Since massages were the key to a healthy body, he would make Raju massage him and sometimes return the favour. Somehow, I felt that Raju might be able to shower some light on this case. I called him to the roof and casually asked him, 'Hey, you've eaten?'

'Yes,' he replied.

'Where did you take the fish from? This one or that?'

He pointed towards the utensil where the special fish had been stored.

'How many did you take? Seven?'

'No, no!' he denied. 'I took two, as Kaku instructed. Two per head.'

'And the other five?'

'Kaku had two and I kept three aside.'

'Where did you keep it?'

'Under Kaku's bed. He asked me to keep it there, so he could have it for dinner.'

And so, the fish was brought back from under the Childhood Friend's bed to the kitchen. I was saved from a really uncomfortable situation. I also managed to clear the allegations on my name. But did I really manage to escape? Could a weakling ever be saved by stepping on the wrong foot of the powerful? By exposing the truth and turning him into a joke, I managed to earn the wrath of the Childhood Friend. I knew that he would definitely avenge himself someday. One opportunity and I would be done for.

* * *

There is a popular saying; 'An apple doesn't fall far from the tree.' The child was bound to pick up traits from his father and his uncle, if not all, at least some of it. The Super's father, a former MLA lord, was a jotedar, a landlord. The jotedars could be compared to the urban nouveau riche. They hankered after money and did not care for ethics or morality. Alcohol, gambling, and adultery were a part of their daily lifestyle.

They shared a quality with leeches; both sucked blood to grow fat. The Naxals had been the true judge of their character, although they too had their reservations about the Naxals. Both of them shared a snake and mongoose relationship, ready to kill each other at any given time.

During the great upheaval of the seventies in the villages of Bengal, this former MLA began fearing that he would not be able to retain his empire. Along with his land, his life was also under threat. The gunpowder lying latent in the hearts of multitudes who had suffered years of oppression and hunger, was just waiting for the right moment to explode. The day it did, everything would turn to ashes. Correctly gauging the pulse of the times, the former MLA found it wise to remove himself to a safer spot while there was still some time. Where else could one find such a place but in Kolkata? Here one could live in anonymity as nobody cared to know about the other. He bought a duplex in Jadavpur and shifted here. Occasionally he would go to his village to ensure that his land was well looked after. Needless to say, this episode created an animosity in his heart against the Naxals.

His son also inherited the same animosity. Congress was the best, CPM was also all right, but the Naxals were horrible. They always resorted to violence. What sort of a party was this! The country had its own legal system in place. One could easily file their complaints with the police or take the assailants to court. Let them be the judges.

People said that Shankar Guha Neogi was a Naxal and that I was his man. I never denied this. I would often get visitors, men with bearded faces, jholas hanging from their shoulders, ones that were filled with books. They clearly bore the Naxal stamp. This made the Super, the former MLA's son, even more averse towards me.

The Super had been in the city for almost thirty years now. Yet he had not been able to mould himself according to the city's customs and mannerisms, save for a slight Babu touch. Despite this, Dasda, one of our guards, refused to treat him like a Babu. He would refer to him as 'Pecho' (Owl). He would look up to the roof and shout out, 'Oye Pecho, a student's guardian has been looking for you.'

The Super initially lived and ate at the hostel. The Warden did not live here, but had his meals here, most of the time. He mainly tasted the food. Like the Super there were ten to twelve more people who lived and ate at the hostel, including the Sports Teacher and the Childhood Friend. All the students and the twelve others washed their own plates after their meals. The rest did not. After their lunch one day, they were about to leave without washing their plates. I said, 'We don't have people to wash them. Please wash your own utensils before leaving.'

It seemed like they couldn't believe their ears. Had they heard right?

Mother came forward to speak on their behalf. 'What are you saying?'

'What?'

'The Super, the Warden and a Teacher: you expect them to wash their own plates?'
'Why, what's the harm? It is their plates after all.'
'Is it prestigious for them to do this task?'
'Of course! What has prestige got to do with washing your own plates?'
'Never! They will never do this.'
'Then let the plates stay unwashed.'
'You won't wash them?'
'I am here to cook. I know how to do that. This, I can't do. How can I do something I don't know.' I paused for a second before adding, 'You are a woman. You are supposed to know how to cook, wash utensils, clean clothes, dust the floors. Why don't you do it?'

All the actual culprits looked uncomfortable. They were at their wit's end. Mother was furious, 'You are asking me to wash utensils. You do think you're very brave, don't you?'

That I would not deny. I did have some amount of bravery. That's how I was. If this were a crime, I would not have a choice. Whenever I went to Dalli, I would observe how Shankar Guha Neogi, Dr. Saibal Jana, Dr. Punyabrata Gun would all wash their own plates. If they could, why couldn't these people who were not half as worthy as them? I would wash all the big greasy pots and pans every day. These plates were not a big deal. But if they found it disrespectful to wash somebody else's used plate, why couldn't I? My political consciousness told me that such a behaviour was the sign of a capitalist society, where one bosses around the other. Only those who were capitalists by nature made others do their own work and lazed around themselves.

It seemed like war was on and I was standing on the battlefield. It was not just a fight between me and them but also between the ruler and the ruled, the oppressor and the oppressed, the higher castes and the Dalits, the capitalists and the communists. I could not bend my knees in front of my opponents. I would have to fight on the offensive. I was an ordinary man. The best I could do was channel my personal rage to a collective one. I could call out on injustice. I did not wash their plates that day. This was my protest against authoritarianism. They too held onto their stubbornness and did not wash the plates. Finally, another female employee, known by the name of Aduri Gosai, was made to wash them.

Aduri had made her way from Bangladesh to West Bengal very recently. She was really lucky. There were so many people in West Bengal who did not have jobs. Even people from the CPM Party, ones who had been beaten up by political opponents, who had had to run away from their neighbourhood, who had served prison terms, even they did not have jobs as yet. But people like Aduri were different. As the saying goes, they came, they saw, they conquered. Be it having their names in the electoral list, or ration cards, or scheduled caste certificates, they had it all. In short, they had all the papers required to prove that a person was an Indian citizen. Some leader had procured all the papers for her with great responsibility. Now, at the age of fifty, she had even managed to get the age on her school certificate as that of thirty and found a job in a government institution as a grade four staff. She would report at eleven, make tea for all the teachers at around 1:40 pm and then spend the rest of the day in the TV room, either watching shows or sleeping. This was her main work, after which she left around 4 pm. Why such generosity towards such people? Can those who are intelligent see it for themselves?

To go back to the story, after the utensil episode the Super got so angry that he stopped eating at the hostel. Aduri might have washed it once; she wouldn't do it every day. The number of working days at the school was almost equal to the list of holidays. As soon as the holidays began, Aduri would also take her leave. So, to preserve his self-esteem, the Super started having his meals at home before coming for work. The Warden, the Sports Teacher and the others got into the practice of washing their plates.

CHAPTER 9

Arm Wrestling

*I*had been promised a helper to assist me with the cooking. I discovered soon that a woman had been hired for the job. When she finally joined, her husband tagged along. Saha informed me that she had come on Boro Sahib's recommendation. From him I heard that the woman used to work at Boro Sahib's place, a job that spanned almost thirty years. She was witness to his rise from a small fenced house in a colony as a poor CPM party member to a palatial bungalow in the rich suburbs as a leader of the CPM Party. Originally, she was the cook at his place but when his mother was down with an illness that would eventually claim her life, Aduri left no stone unturned for her care. On her deathbed, Boro Sahib's mother entreated her son, 'The poor soul has spent her entire life looking after me. Make sure she never goes without food in her old age. If you can, get her a good job.'

There was a lot of work at Boro Sahib's place. Unable to cope with the work pressure, eventually Aduri quit the job to sit at home. She, however, maintained her connection with the family and would often visit them. Many a time she would be handed over rejected old clothes, or money or extra leftover food during her visits. On one of these occasions, Boro Sahib remembered the promise made to his dying mother. He then sent her to this school, with the assurance, 'We already have a cook. You can just assist him.'

She could barely walk. She had also put on a lot of weight. Her body would tilt to one side when she walked. It was difficult for her to sit or get up. But the sharpness of her tongue was intact—once used to keep her neighbours or the women of her household in place, now rerouted to us. 'I used to work at Boro Sahib's place. One word from me and you will see what happens,' she would often threaten, with immense confidence.

In general, she was quite fearless. Her only fear was of her husband. When provoked, there was no end to his verbal abuse; most of which was directed at her character. It was quite intolerable. Even if one ignored his abuses, who would stop the taunt of the neighbours? Some of the flippant neighbourhood wives would say, 'There must be some truth to what Thakurda is saying. Otherwise, who would say such things about his own wife? Thakuma, I hope you haven't done some hanky panky by mistake?'This only made Aduri angrier and she would lash out at all of them. The angrier she got, the more the wives laughed and said, 'Rogues make the most noise. You cannot hide truth with your voice.'

Everybody possesses an inaccessible dark core, impenetrable by even a speck of light. For this woman, whose eldest grandson was old enough to sit for his Class Ten Madhyamaik examinations, it was a past secret dalliance which had inflicted her husband with chronic paranoia. He was constantly scared that somebody would run off with his wife. For the last thirty-forty years, therefore, his sole job had been to keep his wife under his watch. He accompanied her to her workplace and kept a sharp eye on her every move—the way she walked, the way she talked, the way she laughed, everything. This continued even when she went to work at Boro Sahib's place. He would never leave her alone.

When he realized that her co-worker at the school would be a male person, that is, me, his paranoia hit the roof. I stayed alone, away from my wife. Our main workplace was up on the roof, which hardly saw any footfall or light after sunset. What if I used the opportunity to take advantage of the wife? Worse still, what if his wife let me? Saha, the guard, was able to further fuel the jealousy of this half-crazed man towards me. This resulted in him following his wife every day and assuming permanent occupancy of one corner of our roof kitchen to keep a close eye on us.

How tiresome this was! We worked together. How was it possible to do so without talking to each other, without looking at each other? This resulted in a huge fight one day, almost snowballing into a fist-fight. Realizing the potential danger in how the situation was shaping up, the Teacher-in-Charge issued a notice prohibiting bringing one's husband to the workplace. I sighed in relief, hoping for some peace at last, but as it turns out, I wished too soon. The man stopped coming to the school, but he found new means to keep up his surveillance. There was a tall tree right in front of the main gate. Our roof was visible from its top. He would sometimes sit there. At other times he would keep circling around the walls of the building, hoping to catch some part of our conversations. He would squint his eyes to see if we were frolicking around. A three-battery torch was purchased. After sunset, he would use it to see if anything unwarranted was up.

The woman told me she had been married off when she was only seven. Her transition from a young girl to an old woman all happened under the strict surveillance of her husband. Who knew what took place in the journey of this long life? The seed of doubt that had been planted so long back, never disappeared; it only increased with time. The human mind, draped in impregnable mysterious layers, is difficult to understand. Some say, when all goes dark, we light a lamp. But darkness never disappears; it is only suspended for some time. The darkness that engulfs the universe has within its fold mysteries that are incomprehensible even with a lifetime of acquired knowledge. Our knowledge extends only as much as our line of vision. About the rest, who can tell? What suspicions did this septuagenarian man harbour in the dark corners of his heart about his sexagenarian wife was a mystery that had no answers. It was just there and would stay there till his death.

* * *

Hearing a lot of chaos outside, I glanced down from the roof wondering who or what could be causing so much noise in this otherwise 'speech'-less peaceful environment. Being mute did not necessarily mean that one was deaf. The same was, however, not true for somebody who was born deaf. Those who could speak, spoke only through their mouth. The others used their body and facial gestures to express themselves. A large number of the school's deaf and mute kids were trying to say something at the same time. This was the reason behind the chaos.

Watching closely, I realized that a game of arm wrestling was on. It was some holiday or the other and the school was closed. Like every other holiday, the children would all eat late today. Starting with taking a bath to washing dirty clothes to playing the game, everything was happening simultaneously. The Warden had also decided to join in this crowd of arm wrestlers. There were two boys at the school who were of very strong build. Mithun and Somnath. Both of them were dark skinned, tall and had a really good physique. They were battling against each other and their supporters were creating a lot of ruckus on either side. Everybody knew that Mithun would win and that's what happened. He next went up against the Warden. This time, the Warden won. Immediately he broke into a childish banter:

"Arre this is not a hand but a pillar, my dears! To bend this, you will need a bulldozer."

I was laughing at all this when a kid spotted me on the roof. All of them started signalling towards me, asking me to come downstairs and join the game. The Warden looked at me, his face full of nonchalance and said, "Invite whoever you want to! Nobody will be spared. These are not hands but a death trap!"

Then turning directly towards me, he roared, "Come on!"

The Warden was around ten to twelve years younger to me. He had a strong, toned body. In terms of height, he was taller. Both of us knew equally well that there was no way I could win against him—it is human nature to avoid games one might lose, and I did the same. I stayed where I was and nodded my head, indicating a firm no. This seemed to boost the Warden's self-confidence. It was a truth universally known that defeating a person who had accepted his defeat in advance was not very difficult. Moreover, the memory of his own defeat at the chess game against me was still fresh in his mind. Having lost at a mind game, he was now hoping to avenge himself by winning through his physical strength. For people, who had never lost to anybody, a small defeat was much bigger than a big win. The Warden was a living example.

He signalled to a few boys to fetch me from the roof. These boys ran up to where I was and pulled me by my hands. They wouldn't take no for an answer. I had no other choice but to acquiesce. We sat down at the game, with around fifteen children surrounding us as if it were wrestler Dara Singh battling Mukri, the actor. Almost everybody was sure of the outcome and most of them had assembled to have fun at my expense rather than for the game itself.

I forwarded my hand, knowing quite well that I would lose. In my mind, I was determined to put up a good fight at least. If he were an Alexander, I too was man enough. Arm wrestling has some techniques. The first thirty seconds usually go in testing the opponent's strength and the next thirty seconds in letting the opponent exert his strength. If the opponent is too strong, the trick is to just hold the hand in place like a pillar and stall being toppled down for as long as possible. If the opposite is true, the best way is to channel all the body's strength onto the arms and exert pressure on the opponent's arms till it bends.

Like everything else in my life, I had also played arm wrestling at one time. I knew some tricks. All I had to do was apply them well. Shockingly enough, by the end, I had defeated this braggart of a harmad who was ahead of me in all respects of life be it politically, economically or in power. Unbeknownst to me, the kids erupted in wild cheers! It felt like the time when the Indian audience had cheered for the Bangladesh cricket team when they had defeated the world champion team from Pakistan. The Warden was crestfallen. He couldn't believe he had lost. How could he? How could I? I think at that moment my arm had been possessed by the souls of those who had been humiliated by these oppressive abusers created under the long running Left malgovernance. They motivated me not to accept defeat. My loss would have been the loss of the proletariat and the win of a boastful demon. So, I had to win. I had no other way out. The Warden's loss was the loss of Runu Guha Niyogi's savagery. As a representative of the working classes, my victory was the victory of the oppressed.

CHAPTER 10

The Unlettered Are Not Fools

I want a Class Eight-leaving certificate! Some people want a house. Others want a car. Or they want women. Or jobs. So many people have so many wishes, how many of them get truly fulfilled? I wanted a job. To get that one would first require a certificate attesting that I have passed Class Eight successfully. There were indeed people, especially in the era of the Left, who could procure a death certificate for a person who was still alive. Unfortunately, I didn't know where to find them. Among the people I knew, there were many who were educated. Some were educators. They had a major flaw. They did not like being involved in anything that was incorrect. If they found somebody else doing the same, they would take to their pens and fight against it. How could I tell them to get me a Class Eight-leaving certificate! Everyone of them knew that I had not even stepped inside a classroom before.

Kabir had a doha which said, '*Neend na mane murda ka khat / Pyas na mane dhobi ka ghat / Prem na mane jaat paat / Bhukh na mane jhuta bhaat*' (Bier for bed, does sleep even care? / Dhobi Ghat's water to the thirsty seems fair / Love and caste don't pair very well / They who starve did not care if the rice was somebody else's). I was starving. Morals could not drive away the fire of hunger burning in my stomach. My guru had told me, man's biggest crime was to keep himself starving. The soul was where the gods resided. Going without food pained the soul, which in turn pained the gods.

Causing the gods pain was a grave sin and one who did so was relegated to hell forever.

Unlike many people, I could not tolerate hunger. Hunger made my body go numb and start shivering. All my happy thoughts evaporated like camphor. This was another reason why I hadn't been able to become a leader. This subcontinent has seen a man who shook the base of the British Empire just by the power of his hunger strikes. Bengalis have always been anti-Aryans, because of which they have never respected Purushottam Ram Chandra. They have added the epithet of 'Ram' to a variety of billy goats and mocked him. Then how could one expect them to respect Gandhiji, who was an ardent follower of Ram? I was a Bengali and therefore had never been inspired by his hunger strikes to become a political leader.

My fear of hunger made the acquisition of the school-leaving certificate a necessity for me. I had superhuman strength in my body, I could tirelessly work like an ass, I could bear immense amounts of heat, but these were not talents enough. These were not enough to get one a job. What I needed was a document attesting my educational qualification. I started racking my brains over this.

I knew it would be incorrect and illegal, but I did not care. I had lived through the seventies. I would live through this. If I lived, I would have ample time to atone for my sins. I had heard of professors, who acquired their jobs and drew their salaries on showing that they are PhD holders, but the actual PhD happened much later. I, too, would sit for some real exam later. Even Yudhisthira had to lie under dire circumstances. I clearly stated my need to Jogenda, an activist I knew for a long time from my Chhattisgarh days.[1] I said, 'You know a lot of people. Please help me procure this certificate.' The way he looked at me, it seemed like a devout Brahmin had been asked to taste a piece of pork. He replied, 'I won't be able to help you with this. Ask somebody else.'

Whom could I go to? Who would be that practical person for whom morals were secondary to reality? Somebody suggested, 'Go to Boro Sahib. He can do everything.' I went to his place one day. On hearing my problem, he scolded me, 'I have given you the job now I have to arrange for your certificate too? You should leave the job and go. Don't even have the capability of arranging for a simple paper! Get lost.'

Almost in tears, as I was returning back, I bumped into Aduri Gosai on the road. She had gone to the ration office after giving her attendance at the school and was now returning back. She heard everything and burst out laughing. Then she said in her thick Bangal accent, 'I have not seen such an imbecile like you. You had gone to the palace to ask for stale bread! Why would somebody go to Boro Sahib with such an insignificant task? Had you been sent to the gallows for murdering somebody that would have been a different deal! But no! You go there to ask for a simple certificate? Is this even worthy of his stature?'

I replied, 'It might be a small deal for him, but for me it is a mountainous task.'

She laughed again and said, 'You should have come to me.'

'What!!'

'What, what? Give me the money, I will get you your certificate. Five hundred rupees would go to the person making it and I would need two hundred more for the commute.'

Humans! It was not easy to understand them. Ramakrishna had rightly said that it was not easy to detect which pebbles had God in them. Who knew that the Aduri, who had made her way to India just the other day, would be so powerful! Even after going to countless people, I had completely missed Aduri. Who knew that I would find the person I was looking for right at my doorstep!

Aduri was one of the bravest people I had ever met—together with two of her sons and two daughters, she had left for India solely on the basis of her courage. It is a grave mistake to assume that the unlettered are fools. Based on her limited knowledge, she had realized that the best way to a person's heart is through his stomach, and so, she had bought a large tiffin carrier, with four separate containers, each of which she filled up carefully with cooked dishes. She would take these to a married orphaned female leader's house. Satisfied with her services, this woman asked her one day, 'Tell me what do you want?'

'I am very poor. Please give me a good job.'
'Done. Anything more?'
'Just that. If I need anything more, I will definitely come to you again.'
'What will you give me in return?'
'Whatever you want.'
'Let's say the day you stop serving me, you will lose your job.'
'Don't worry about that. I have two daughters. If a time comes when I cannot, one of them will surely come with the food.'

The same tiffin box had now accompanied Aduri to this school. One of its containers was reserved for Bordi, while the rest would be reserved for different people each day, provided they were useful to her. She seemed well settled now; her shift to India had been successful. This was the same Aduri who brought me my Class Eight-leaving certificate from a school in South Bengal. Thanks to Aduri, I learnt that I had earned a couple of new classmates. A CPM leader, out of the goodness of his heart, had distributed hundreds of such certificates for a very low price.

Finally, I submitted the certificate at the school and eagerly waited for my appointment letter—my salary was still due. Days would pass, I would get my meals but nothing else. Food was surely important but one also needed some money for one's daily expenses. My literary pursuits required me to buy writing materials; one needed money to travel; even for basic hair oil and soap—cash in hand was a basic necessity. I did try to use the mustard oil reserved for cooking as an alternative to hair oil, but was soon caught by the Hostel Super who ticked me off, saying, 'This oil is reserved for the kids. Don't you dare use it for your own personal needs.' These people did not even provide me with breakfast or evening snacks. It was strictly forbidden. I was only entitled to the lunches and dinners. The number of students had now gone up to sixty. Besides, admissions were going on, and more kids would join soon. Everybody was offered tiffin meals, except me, because I was an adult not a child, because I was an employee not a student. It was highly uncharacteristic of me to grovel for food.

I have written elsewhere that the mark of being cultured was to offer your own food to somebody else. To eat when hungry was natural, and to eat when not hungry was perversion. But the one who snatched somebody else's food, was a criminal. It was definitely a crime to eat from the food reserved for the deaf and mute children, so I had been kept away from two meals.

It does not feel nice to write about all this. People view the world through their own lenses. Nobody will want to believe that real human beings can harbour such violent mentality. In some years, these same people I'm talking about would be known around the country by the single name of harmad—the land, trees and waters of Marichjhapi would witness how low they could stoop. Lalgarh would attest how heinous they could be. These people would defile their own drinking water with their own shit—Singur and Nandigram would also know.[2] All this would, however, take some more time.

* * *

An entire year passed by with my hoping that I would get my appointment letter in hand today. Anu would send me letters from Bastar. She would write, 'What are you doing? How have you been? It is becoming more and more difficult for me to sustain the family. The prices of things have shot up, so have the educational expenses of our kids. How long can we continue on my meagre salary!'

I would reply back, 'I know you have suffered a lot. Please just be patient for some more months. I want to wait till June 10. If the situation does not change by then, I will return back to Bastar. Then we will see what to do.' Thankfully, I did not have to wait till June. My appointment letter reached me in April. This meant that I finally had a job. That, however, did not solve the problem of money as my salary was yet to come. At the end of almost one year, I finally received my entire salary at two thousand and five hundred rupees a month.

The first year's money was counted as voluntary work. From the second year's salary of thirty thousand rupees, too, around two thousand and two hundred rupees were deducted as donation money. I was not alone in this. Everybody had to go through the same ordeal. Huge chunks of their salary were deducted in exchange for their jobs. We all received a signed bill from the school's chairman as proof, to preserve as memory.

Paying a donation was a must. There was nobody in the school with enough courage to stand up to this unwritten order. That the 'voluntary' donation amount would be filled in by the chairman himself was also unanimously accepted. We knew that for the rest of our lives now, the money from our salaries would be deducted to be donated to the school's development fund or the Chief Minister's relief fund or election funds or for whatever other purposes as deemed by the chairman and everybody else would have to happily oblige.

From the eight thousand rupees that was left with me, some was deducted for my provident fund, some to pay my professional tax and some as payment for the food I had consumed at the school. For my long two years of labour, I received only two thousand rupees. Of this, I kept a grand and sent the rest to Anu as a money order.

That night, the Warden came to me with around six deaf and mute children. In my long life, I had come across all sorts of people. Thanks to my time in the jail, I also knew a lot of thieves and murderers. Never once though had I met anyone who was as cunning and cruel as the Warden. The biggest irony was that this person who knew nothing better than to harm others, was actually a member of the Communist Party. Such communists made fascists look much better—at least fascists do not hide behind false ideals!

It was already quite dark on the roof. One could not make out the traces of the crafty laughter on the Warden's face. He said, 'So, finally the wait is over. Right? Now you will get a monthly salary. It's a joyous occasion for you. Isn't it? We stay with these children. In fact, we have our jobs because of them. The kids have requested, and not unjustly so, for a nice treat from you. Hence, I brought them here. Why should I speak on their behalf? It's their demand. They should convey this to you in person.'

The kids also joined in with sounds and gestures. It seemed like they had been prepared well in advance. The Warden also did not fail to remind me, from time to time, that this was also what Boro Sahib wanted. He would get angry otherwise. That his anger was a thing of legends, only somebody who had borne the brunt of it in the past would know. Now that the Warden had taken a personal initiative in this, there was no way I could escape. Shielding him from all sides were the deaf and mute children.

A couple of days before this incident, I had come across a piece that had been written by a teacher for a magazine, probably for *Dhrubapad*. He had worked as a teacher for almost thirty years at another such school for deaf and mute children. In his long diatribe, there was not a single line that could be seen as positive. His thirty years' worth of experience had ended with him coming to the conclusion that these disabled children were akin to a different species, whose cruelty and selfishness knew no bounds. They viewed any able-bodied person as an enemy. The day that I treated the kids from my own money, I realized somewhat what this teacher might have felt.

It had been decided upon that I would treat them to parathas and egg curry. The total headcount at that time was around seventy. According to my calculations, I would need around ten kilos of flour, eighty eggs and around ten to twelve kilos of potatoes. To go with it, I would need around three kilos of dalda or hydrogenated vegetable oil, a few litres of oil and spices. I had carefully arranged for everything in advance. The egg curry was prepared on time. Only the frying of the paranthas was left. Around 8 o'clock in the evening, the first batch of roughly thirty children, sat down to dinner. My helper was preparing the paranthas while I was frying them. The children were given the charge of serving the food.

After some time had passed, I began to notice that I had been frying non-stop for quite some time now, but the first batch was still not done eating. In fact, I was getting repeated requests for more paranthas. I was seated in front of the frying pan all this while, and had no idea what was happening outside in the serving area. When the first batch finally finished eating, almost three-fourths of the flour was over. There were no eggs remaining in the egg curry, only the curry! Perforce I had to rush to the grocery shop once more.

Life is all about experiences. There was so much I had learnt from this life. I had seen the different shades of a human being. If there was one thing that I loved most in this life, it was people. Not mountains or rivers, not fields filled with golden harvest, not the songs of the birds, not the forests or its fruit-laden trees, only people and their needs. Nothing was as precious to me as people. At the same time, if there were something that had caused me the utmost pain and anger: if there had been something that I have felt was the worst creation on earth that too had been people.

I am the son of a man who had spent countless nights without food. Yet the very same man would eagerly wait for guests to share his food with on days that we managed to find something good to eat. He would be the happiest feeding others rather than eating himself. On that day, his son, me, experienced so much wastage of food by a group of greedy monsters that for the rest of his life he would shudder at the saying that god resides in guests.

The same thing was repeated with the next batch. More than they ate, they wasted. A lot of food had been smuggled out of the eating area to be hidden under their beds so that they could eat it the next day. But what was even worse and reprehensible was the fact that an immense amount of food had been flung across the roof into a rotting dead pond behind the school. When I got to see the damage under the morning sun the next day, it felt like something my heart would break. I had gone without food for days. Food was my god. It pained me to see it treated this way.

This did not end here. The kids who had hidden the food under their beds got severe food poisoning from the stale parathas and started puking and shitting since the evening. The queue in front of the bathroom kept increasing as the night progressed. Around ten to twelve of them got totally bedridden, out of whom four looked critical. No amount of electrolyte water seemed to work and finally the doctor had to be called for.

In any case, these kids were not too happy with me. I could not indulge any of their requests, even if it were for something as basic as onions, or green chillies, or a little oil. How could I? The provisions supplied to me by the Hostel Super were never enough. If I gave these away, how was I to cook? Even if I did, there was no way I could satisfy them all. The ones who would not get their demands fulfilled would only get angrier. The best way was to not give anything at all.

The Childhood Friend managed to supply more fuel to this latent anger. He suggested to the boys, 'Don't you understand why this happened? How would you? I have been in the medical line for a long time, so I know. He must have spilled some of his tobacco into the food. Boro Sahib forced him to treat you all, draining a lot of money from his own pocket. Hence, the anger.'

In the scriptures, a word is referred to as Brahma. Anybody who is deprived of words, is deprived of Brahma. These deaf and mute kids were quite unfortunate. They had neither heard any mantras being chanted, nor any poems recited, nor the note of any melodious music. Being far away from the medium of sound used to express the well-meant intentions of the heart, a thick layer had formed on the discerning ability of these kids, making it impossible for the finer senses to penetrate. Whatever managed to enter this space was gross and ugly and difficult to extract. Treading on this linear path of simple truths, the deaf and mute children ended up buying the Childhood Friend's lies. They already knew that I was a regular consumer of tobacco and carried an ample amount with me every day. Hence, they were furious at me.

Gratefulness—in the dictionary of the disabled people, this was a sickly under-valued word. The word did not manage to scratch a mark on their minds. All people, starting with their neighbours, to the society, to the state and the country, were their opponents. What the Warden or the Childhood Friend or those many others had desired came to happen. The whole atmosphere changed in an instant. I felt like I was hurled into the mouth of a volcano, with fiery flames surrounding me from all sides. There was nobody beside me, I was burning all alone. Like Ravana's pyre, this would burn eternally. The moment it would be on the verge of dying out, somebody would push more fuel into it.

China was India's neighbouring country. Both the countries were bonded by culture for thousands of years. Just two bullets had been fired at the borders by the two countries on each other for some misunderstanding and the years of friendship had crumbled down. Fifty to sixty years had passed, but the crack had not been healed. Even after working for eighteen to twenty long years at the school, long after this batch of students had already left, whenever anybody at the school suffered from a stomach upset, fingers would be pointed at me and my tobacco.

NOTES

[1] See *Interrogating My Chandal Life*, p 281. An intellectual and activist whom the author met when he was in Dalli, with the Chhattisgarh Mukhti Morcha (see also Part II).

[2] Areas of conflict between rural people and the Left Front government that eventually played a considerable role in ending their rule of thirty-four years.

CHAPTER 11

Lessons in Morality

Once, the Teacher-in-Charge found herself in a greatly embarrassing situation, although some people would tag it as an attempt to defame her. Self-respect entirely depends on an individual's attitude. What might be humiliating for some might not be so for others. The Warden would frequently say, 'Honour is not a glass bowl that can be easily broken. It is like solid iron, strong and long lasting. It can be corrupted only if the self allows itself to feel humiliated.' A valuable piece of advice from him! In this regard, I also remember a rogue once telling me, 'You won't believe me, brother, they kept hitting me with their sandals till these tore to shreds. They were still not able to humiliate me.'

Sometimes, however, the same humiliation boomerangs as great respect. I was privy to such an incident. It was from when I was still in Bastar. The district magistrate at that time was Dr. Brahmadeo Sharma. The region was known for its production of tendu leaves, used to make bidis. Dr. Sharma got into a huge debate with Arjun Singh, the then Chief Minister of Madhya Pradesh, over the increase in labour cost of these leaves. According to Singh, the contractors were fully justified in paying twelve rupees for preparing every hundred bundles of the Indian Ebony leaves. Sharma, on the other hand, was of the belief that the contractors were exploiting the goodness of the innocent Adivasi people. When their fight escalated, Sharma resigned from his post and gathered the Adivasis of the region into a collective known as the Bharat Jan Andolan. Many other organizations lent their support to this collective, especially the Chhattisgarh Mukti Morcha and the Janyuddha Goshti. With the motto of acquiring back jal-jangal-jameen—the forests, waters and lands—for the people, the movement gained momentum in all the districts of Madhya Pradesh. This eventually ended the regime of the contractors in the production of tendu leaves and led to an increase in the labour cost to fifty rupees.

Arjun Singh was a Congress leader, but none of the contractors were so. They were initially all members of the Jan Sangh, after which they shifted to BJP. They had a huge base in Jagdalpur, one of the biggest towns of Bastar. None of them were happy with Sharma, who was the person responsible for ending the lease of the contractors and for spreading awareness among the Adivasis through the Bharat Jan Andolan. One day, finding him alone, they decided to teach him a lesson. They stripped him naked, doused him in cow dung and paraded him through the town with a rope tied to his waist. These pictures made headlines in all the leading dailies of Madhya Pradesh the very next day. Sitting in Delhi, Swami Agnivesh, a leader of the Arya Samaj, read this news. He immediately sat down on a strike in front of the Parliament with four hundred of his followers, demanding the culprit's arrest. Atal Bihari Vajpayee, the topmost leader of the same party whose Madhya Pradesh unit had been so overjoyed at this incident, had to apologize on behalf of his party cadres. He promised to make sure that this would not be repeated. The incident which caused so much humiliation for Sharma, ended up earning him a Gandhi-like position of respect.

With the Teacher-in-Charge, however, the case turned out quite differently. She didn't let the humiliation get to her, as the Warden would advise. Although it was true that people made fun of her and cracked nasty jokes about her, nothing really bothered her. What bothered her was the fact that certain kids in the school, whose age had crossed the twenties, would check her out in a cringe-worthy manner these days. It was as if all their fear and respect towards her was fizzling out. This was not a good sign. Just a couple of days back, she landed a slap on a Class Seven student totally forgetting that by age he was not a 'Class Seven kid', but much older. In response, the student did something unimaginable and unheard of. He pulled her hand in reflex, and with such force that it went and hit Bordi's own cheeks. Her posh spectacles was knocked off, breaking into a thousand pieces. A similar behavioural pattern was observed in another student, much younger than the first, making it a just cause of worry.

There were many people and social service organizations, who often sent toys, food, clothes, blankets, and so on, for the disabled children of the school. In Indian culture, donating things for the needy is seen as a way of earning blessings. But many of these benefactors did not know that not all the children at the school were from poor families. Some of them came from such affluent backgrounds that even the benefactors would seem worthy of their donations. The trouble was these kids could not show off their wealth around here. They lived ordinary lives like the others and accepted these donations as their needy counterparts. Also, not everybody donated to be in Boro Sahib's good books. There were many others, including international organizations, who donated out of their own volition and quite expensive stuff at that. They left it with Bordi hoping that it would reach its due destination. Some of it did of course reach the kids, but not everything. The rest was either distributed among her favourites or carried back to her hometown to be donated. This was a usual routine for her. School teachers, in any case, did not get enough salary. Most of the extra income had to be arranged in this fashion. As for instance, the hearing-aid machine came for came to around six to seven thousand rupees each. Even if around four to five of them could be resold back each month, the money would be enough. She had recently bought a car. Its maintenance had its own cost. Save for such practices, how else would she arrange for all the extra expenses?

As every day, she was arranging her bags at the end of the day, behind shut office doors. Her office had around four to six big almirahs. All the donations received were carefully stored in these. Bordi would extract the choicest of things from these almirahs and stuff them into her bag. She lived far away and had to change her mode of transport thrice—first a bus, then the train, then a bus again. Public transport nowadays was extremely crowded. It was difficult to carry the bag if it were too heavy, so she carried the items in instalments. This reduced her load and made her travel comfortably. That day, the bag must have been really heavy. Bihari, one of her trusted guards, had to be summoned to help her with it. Nobody knows whether he was the one to betray her or the kids. While on the way out, Bordi fell behind by a bit with Bihari walking in front of her. Suddenly, a couple of kids appeared and blocked the main entrance. Disregarding Bihari's repeated warnings that the bag was not his but Bordi's, they zipped it open. The Teacher-in-Charge was highly embarrassed. She tried to explain that she was not stealing them, but who was to believe her! Thankfully, her colleagues were more understanding of her explanations.

What does it mean to steal something? It means to take someone else's things without their permission. One should specifically note the 'someone else's things' here. If the things were one's own, that did not qualify as stealing. Bordi was the main in-charge of this place. Her taking things from her own workplace might be anything else but not what the students were accusing it to be. At the most, it could be seen as her giving those things to others instead of her own school kids. Yes, there was definitely an error in choosing the recipients, but it still did not make her a thief. Making an error and stealing were not the same thing. Everybody made such errors. This was especially true for all the people working in the school. People made mistakes according to their own capacities. The person in charge of the vegetable garden would sometimes 'by mistake' send the vegetables back to his own house instead of the school kitchen. The one in charge of buying groceries, would buy rice for twelve rupees per kilo, but end up logging rupees sixteen per kilo for the same. Of course, 'by mistake'! Same was true for the person in charge of supplying the electrical goods and furniture for the school. He was sitting on a mound of such mistakes. It was difficult to find anybody who had not made any mistakes here. Then how was it Bordi's fault alone? At this, everybody finally understood what their madam was trying to tell them and started laughing.

I had to go to madam's room one day. Some serious allegations against me were doing the rounds. Apparently, all the children were falling sick because of me—because of my tobacco. At that time, there was another person in her room with her, someone who hailed from Bordi's neighbouring village. This boy was really talented. Not only was he a great singer, he also had a great smile. Painting was another of his talents. In short, he was a true artist! The Teacher-in-Charge had brought him to the school to teach the kids how to paint as his other talent was wasted on them. Two others had been hired before him, a mime teacher and a dance teacher. That the both of them had already attracted a lot of attention in the faculty circuit of the school by trying to impress each other with their individual talents, was a different matter altogether. This boy was here to teach the students a new skill, the art of painting, as most of them had already become quite adept at the other two skills. So, the boy came twice a week and returned back with Bordi on those days. Even though he referred to her as Bordi in front of people, in reality there was a distant connection, she was like a sister-in-law. When I entered, they were engrossed in an important discussion over painting brushes. The dilemma was whether to get it from Burrabazar in Kolkata or Baruipur? It was the season for litchi and Baruipur was renowned for the fruit. What if the price for buying litchis could be included within the expenses set aside for buying what was required for the painting classes? It would be like killing two birds with one stone. It was at this very inopportune moment that I interrupted their discussion with, 'Bordi, may I please come in?'

'Come in,' Bordi shifted her gaze to me and said. 'I hear you had once served a term in jail in the name of revolution. How can a person who has no compassion for people be a revolutionary?'

I answered back, 'Do you believe that I could add tobacco in the children's food?'

'I am not saying you did it intentionally. It might have also been a mistake. It's not a big deal in general. The bigger thing is in having compassion for people. Anything served by a person with a compassionate heart, even if it might be bitter, will taste sweet. Whatever has happened in the past let it remain in the past. You were working without any salary and I did not have the place to say anything. But now if I see any neglect in your work, I will be forced to take a step. I will straightaway suspend you.'

Hearing these maxims coming out of her mouth, I looked up at the ceiling in fear that it might collapse on us out of the weight of the absurdity in this situation. I remembered an accident, when an airplane crashed on the ground despite the skies being clear and the machinery in robust health. Later, when the black box was secured from the site of the crash, a conversation between two co-passengers—a moneylender and a butcher—surfaced. They had been discussing things like humanity, non-violence and having compassion for living beings. The peaceful weather must have got so shocked by their conversation that it made the airplane to crash with all its passengers! Bordi's words made me fear a similar backlash from nature. What if an earthquake ensued at this moment?

* * *

On receiving the one thousand rupees I had sent Anu, she decided to take a much-needed break from her year-long exile to visit me. She arrived at my place in Kolkata with a month's leave from her ICDS job. Kenaram, the person who personally guided her to my workplace, didn't do it as a favour. The entire travel fare had already been extracted from me. His work was to get Anu to my school, put her under my charge and then leave. He owned a garments shop in Kapsi and had plans to buy some merchandise at wholesale price from Burrabazar before heading back in the night train. So, he declined my invitation to stay on for the night. To be honest, I would have landed in trouble had he agreed to stay back and with him gone, the arrangement seemed perfect.

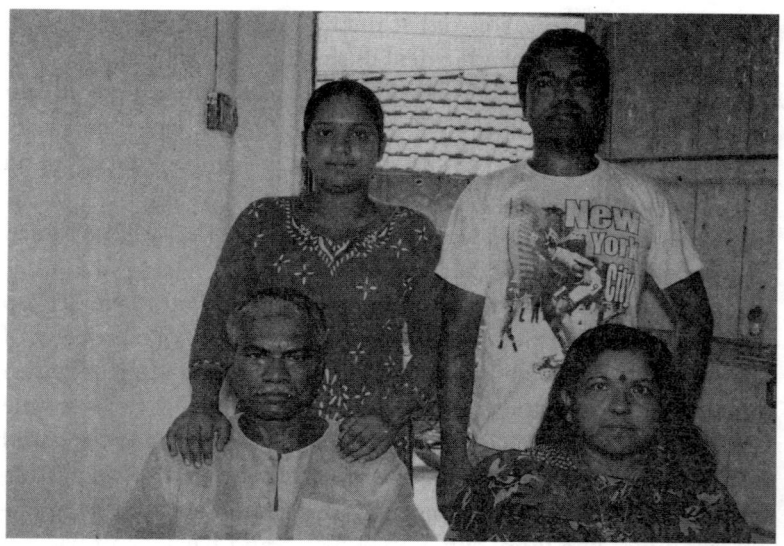

Manoranjan Byapari with wife, Anu, daughter, Mahasweta and son, Manik.

It was around 10 am when Anu finally reached the school entrance. On being informed by somebody, I quickly went down to receive her. After bidding farewell to Kenaram, I was just about to take Anu inside when Das obstructed my way. This was the same person who read at least four magazines a day. Usually, education turned a person into a scholar. Surely, it was unlikely for a person of such scholarly nature to behave like a fool, since they usually got into the habit of putting a lot of thought behind each action.

If a stranger came up to the door and said 'I am thirsty, give me a glass of water', the fool would immediately hand out a glass. The scholar would first gauge if the person was really thirsty or pretending to be thirsty for some ulterior motive. Did he want to use the opportunity to peep around and make a mental note of the residents of the house and what possessions they had? Why would he specifically come up to *their* door, when there were so many other houses to go to? Was there any conspiracy behind this? Would an act of kindness today lead the person to make it into a regular habit? Or worse still, would the act of kindness make the person more confident to request for bigger favours? A person who could use that fraction of time to mull over all these possibilities and reach a conclusion was a true scholar. Our guard Das was a person like that.

He said, 'Manoranjanda, don't mind my saying but since you still don't know all the rules around here, I thought of informing you in advance. Bordi has given me strict orders not to let any outsider to enter the school premises without proper permission. I hope you haven't forgotten the storm your assistant's husband had brewed up. If I let your wife enter the school now and later Bordi asks me on whose permission I have done so, I would have nothing to say in my defence. So, I would say, let her and the kids wait here. Be it Bordi or the Super, let any one of them give the green signal and you may do whatever you want. In any case, they are almost about to reach any time now. If, however, you are insistent on taking them in now, the entire responsibility will be on you. If Bordi asks something, I will straightaway say I had forewarned you. Now you decide what you want to do. That's all I had to say.'

They, Anu and our two kids, had spent an entire day travelling, in buses, rickshaws, and trains to traverse these long miles. They were exhausted and needed a bath and to get some sleep. But, I had no choice except to keep them waiting. Finally, only after Bordi came and gave her permission was I able to ask them in.

She said, 'We don't have permission to let outsiders stay. But they have come from far away. Let them stay the night. But from tomorrow, please make some alternative arrangements.' I would have done that even had she not told me. My mother-in-law now stayed in a rented place in Taldi where I was planning to take them. I took them upstairs and made seating arrangements for them on the stairway to the roof. The roof had a water supply and they could easily have a wash there. A request to the Hostel Super made it possible to arrange for their food and other basic necessities.

The children had classes in the afternoon. Even when they did not have any class, they were not allowed to come to the roof. The orders were relaxed only during lunch and dinner hours.

In case of good weather, they also had the provision of having their lunches on the stairs and their dinners on the roof. Until the kitchen and dining space downstairs were ready— it would take one or two more years still—this was the temporary arrangement. As a general rule, after dinner, the gate of the children's hostel was locked, leaving the roof entirely to me. I stayed on the roof. My helper came in the morning, finished her chores and left in the afternoon. She would be back in the evening and finally leave by around ten or ten-thirty in the night. I generally found time to write in the afternoons or in the night, sometimes on these stairs and sometimes on the roof itself.

Once these elementary problems were solved, I finally found the time to properly look at my wife and children. After two long years of absence, I was like a stranger to my own kids. They had always found their mother near them and only knew her well. So, they preferred to stay close to her instead of coming to me. They were unused to a crowd, so many buildings and vehicles, having grown up among Bastar's hills and forests. The crowd and the noise here partly scared them and partly overwhelmed them.

The afternoon passed in great happiness. My heart was overjoyed to find my family with me. I gladly finished my nightly duties of feeding the students, after which they all left for their dorm. My helper left for the day. We, too, quickly finished our dinner and got ready for bed.When Anu asked me about the sleeping arrangements, I pointed to the roof and said, 'This is such a huge place. We can sleep anywhere we want.' I was soon to realize that I had spoken too soon, having completely forgotten that there was an extremely perverted man around who could cross all limits of decency simply to show off his power. Whether he had kept his trump card saved for the last minute or whether it came to him late, I couldn't say. He initially did not say anything. He even started walking down the stairs, when he retraced his steps and dropped the bomb.

There would soon be complete silence around the school. Not just the school, the entire universe would slip into deep slumber and silence would reign. The moon was up. The full moon was due tomorrow or the day after, so it already looked quite full. The surrounding fields and rocks of this suburban place were flooded in its bright silver shine. A low breeze was flowing from the south. After a full day's work under the sun, this felt blissful. All of it put together had created an environment that was making the heart flutter. After being separated from his wife for so long, such weather was bound to drive a man crazy with passion. The veins of his body would have electric currents flowing through them. It would be no different for me or Anu. We had been away from each other for almost two years. Given this situation, her mind too, like mine, must have been weaving rainbow-coloured dreams in anticipation of our imminent togetherness.

The Warden must have discovered the possibility of his next source of entertainment in puncturing this dream. So, he rushed back to the roof. He knew that this couple had fasted for long and were now longing for each other. What fun it would be to separate them and put them in two different beds! They would spend a restless night. Their starving stomachs burning with the hunger of a lifetime, would be disappointed to find food within their reach but inaccessible. Their selves would burn, turning them insomniacs. What fun that would be!

I was just making my way from the kitchen to one corner of the roof, where Anu was sleeping with our kids. The Warden called me, 'Listen, I want to have a word with you.'

'Yes, tell me?'

'Where will your wife sleep?'

'She has already made her bed over there. It's just a matter of one night. No worries!'

'No, don't let her sleep here. You stay here like every day. Send your wife to a hostel room. There are so many beds empty. Let her sleep on one of them.' His voice sounded soft but the sharpness of his orders was unmistakable. His eyes were glowing even in the darkness, in whose depths one could detect the serpentine hiss. I knew exactly what was going on behind those eyes, which is why my whole body started fuming in rage.

His brothers were all political leaders. He drew his power from their position. But that did not give him the right to show off his power all the time. He might have been my boss, but did he really have the right of not letting me stay with my wife and two children? He did; not because he was my superior but because he was Boro Sahib's favourite.

I still tried my best to fight back. 'Why? Why will my wife go downstairs?' I said. 'What would be the problem if she stays here?'

In 1977, when the Left government came to power, he must have still been in his knickers. His brothers had established their position in the area around that time. He grew up seeing how people treated his brothers obsequiously. They would get beaten by them in silence, not say a word back when verbally abused. He never did get the chance to realize that these other people also needed to be treated with respect and honour. Having bullied them for ages, he had by now forgotten what was appropriate and what not.

In response to my question, he now said, 'Some of the boys in the hostel are quite old. They can't speak, but they understand everything. They are also aware of everything. If you and your wife spend the night on the roof, they will very well understand what it means. This might have adverse effects on their character.'

I realized that I was burning with rage. Soon I would have no control over it. I replied, 'They are old enough. They know everything and understand everything. They have their mothers and fathers, brothers and sisters. They know very well how their siblings were born, how they were born. Doesn't that ruin their character? But if I stay with my wife on the roof, the children sleeping downstairs will have their characters spoilt?'

The Warden was stupefied for a moment. He had not come here to listen to counter arguments. His sole intention had been to disturb my mental peace and gain his own succour from that. He said, 'I don't want any excuses. Just follow my orders. This is a hostel, not a hotel. That which is allowed in a hotel, will not be allowed here. Send your wife downstairs.'

Anu was extremely embarrassed. I was not able to see her face, but it was evident that the entire episode was making her uncomfortable. The subject matter was bordering on the indecent. Naturally, a woman who was not so modern in her approach, having been brought up in the simple traditions of the Indian villages, would find it unbearable and unwelcome. She wanted me to draw an end to the conversation. We had spent so many nights apart, what was one more night? I, too, had no intention of prolonging the debate. There was no sense in doing that. This man who was standing here and talking to me was not alone but backed by his political and financial affluence in society. Everything—his education, his culture, his blood group, his genealogy—everything was fuelled by this privilege. The language that was needed to argue back with him was not something I possessed.

Finding no other way, I settled Anu in one of the hostel beds for the night. I knew that making a woman sleep among thirty to forty boys so well advanced in age was improper. Her sari might get displaced in her sleep. This might titillate the boys. She might be improperly touched. But I was forced to submit to such an unjust demand. I felt the stirrings of a fire burning in my heart. It was the fire of humiliation. This fire, which incessantly burnt in the heart of those who are eternally oppressed, would turn into a forest fire any of these days. Ones blinded by their own arrogance did not realize this.

Standing alone under the starlit night that day I was reminded of my wise master. He had said, 'Practice caution everywhere. Be it in this country or abroad, the weak have been oppressed by the high and mighty, the poor by the rich and the common man by those in power. This has happened for generations and will never end.' Our scriptures say that each time the earth gets overpowered by sin and the devout becomes a victim of the heretic, the gods descend in a new avatar to drive off the troublesome elements and restore order and peace. They have been forced to come back again and again, because even the gods don't have the power to eternally eradicate the sinners. Some of their remnants always stay back, lying dormant like seeds to blossom into a plant when the appropriate time comes. As they grow, they make the world unliveable again.

Parshuram had cleansed the earth of the kshatriyas not once but twenty-one times. Why twenty-one? Because of this very reason. The dinosaurs would not resurface because their seeds were extinct, but the same was not true for the oppressors. Thus, to live, man has to be able to pick up the axe time and again. They will have to take up the role of Parshuram, of the gods. This struggle is ongoing and will continue.

I am an extremely ordinary man. I have heard that this subcontinent was once under the rule of the British, who were known for torturing people. People came together and finally drove them out. The ones who assumed their place also picked up the same traits with time. I have been a witness to those dark days in the decade of the seventies when people rose in revolt against them and helped establish a new rule. As soon as these new rulers came to power, they started their journey through the cruel murders and rapes at Marichjhapi. Their journey would end only after their autocratic chariot had trampled over the bodies of thousands of starving protestors and reached Netai.[1] Once again, it would be the people stopping them.

Once again, somebody new would replace them. Nobody would have any prior inkling who or how these new rulers would be. Nobody would be able to tell for sure if man would finally be able to give up his weapon or not. Only time would tell. That time was far ahead in the future while I stood helpless under the open sky that midnight. Moreover, I did not have a sword in my hand but just a flimsy pen.

NOTE

[1] On 7 January 2011 there was indiscriminate firing allegedly from a CPI (M activist's house that killed 9 people in Netai village. CBI filed charge sheets against 20 people in May 2014, among whom 12 arrested were linked to CPI(M).

CHAPTER 12

Embattling Superiors

*P*alda was one of our guards. He had been afflicted with polio at a very young age. The disease had left one side of his body totally numb. Even though he did not need the wheelchair, he walked with much difficulty. His body was bent on one side and he had to drag himself forward with a lot of effort. He was quiet and restrained—an extremely good person. Nobody had any trouble with him. He came to do his duty and went straight back home. But the oppressive Warden did not spare even him. Instead of showing him compassion, the Warden would seize every opportunity to torment him. In the absence of opportunities, he created new ones. The Warden would come for his daily attendance on a bicycle. The road he came by was flanked on both sides with paan, bidi and cigarette shops. Had he so desired, he could have easily picked up some on his way. Instead, he would reach the school gate and then order someone to fetch him some Flakes.

He was a frequent smoker, but he would never buy an entire packet at one go. The moment he started craving for a smoke, he would send somebody to fetch him cigarettes. He would justify that having more would lead to smoking more. During the two hours he spent at the school, he needed somebody to run and help him with his addiction at least four times in between. I too had fallen a victim to this, multiple times. Just because he refused to stop his bicycle for two minutes and pick up his own cigarettes on the way,

I would have to climb down three flights of stairs, walk half a mile to the shop, and then climb up the steep stairs again. My pain did not bother him as much as alighting from his bicycle did.

There was a time when people would feel each other's pain, but such compassion seemed to be dead now. West Bengal was full of a bunch of inhuman people romping all over the place. In the passage of time, there would come periods which would go down in history as the dark ages, and West Bengal was currently under such an age of anarchy. Crushed under the weight of miscreants who had appropriated power, there were people shouting for help. Who would save whom? Fear had robbed every one of their power of speech.

It was early on in the year, around eight in the night. The sky had been overcast all day, and had broken into a light shower, accompanied by cold winds. The entire area had literally curled up in the biting cold. A single icy raindrop on the body felt like it would pierce through the pores of the skin and bite the bones. Fingers seemed to be bending. In the midst of such weather, the Warden made his entrance. As usual, he hunted around in his pocket and fished out some change. Hurling expletives at the cold air, he then turned to Palda and said, 'Palda, get me a Flake. If I don't get a puff, this weather will get to me.' Saying so, he extended the change to him.

The Warden had his raincoat on, having left home in the rain. Palda, on the other hand, had come when the skies were clear. He had not brought any umbrella or raincoat with him. His eyes seemed to fill with dread at the prospect of venturing out in this weather without any protection, especially with his polio-ridden body that had to be dragged like a snail's. It was clear from his looks that he was praying to the higher powers for some compassion. But 'compassion' was not a word present in the Warden's vocabulary. Even a butcher might let a goat kid off, but for the Warden it was unimaginable. Like a crab which would exert more pressure on its prey on realizing its attempt to escape, the Warden got more titillated when anybody said no to him—there was no way he would let him go until he had his way, even if his victim died in the process.

It was the same with Palda who could not say no to him. In that extreme cold and rain, he started dragging himself to the nearby cigarette shop. He still had two hours to go before his shift ended and he would have to stay in his damp clothes till almost 10 pm. The Warden was well aware of this. Perhaps this was why he was unable to hide the demonic happiness reflecting on his face. Leaning against the gate he looked on in relish as Palda dragged himself in the rain.

Watching him struggle, I felt like it was not Palda but my own self which was being crushed. Something in my heart rumbled, an inexplicable rage woke up in my heart. I remembered a dialogue from the Amitabh Bacchan starrer *Deewar*, 'Next week, somebody else will say no!' The scene depicts Vijay, a worker who has recently joined a factory, observing as workers line up to pick up their salary where a part of their wages is deducted as payment to be handed over to the gang leader of the area. An old worker expresses his reluctance to pay the money that day, citing some familial issues. He pleads for mercy. The gang instead beats him black and blue. Everybody else watches, but nobody comes to help.

This is how society operated. Even though the unjust were few in number, their tyranny was widespread. That was mainly because nobody protested. I didn't care for anyone, but decided that I would protest. The Warden seemed to me like an evil reincarnated. I promised myself that next time there would be somebody to say no.

* * *

Boro Sahib usually came in the evenings. The moment he landed here, a huge chaos would ensue. Everybody would line up against each other to vie for his attention. He would hardly have the chance to open his mouth as these people literally scrambled over each other to serve him. The Warden too might have been inspired by such fervour. In fact, there were many people who loved sucking up to those in power. This ensured that the Warden also got his own share of devotees. When he reached the school, some people would be on high alert—their sole desire was to please him. As soon as he entered the gate, somebody would inevitably call out to me urgently, 'Ranjanda, get some tea ready. Dada has come.' As if, a minute's delay in serving tea would cost the Warden his life.

Once, after drinking his tea, he started fiddling around in his pocket. Handing me some change, he ordered, 'Hurry and get me a Flake.' I stayed rooted to my place like Ghatotkacha,[1] unlike other days when I would take the money and rush out to carry his orders. I knew what was in store for me, but I was determined to not budge.

I replied, 'I won't be able to go now.'

'What do you mean you can't go?'

'The rice is almost done. If I don't tend to it now, it will be overdone.'

'How much time does it take to fetch a cigarette? You will be back in no time. Now hurry and get me my cigarette before I lose my cool.'

I replied, 'If you are so addicted why didn't you get one on your way here? There are so many shops on both sides of the road.'

The Warden stared at my face in disbelief. I continued, 'I can understand getting you cigarettes now and then. Who has so much time to leave their work and serve you every day? If somebody else wants to go, let him. I will not. Don't ever ask me for this favour.'

'Don't you work under me?'

'I do.'

'Then you are bound to do as I want.'

'Not at all. The demands have to be justified. This is your personal matter, nothing to do with the school. You cannot force me to do this. That is illegal.'

The Warden seemed to have seen a ghost. His flatterers also looked shocked. There comes a time in everybody's life, when people are forced to turn the course of their actions, to counter evil. Even though it brings more losses than gains, at least it keeps one's self-respect intact. One feels proud of oneself. I felt the same. It was a small blow to his ego, but a blow nonetheless. That was enough.

* * *

Another battle raged between me and the Childhood Friend. After the case of fish theft, he would be perennially angry with me and nitpick on every small or big thing to get back at me. On that particular day, however, the fault was completely mine. He had come to the roof for his bath. During winters, he would hardly take a bath. On the rare days that he would, he would get some water pre-heated. But it was summer and as far as he was concerned, there was no problem in taking a bath now and for as many times as needed.

The tap which he used to take a bath whenever he so desired was used to wash the kitchen utensils. It was his childhood friend's school. There was hardly anybody bold enough to stop him. The one time that the Teacher-in-Charge had showed displeasure at the reckless way he used the phone, he had launched into such a tirade that she had no other way left but to flee from his sight.

There were some poor but extremely meritorious boys from the village who lived in the same room as him. The parents of these boys did not have enough means to educate their children. They had approached Boro Sahib for help, pleading with him to let them stay and eat at the hostel. All of them went to different colleges in Kolkata. Before their exams they would sometimes stay up late in the night for preparation's sake. On those very nights, the Childhood Friend would suddenly feel like listening to Rabindrasangeet in Debabrata Biswas' voice. He had a recorder and a few cassettes with him. He would put the song on full volume without caring for the others. The boys would be left with only two choices. To put an end to their studies and appreciate the music or to take their books with them and leave the room. They could have put in a complaint. But to whom? The Teacher-in-Charge? After the phone incident, she herself had to run to Boro Sahib with her own complaints.

The Childhood Friend relished his bath that day, after which he promptly went downstairs leaving his towel, dirty clothes and underwear in the wash basin under the tap. His order was, 'Wash them properly and spread them out to dry on the roof. Once it dries, bring it to my room.'

I heard his orders but completely forgot about them, as a result, his clothes remained soaked in the basin, unwashed. In the evening, not finding his towel, he came up to the roof again to check for himself.

'Manoranjan,' he said.

'Yes?'

'Where are my clothes and towel?'

'Exactly where you had left them.'

'Why didn't you wash them?'

'I feel disgusted washing somebody else's used underwear.'

'Disgusted?' the man was both surprised and furious. His eyes started burning like fire. He said very seriously, 'I am a Brahmin from the Chakraborty clan.'

'I know.'

'What do you know?'

'That you are a Brahmin from the Chakraborty clan. So what? Your underwear is not the same. I will not wash it. I am a cook, washing clothes is not part of my duties.'

Naturally enough, we got into a huge altercation over this. The Childhood Friend ended it with his final blow, 'I will convey this to Kestho (Boro Sahib's nick name). You have put on a lot of airs. You don't know what to say to whom. What is wrong with you!'

The next incident happened with the Teacher-in-Charge. It was around 2.30 pm and I was resting on the stairs after my lunch—resting in the sense of devoting some time to my own reading and writing. I had started writing with a renewed vigour again, contributing a story to the magazine *Adal Badal* almost every month. At the same time, my novel *Jibon Chandal* was being serialised in the weekly subscription of *Bahujan Nayak*. I was also writing for many new magazines—in short, it was a very productive time in terms of my literary output.

A well-known TV soap opera director had his palatial home nearby. He would often land up at the school for shoots with his entire crew. Boro Sahib had already given his permission for this. On those days, the entire school would turn into a studio. Royda, a clerk, got acquainted with him during one of these shoots. One day, he started pestering him to give him a role in his production.

'Have you acted before?' the director wanted to know.
'Not at all. But I have watched a lot of theatre and cinema. Give me a chance, I will not disappoint you.'
The director was unable to turn down his request. He offered a part to him that very day, the role of a doctor. The make-up artist took almost two-and-a-half hours to make him look like one, after which Royda waited for one more hour in his costume. Finally, the time came for his shot. He reached the movie set in high spirits. A man was lying flat on the ground. Royda checked his pulse, then proclaimed, 'He is dead'. Immediately the director went 'Cut!' This was his first and last acting venture. This episode earned him a new name of Dr. Bidhan Chandra Roy, a former Chief Minister who had been a famous physician. People would call him 'Dr. Roy' in short.

The fact that I had a separate literary life was not to everyone's liking. Dr. Roy was one of them. He would make the unforgettable comment comparing my ambition to a hunchback wanting to lie down straight on his back—a statement that would be later immortalized by journalist Riju Basu in an article for *Anandabazar Patrika*. Dr. Roy felt that instead of wasting my time on these academic pursuits, if I devoted more time to the school and to serving him or the Teacher-in-Charge, that would be more worthwhile. This included, serving them tea at frequent intervals, refilling their bottles with drinking water and delivering it to their respective rooms, or fetching them paan and cigarettes from the shop outside. None of the other Group IV staff said no to these, except me. Hence the anger! This anger would be vented out in various ways, through mockery or ridicule. He didn't know that if there were a will, even the hunchback could sleep straight on his back. I belonged to that category. There were many respected people who were impressed with my life's struggles and writing. This had also harmed me by inflating my self-esteem. I had started considering myself as a creator, an artist, a representative of the eternally-oppressed Dalits. The creator and his creation had merged in my subconscious as one.

That afternoon on the stairs, I was trying to write a story when Dr. Roy came looking for me. Seeing what I was doing, he gave a sarcastic smile and then asked, 'What is happening?'

I said, 'I am writing a story.'

Dr. Roy lashed at me with his sharp tongue, 'How will this help? You will be an author? A writer?'

'If that happens, would you have any objection?'

With a crooked smile, Dr. Roy said, 'Your back breaks just to write your name and you want to be a writer! Go and make some tea. Bordi's guests have come. Serve them some water first. All this writing can happen later.'

I had not noticed that another person had been standing behind him all this while and having fun at my expense. My body started burning up in rage. I said, 'Please go and inform Bordi that I won't be able to make tea now. This is my break time. My morning shift is over. When my evening shift begins, I will happily oblige.'

What I said and the way I said it was comparable to sedition. Dr. Roy immediately took to the stairs to report against me. Why would he let this golden opportunity pass? I knew very well that this matter would not be taken lightly. Why would Bordi also let this pass? Especially when she could use it to show off her power in front of her relatives.

I heard her roar from the stairs itself, 'Somebody ask him to report to me.'

Bihari, our guard, came to call me. He was among Bordi's loyal entourage, her source for every campus gossip. At present, Bihari was a permanent resident on campus. He would be shifting out in some days. He knew that the best way to keep one's job was to stay in the boss' good books. Needless to say, I had to report to the Teacher-in-Charge. Her room was full of people; her daughter, her son-in-law, and another man who was perhaps her younger brother. Muttering furiously, she asked, 'Royda asked you to make tea and you refused. Is that right?

I answered in the affirmative without an iota of tremor in my voice. I did what a representative of the working class would do had it been within the world of one of my own stories. The way Bordi, like one of the overlords, had called me forth to show off her positional power in front of her people, I too, was eager to show her that I was a knowledgeable and brave representative of my class of people. I said, 'From the break of dawn to about two in the afternoon I toil in front of the oven for almost six to seven hours. Come evening, this process is repeated till late in the night. I just get a few hours in the afternoon for my own work. If you take that too from me, how am I supposed to survive?'

Bordi was angry in any case. Hearing my explanation, she got even more enraged. She said, 'Don't give me these pointless excuses. It will not help. Cooks are supposed to be working for twenty-four hours. You knew this when you joined the job. You are expected to work as you are told.'

'Who has fed this information to you that cooking is a twenty-four-hour job? Which book? Please show me.'

'I am telling you.'

'You are incorrect. There is no law in India that sanctions work time beyond eight hours.'

'Your job falls under the emergency category. The rules of other positions will not work in your case.'

'Healthcare facilities, fire service, police, army, these are all emergency departments. They are available for twenty-four hours. But remember this; their departments might be under the emergency category but this does not extend to the staff. All the staff has eight-hour long shifts. If due to some urgent matter someone has to stay for more than eight hours, he is paid an overtime amount for his additional services. For me, the work hours, in any case, are five to six hours more—I cannot devote any more time.'

'You will have to. If you want to stay here that is. Otherwise, you are free to leave this job.'

'I will. You do not have to remind me time and again. If I can't continue, I will have to leave it. But till then don't assume that you can monkey me around.'

Bordi was rendered speechless. She was not being able to decide what to say next.

Using this opportunity, I continued, 'I think you don't remember, but many years ago in the city of Chicago in the country known as the United States, a group of workers fought for the right to work for only eight hours. To disband the movement, police fired guns. A lot of workers lost their lives. This did not deter the rest of them. They joined the movement with further gusto, flying the blood-soaked clothes of their martyred comrades as flags. A heap of losses later, they also managed to secure victory. Since then, the eight-hour working day has become a worldwide norm.'

Bordi had a cook at her own place. Many people within her circuit also had cooks. All of them were timid by nature, ones who hardly made any noise. For her this was a new kind of experience. A cook was teaching her politics, that too world politics.

Meanwhile, I continued my tirade, 'Later, when the Communist Party or the party dedicated to the working classes was formed, red was chosen as the colour of its flag in memory of the blood-soaked clothes of those workers who lost their lives to the cause. Boro Sahib was the leader of one such party in West Bengal, whose colour was red. He is the founder of this schoolAs the head of such a school you are telling me that I have a twenty-four-hour shift? This is very surprising.'

I paused for breath, and then said, 'This is a residential school. According to the government orders, you, me, the Hostel Super, the guards, the sweeper, the Warden, all six of us—are supposed to be here for twenty-four hours. Just like the police or army are supposed to hold posts at their respective barracks, to be available whenever required. But their shift is not supposed to exceed the eight-hour time slot. You are exempted from this. By virtue of the Managing Committee's permission, you can stay elsewhere, but even so you need to be within 3-kms radius of the school.'

I smiled. 'Bordi, but you travel from Jaynagar. It is so far off. But nobody says anything to you. You have been given full freedom in this matter.'

Bordi finally lost her patience and retorted back, 'Where did you hear all this? Who said so?'

'Books. Books say so. Nobody has told you, but I know because I read books. I not only read, but I also write them. So, I have to read.'

Nobody here really believed that I could write. They felt that the writer Manoranjan was some other person or maybe I was plagiarizing somebody else's works. It was, indeed, difficult for people to believe. I had forged a false academic certificate, my handwriting looked like a bird's footprint, and my spellings were haywire. If I were a writer then the bat was a bird. The fair face of the Teacher-in-Charge turned red at being insulted in front of her family members. Not being able to argue back, she launched that missile on me which was fatal for people like us.

'I will have to take this up with Boro Sahib. He has ordered that nobody should clock their time while working in this school.'

I replied, 'Of course! You should definitely inform him. It is his school. His word will be the last word. We all are ultimately his slaves, despite the disparity in our positions and salaries. Nobody is above him. He has also said that everybody should do everything. Does everybody do that? He is a big leader, but does not think twice about manual labour. His employees, on the other hand, can't even pour themselves a glass of water. Apparently, it is disrespectful for them. Please tell him whatever you want. I will also share my own version of the story.'

Having said whatever I had to, I was just about to put my foot on the first step of the stairs to climb back to the roof when Dasda came running. 'I remember you telling me that you do not like keeping a debt,' he said. 'That you would pay back so soon was completely unexpected.'

According to materialist philosophy, this was probably how people discovered conflict in unity, and unity in conflict. Dasda had been censured by Bordi once. He had not been able to give a befitting response. Finding a fellow Group IV staff giving it back to her had made him happy. All past battles were forgotten and I no longer remained an enemy. I became his comrade. Yet he couldn't hold his smile for long. He said, 'But I still think you shouldn't have spoken to Bordi that way. After all she is our superior. Her post demands that respect.'

I replied, 'Do you know the mouse story?'

'I know, I know,' he replied. 'Being chased by a cat, a mouse went and hid in a hermit's lap. The hermit turned the mouse into a cat. When the mouse-cat was chased by a dog, the hermit turned it into a dog. In this manner, the hermit turned it into a tiger one day only to be devoured by it. That story, right?'

I said, 'Yes, but mine is slightly different—the hermit in my story had turned a bunch of mice into different animals—some, into cats, while others were turned into tigers, and so on. Still, in reality, they were all mice underneath. They found their new identities solely because of the hermit. For outsiders, the reality might be different but why us? We know that it is their having money that makes them superior to us. Just by the power of money! If I had the ability to spend lakhs of money, I would also have bought myself an MA certificate. Who knows if I would have been sitting on her chair then?'

Dasda was shocked. He said, 'Don't say such things. You will land into trouble.'

NOTE

[1] Ghatotkacha in the epic *Mahabharata*, was the son of one of the Pandavas, Bhima, and a rakshaha Hidimba, through whom he inherited special magical powers, He fought on the side of the Pandavas against their cousins, the Kauravas. He was killed by Karna, the supreme fighter of the Kauravas (and the unacknowledged eldest brother of the Pandavas).

CHAPTER 13

Mother Killer

One day, Mother Killer—as a way of protecting her caste from food touched by me—was preparing her rice on the smaller stove and re-boiling the dal and fish curry on the other one. Her relationship with me at that time was like the one between the clouds and the sun. On some days it felt like the sky was overcast with clouds, while on others it appeared bright and sunny.

I felt compelled to ask her, 'Do you want to listen to a story? It bears close similarities with your story.'

Looking at me from the top of her spectacles, she answered, 'Tell me. Let me see what similarities you are talking about?'

'A man spent twelve years in a cave in the Himalayas immersed in deep meditation.'

'When have I done so?'

'Listen to the whole story first. Meditation bestowed him with powers that were not available to ordinary people. To test his powers, he landed in the plains one day.'

'Then?'

'He called out the people from a village and said, 'I have now gained yogic powers with which I can make the impossible possible. Do you want proof? By my powers, I can make fire from straw.' A fool asked him, 'What else can you do? Can you do something bigger than this?' The yogi was furious. 'Do you think making fire from dry grass just with the power of the mind is a small thing? Can anybody else do this?' The fool continued in his foolish tone, 'You wasted twelve years of your life on this insignificant thing? Nobody would even want to do this.' 'What do you mean?' the yogi asked. 'A box of matches can be purchased for a paisa. It can last for a month. You wasted twelve years just to save a penny? There is no other bigger fool than you."

Mother was rendered speechless by my tale. She said, 'You said that this story has resonances with my life. Where is that similarity?'

'There is,' I said. 'The house in which you spent your entire life is a well-known one in West Bengal with many influential people frequenting it. Wasn't it so?'

'That's where I met Jyoti Basu. At the time, he was the opposition leader at Vidhan Sabha and a regular at the house. I have served him tea umpteen numbers of times. Jyoti Basu, Harekrishna Konar, Promode Dasgupta, all of them have tasted cups of tea brewed by these very hands.'

I said, 'If you had been able to learn anything from them, you would have been a female leader by now. But you did not learn anything! You spent your entire life toiling in the kitchen and guarding the larder!'

'This place where our school is located is also the home to a political leader: Bappa, the Thief. His epithet is an inheritance from the time before he joined the party. He also has a history of being thrashed by the CPM goons a number of times. Eventually, one of the leaders employed him for dusting, preparing tea and other such odd tasks for a petty salary. During his time there, he became a lackey in Buddhadeb Bhattacharjee's office. Finally, he moved to this place when it started developing and rose to the rank of a leader himself. He seized a two-storey building from Amulya Majhi, a hotel owner in this area, and became its new owner. Presently, he is living a comfortable life. Nobody calls him Bappa the Thief anymore. He is now known as Comrade Bappa. Finally, people have begun to realize the true meaning of the word "Comrade"!'

My words seemed to enrage Mother. She replied, 'Examples are better than advice. Instead of listing out what others have done or not, why don't you try and do something yourself?'

I said, 'That's exactly what I am doing.'
'And? What feat have you achieved?'
'You will discover that for yourself one day. When a flower blooms, no one can hide its scent.'
'All that I can smell is a rotting rat.'
She was right. I had become rotten for a group of people. My behaviour had undergone a drastic change. My traditional identity as a lower caste had found a new consciousness, and this newfound sense of awareness within me was slowly emerging to be a source of my own destruction. This newly acquired knowledge had turned me anti-traditional and anti-establishment. There are three levels to such an anti-establishment education. Firstly, there is no guide book or literature. Secondly, there are no exams, no pass or fail and no Diploma or Degree certificate that comes with it. Thirdly, it has no practical usage in terms of finding a job or upgrading one's social status. My learning, therefore, had solely been to widen my own extent of knowledge. It had brought me back from isolation and integrated me with the whole. It had made me see my personal pain in relation to that of the entire community. My life had been my biggest teacher in this path of knowledge acquisition. This was why I couldn't slave away to somebody else's orders. I was a slave only and only to knowledge, wisdom and my own conscience. All working-class people have always been expected to obey, or else be tagged as arrogant. In a world where expectations are that we spend an entire life as Keshta, the obedient servant from Tagore's 'Puraton Bhrittyo' ('The Faithful Old Servant'), my refusal to comply was making these people angry.

But not without putting them slightly in a fix, given the fact that it was Boro Sahib himself who had hired me. There was nobody who could ask him to take that back. Would he even do that? Who would cook for so many children? There was just one way—to consistently torment me so that I would resign. It would be like killing two birds with one stone: nobody would be put to blame. Mother was the favourite target of all those people who wanted me out. They would provoke her and she would in turn use every opportunity to channel her frustrations onto me. The knowledge that

Boro Sahib was her rakhi-brother—her adopted-brother—made her feel like she owned the school, turning her into terror personified. She wanted to use that to terrorize me too.

* * *

A conspiracy was brewing up against me at my workplace, similar to the one against Sandip Master, the former Teacher-in-Charge, who had been forced to resign because of his idealistic work ethics. I had not seen him, but I had met a person named Niloy. He had also been an employee at the school. His biggest strength, however, was that he was a brilliant chess player. He had won awards at various tournaments around India and also found recognition as an internationally ranked player. He had won the first prize at the England Christmas Morning Championship and the third prize at the Blitz Chase Tournament. However, his brilliance became his biggest bane at the workplace. The vicious circle over here found every opportunity to ridicule him as a collective and by the end of it, Niloy started losing his cool. Chess is a game for the calm minded. He was, thus, forced to quit the job and leave.

Chess is a game. Although it is garbed in the guise of war, it is ultimately a game. Even if a number of horses and elephants are killed, it does not cause any real harm. But writing is a different ball game altogether, which I gradually started realizing as I began my second innings with writing. The pen is sometimes deemed mightier than the sword. The tip of my pen was dipped in the venom of life's intense suffering. Capitalism and Brahminism were my opponents. The people who were directly affected by my writing would obviously retaliate. They would want to stop me from writing. Those very people, who once sang the Black American song that 'They don't let us sing our songs', didn't want a working-class person to disclose the truth today.

My work began every morning at six. I had to wash utensils, wash and chop vegetables, clean the fish, prepare the spices, cook, serve and then clean the entire kitchen and eating area. The same cycle was repeated again in the night. Added to that was the task of procuring the grains and spices from the storage for the next day. I had to finish all this with the help of an almost invalid woman. The morning meal had to be served by nine-thirty. The menu would consist of rice, dal, fried potato, fish or eggs. Luchi and potato curry would get added to the breakfast menu on Sundays and the fish would be replaced with meat. Dinner would usually have two kinds of accompaniment along with rice and dal. The timing was fixed at eight-thirty. Be it storms, or floods, or an absent assistant, there was no chance of deviating from this schedule. If I did, a backlash was inevitable, with dangling threats of show cause notices.

The main agenda was to keep me under immense pressure. To not leave me with any time to write. I had been hired on the pretext of cooking for fifty people. Now, the numbers had escalated to around one hundred and fifty. Even though the numbers had risen exponentially, no attempts had been taken to hire new hands. It was impossible for two people to provide hay to one hundred and fifty cows—and these were humans! As could be expected, there was always some shortcoming or the other. The children would be perpetually fuming.

Whatever be the hidden agenda, such problems could still be dealt with. What was impossible was to deal with situations that had been intentionally created to embarrass me. There were incidents when a fistful of dirt would be dumped into cooked rice when I was not looking. Mother had done something like this once. Or maybe, somebody would plonk extra salt into the vegetable. The Childhood Friend had been responsible for something like this. I used to go home for lunch. Boro Sahib had strictly forbidden me from eating the food that had been cooked for the children as apparently it was illegal. On my return one day, I discovered that somebody had toyed around with the gas stove. Only a disaster would probably soothe their toxic hearts. If not a disaster, chaos was inevitable. The cooking would get delayed, and the hungry kids would fume at me. Such pettiness would bring my perpetrators happiness and gain.

I had a bicycle on which I travelled from my home to the school and back. No other vehicle ferried on that route. There would be days, when while getting ready to leave for home after an entire day's gruelling work, I would find that the air from the bicycle tires had been drawn out or it had been damaged with a pin or a blade. No mechanic shop would be open at that odd hour, forcing me to walk back around five kilometres on foot and repeat the exercise again the next morning.

I owned a mobile phone. My house was far off and the road was quite scary. What if somebody wanted to find my address? Say the peon was looking for me to deliver an important letter? So, I had to take a mobile connection. I started getting constant missed calls on my phone and if I dared to receive them, I would be subjected to filthy abuses of the mother and sister variety. Eventually, I had no other choice but to note down the numbers on a piece of paper and report it to Boro Sahib, and along with it a petition.

I wrote:

> I work as a cook at your school for the deaf and the mute. Because of reasons unknown, there are some people who have been mentally harassing me. I have been getting calls from around twenty-five to thirty unknown numbers and if I happen to receive them, I am being subjected to filthy abuse. I have no clue as to their identity or reason for acting in this fashion. I have a feeling that they are all associated with the school in some way. I just wanted to bring this to your notice, with the request for help.
>
> These people are making it impossible for me to sleep at night or perform my duties during the day. They call me throughout the day and torment me, which hampers my mental peace. Such is the nature of my work that many people from West Bengal as well as the other states of India want to stay in touch with me. So, it is not even possible for me to change the number suddenly. If you look into it, I am sure a solution can be reached.

The phone calls stopped, but the other things did not. I was compelled to submit a written complaint to the Teacher-in-Charge.

CHAPTER 14

The Secretary of the Organization for Disabled People

*W*hile working as a cook, as I have said, I was writing. The history behind the publication of my collection of short stories, *The Final Turn of the Circle*, marred by the inhuman extortion by De babu and and his colleague Biswas babu, was something that I was unable to forget. To lighten the burden on my heart, I ended up sharing the incident with a few others, one of whom took it up with De babu. This infuriated him. He was the secretary of the organization for disabled people, an organization spread out over eighteen districts. He was entrusted with a lot of responsibilities, which had earned him wealth, power and prestige. That one had to obey his orders without any questions was an unwritten law. And here was I, openly expressing my displeasure against his actions. I was ruining his reputation. This was intolerable! Nobody in power would silently accept such behaviour from the weak.

One day, he landed up at the school. Calling for me, he said, 'What are these rumours you are spreading? We have sacrificed you like a goat? Like a sugar cane, we have squeezed out your juices and reduced you to crap?'

I stood with my head hanging low, not knowing what to say.

Suddenly his voice turned extremely calm. In a manner of a wise person explaining to a fool, he said, 'Have you ever drunk tea at a big shop? One cup will cost you a hundred rupees. Now go to the tea shop right across the street. Over there a cup of tea will come for just two rupees. Are they then cheating people? Not at all. It depends on their individual rates. Did you understand?'

'Yes,' I nodded my head.

'Why are you standing? Sit down.'

I sat.

'Pass me a little tobacco.'

I did.

Stuffing the tobacco into his mouth he said, 'I heard you have been to jail. Have you?'

'Yes.'

'Why didn't you tell me earlier? Which jail? What was the case? Tell me everything. We will have to get a police verification done. It has to be properly investigated how a person with a criminal record could become a government employee.'

By now I was feeling quite intimidated. Beads of sweat had started forming on my forehead. Times were dangerous. People were being witch-hunted as Mao supporters. Just recently, a couple of young boys distributing leaflets at Nandan had been taken into police custody and passed off as Mao's sympathizers. My own past record was not blemish-free. If one so wanted, it would be very easy to make a mountain out of a molehill.

'So, when will you give it to me?'

'What?'

'Your complete biodata. How many murders? How many police cases? How many for CPM? I want everything. The outcome of the cases, everything.'

De babu said a lot of other things that day by the end of which my head and ears were buzzing. I understood that my reverse countdown had begun. I would have to leave soon. De babu had rung the death knell on my job. I returned home, but did not find any respite. Food wouldn't go down my throat and sleep refused to come. My son and daughter were sleeping on the bed and my wife Anu, below. All of them were in a carefree deep sleep. Their faces looked calm and relaxed. None of them had any inkling of what was about to descend on our lives. The cage called employment, which had securely stored their dreams and aspirations, was about to be snatched away from them in the coming days. We would soon be hurled onto another unknown path.

Around that time, I went to meet Jogenda at his Sodepur address. He had taken me to Salt Lake, to the house of Dr Ilina Sen. She was the wife of the internationally acclaimed doctor Binayak Sen and a professor at Mahatma Gandhi International Hindi University in Wardha, Maharashtra.

Binayak Sen, Ilina Sen and the author.

At one time, Binayak Sen had strong ties with Dalli's labour leader Shankar Guha Neogi. Their combined efforts led to the establishment of the Shaheed Hospital, the first initiative under the Chhattisgarh Mukti Morcha's historical public health awareness programme.

Amidst tea and conversations, when Ilina Sen got to know that I had been part of the Chhattisgarh Mukti Morcha and how I was presently stuck in a violent work environment in Kolkata, she laughed it off and said, 'Why would you live in such perennial fright? Leave the place and join something that you are made for—a job among people and for people. Do you want to go to Raipur?

You very well know the kind of work Binayak is involved with in Raipur. Go to Raipur.' I did not give my word to her, but neither did I say a clear no. I left and waited for De babu to issue my death summons. Here I would lose my job; there a call would go informing her that 'I am coming.'

After a few months of waiting, I was the one to receive the terrible news that nobody was prepared for, including myself—De babu had passed away. When the news reached the school from the office for disabled people, I could not believe my ears. Was this possible? How was this possible? De babu was no more!

He had been in the pink of health. Even the day before he had been to his office, met everybody, drunk black tea and chewed on tobacco. Somebody was patted on the back, while somebody else was at the receiving end of his displeasure. There had been no deviation from his daily routine. And now suddenly this bolt out of the blue!

Apparently, the previous night, at around two, he had complained of an excruciating headache. His son, a doctor and a good one at that, had tried his best to cure his headache, but to no effect. Ultimately, he had to be admitted to one of Kolkata's most luxurious private nursing homes. Despite the efforts of five doctors working at a stretch for five hours, he found no respite. What would one call this? Fate? Or the rich people's disease? Where a poor person's headache would look for ways to escape on a single Disprin, a rich person's headache left him completely bedridden. Five doctors were rendered totally clueless. Advanced medical science was proven useless. He left for his heavenly abode around ten in the morning, leaving his loved ones in tears. Upon hearing this news, a sigh ensued from my heart. Whether it was out of relief or pain, who knows!

* * *

Indians consider it improper to talk ill of the dead. People feel it to be disrespectful towards the soul of the dead. The dead are above all criticism. Hence, the death of De babu, who was busy planning my doom, left me grief-stricken by all measures of tradition. By this time there was no one in the school who did not know that I was actually an author. At this painful hour, I received an invitation from the grieving school authorities. 'Dada's body will be brought to the school to pay our last respects. The body will be taken to other places too, so it will reach our school at around eight to nine in the night. In the meantime, compose a poem in his honour. Write it in a fashion that people are reduced to tears.'

A poem that will reduce people to tears? For a death where even the actual body would not be able to bring tears to my eyes, I was being asked to do the impossible with a poem. What did they think poetry was? Chilli powder? Or onions? Or mustard oil? For these were things that even made a poet shed tears! Returning home, I frantically started going through my diaries and notebooks in the hope of locating something that could be tweaked for the occasion. Somebody had once told me about a Krishna devotee who had been forced to convert to Christianity. The bhajans he had sung previously in praise of Krishna, were now readjusted to replace the 'Krishna' with 'Christ'. My case was somewhat similar. Grief, sadness and other such emotional excesses had made me pen down so many things. Would it not be easiest to find one of those to rescue me from this situation?

It did not take me too much time to find one. In a diary from the previous year, I found a poem that was apt for the occasion. The name of the poem was 'Brikshyo Jibon' ('The Life of a Tree'). I had written this on request by Poly Das, one of my wife's friends, as a farewell gift for a supervisor at her workplace which had ultimately come to no use. The poem was a special kind of verse which could only serve on occasions like funeral or farewells. It was not suitable for the living. That day, the same poem came to my rescue as I decided to use it for the occasion of De babu's demise.

It was already eight in the night. Dada's dead body had still not reached the school. The sky was overcast. The sound of incessant thunder followed by lightning was hinting the onset of heavy rains. The nearby trees were moving in the strong breeze and shedding off dead leaves. Given the late hour, it had not been possible for the teachers to stay back. All of them had classes the next day. To take classes, one had to keep one's cool, and to keep one's cool, ample sleep was required. The school usually closed at four. But to reach home and finally retire for the night took so long that rising in the morning got delayed. As a result, most of them reached school quite late, almost regularly. Now that their departure had been further delayed, it was difficult to say if they could even make it the next day. The one who was no more was no more, but those who were still alive, had their future to think about. One day of no classes for them could cause great losses.

There was just one teacher who stayed back, somebody who was more successful as a photographer with knowledge about all the clever angles for a good shot—the reason he was favoured most by the Teacher-in-Charge. When the Governor and the Chief Minister had visited the school, his brilliant techniques came handy in ensuring that Bordi was in all the photos clicked that day. This teacher had another talent. He wrote poetry. I showed him my poem and asked him for his opinion. After reading the poem, he said, 'What do I say? This poem has not been written with a pen but from the heart—only a person overwhelmed with grief can write such lines—I can say for certain that nobody else would have felt the same way about Dada.'

What he left unsaid by this, said more than what was said. He had known Dada quite well!

* * *

Fame is always followed by shame. Thanks to *Khas Khobor*, which had covered a feature on *Brittyer Sesh Parba* and its author by then, I had already started experiencing some fame. Now it was time for the consequences. The people at work who were already fuming because of me, were now on the verge of bursting like a volcano. It was a wonder for them that I had joined as a cook and was now an author. What was the need for such misplaced ambition? One did not have the power to change one's destiny. Just having one's face appear on TV was not going to turn the person into a big shot.

They were all members and leaders of the CPM Party, and distant relatives of the LCM. Their reach was not just limited to the school but spread all over the state. The disabled kids at the school further shielded them. People in general sympathized with them, so it was easy to shoot off their shoulders. The Warden called me one day, 'Listen Manoranjanda. That you are writing stories and becoming an author is a good thing. But make sure to do your actual work, for which you are drawing your salary, properly. The kids are complaining of gravel in the rice every day. Do clean the grains properly before cooking. How much time does it take to spread it on the floor of the roof and sift through it?'

They started increasing my workload through such excuses, almost as if challenging me to continue writing. Soon, a new order was passed out of the blue—no rice, from now onwards the kids would only have roti.

When we first joined, we had been told that two would have to cook for fifty kids. The numbers, as mentioned earlier, had since increased to one hundred and fifty. A ladies' hostel had also come into operation. Two staff to cook, wash, prepare and serve twice a day for so many kids was itself a tall task. Now roti had been added to it. How much time would it take to prepare the dough, roll it into shape and then roast it? On top of that flour would have to be fetched from the grinders and the wheat required for the grinding, too, would have to be procured personally from the ration shop.

Carrying out this amount of work was impossible. I took it up with the Teacher-in-Charge and told her, 'Now that the numbers of people have increased, hire one or two more helpers.'

'Where do we find helpers? There are no helpers. The government won't give us more staff.'

I said, 'Then ask those government recruits who sit idle all day to come and help.'

'Who? Who sits idle? Give me the names?'

'So many people. For instance, Aduri Gosai.'

'Aduridi sits idle? She does nothing?'

'She does. She makes the tea in the afternoon and serves a bowlful of puffed rice to the children in the evening. But the rest of the time, she sleeps and watches television.'

'Why did you leave all other names and take hers alone?'

'The rest are all men. I don't know if they can cook. She is a woman. Even if she helps prepare two rotis or peel the potatoes, the pressure on me will lessen.'

'All right, you go ahead. Let me look into this.'

She did look into the matter. After school, she left a letter on my name with the guard. From now onwards, preparing the evening snack was also my responsibility. Aduri Gosai would not help.

As luck would have it, the order for making roti was eventually withdrawn. Bordi's plan to harass me failed completely when the kids boycotted roti after a year and started starving themselves. The evening snack was also reassigned to Aduri Gosai. It did not look nice to have her make only ten cups of tea a day.

CHAPTER 15

Boro Sahib

A team from a local television channel landed at my school for a half an hour's programme with me. Realizing its intentions, the Teacher-in-Charge roared out her orders, 'Do whatever you want with him but you do not have permission to enter the kitchen. Neither do you have permission to click photographs!' Her stance was such that the TV crew immediately understood that the school authorities were not favourable towards me.

The crew leader said, 'That's all. Let's go to your place.'

As soon as the camera started rolling, he directed his first question towards me, 'Why do you write?'

I answered, 'I can't live without writing, like we can't live without breathing.'

'What do you write? Story? Poetry? Novels?'

'I write about life. The inspiration for my writing is people who do not accept defeat.'

'Do you write about anything other than people? Like nature?'

'No, only people. People alone. My writing begins and ends with people. People who revolt and rebel.'

Around a lakh of subscribers of this cable network, Sukanta Satellite, also resided around the Jadavpur area. The day this programme was telecast, people in and around Jadavpur saw me. Bordi or Royda did not. The Warden accompanied by a few others landed up at the Teacher-in-Charge's room the next day to complain about me. 'Did you see, Bordi? He is so ungrateful. In a half-hour long interview, he never once mentioned Boro Sahib or you or the school.'

This was a major goof-up on my part, which I ended up repeating for both the *Khas Khobor* interview and an interview I had done with *Anandabazar Patrika*. I spoke about so many things, but not once did I mention the contribution of Boro Sahib or the school. I realized that slowly the tide was turning against me. Nobody at the school spoke to me properly, and if I ever happened to ask something, I always got a crooked reply. I was ridiculed. Everybody knew that this was the way to please Bordi, the Super and the Warden: keeping the superiors happy was always beneficial. But I could never master this art. What can be done! I was like a crow who had found a peacock's feather on its wings. The feather had slowly penetrated into my very being. It did not feel like the feather was not mine anymore. People around made fun of it and laughed. But for me, the feather occupied my whole heart. It hurt to sever it. There was blood loss.

* * *

My life had been a failure so far. I did not have any support to pull me through. Time had gifted me with a mere pen. All I wanted to do was to hold onto it with all my might, just like a small dinghy on a vast ocean, a lamp on a dark night, or a stick in a blind man's hand. I wanted to fathom the real meaning of *jijibisha*—the will to live. If my pen was snatched away from me, I would also cease to exist as a human being. Instead of living the day when I would become incapable of writing—because that would kill me from within—I would rather commit suicide.

These times of adversity were trying to put a chain on my hands. There were attempts to prevent me from writing. Conspiracies were building walls on all sides. In the era of the *Mahabharata,* Eklavya's thumb was snatched away from him. Closer to our times, Etoyar from Mahasweta Devi's story suffered the same fate. How would I save myself? If somebody blocked your mouth and nose with all their strength, how would you escape? The victim would try to breathe through the gaps in between the fingers. Would there be any air to breathe? None. But that would not deter the victim from trying, in the hope of staying alive a few seconds longer. To snatch away a few seconds from eternity. Writing was not a hobby for me. It never had been. It was jijibisha. It was my way of transforming society, of protesting against oppression, deprivation, injustice and torture. It is said that one can sacrifice everything for truth. For me writing was my truth, my god, my everything. I could not leave it for anything!

The secretary of the school knew in his heart that our school was miles apart from any other school. The educational standards at this school were so high, that even a mere cook could become an author. If a cook could write, one could well imagine the level of the teachers. Whenever a distinguished guest came to visit the school, I was beckoned from the kitchen and showcased in front of the guest. Robin Dev, Meera Bhattacharjee, Alapan Bandyopadhyay, Azizul Haque, the list was never ending. Boro Sahib flaunted me before them and said, 'See, he is a cook at our school. He also writes. Manoranjan, why don't you show a couple of your books to them? You need to read them to know what a talent he is. The day he came to me and said that he wrote, I gave him a task. I asked him to write about people and he has been doing just that.'

With wealth, came fancy hobbies. Some people acquired expensive breeds of dogs as pets, some got tigers, others set up aquariums. Boro Sahib had a feeling that he had a writer for a pet. In that moment of excitement, like parents had while showing their children around a zoo, he would display a live author to his guests. He would show how domesticated I was. After being thus displayed to about twenty to twenty-five people, each time losing a couple of my books as free donations, I started feeling irritated. Each book usually cost me around forty rupees for publication. Boro Sahib might be benefitting this way, but what use was it to me? Be it a minister or an MLA or a District Magistrate, everybody forgot me the moment they stepped out of the school. Maybe they dumped my book into a waste basket. I did not want to dole out my books unnecessarily. Initially I used to hope that perhaps they would read my book and think about me. Possibly that would bring about a change in my life; I would find respite from this laborious job and more time to write. But it was all pointless. Nothing changed. I was becoming like a spinster who had lost all will to dress up or impress after being paraded off in front of the family of potential grooms numerous times without a wedding materializing.

When he said, 'He is a cook here. He also writes. Go and get one of your books,' I would nod my head and say, 'I don't have any more books left.' Boro Sahib was not a fool. Had he been a fool, he wouldn't have been able to rise to his present position from where he could touch the skies. So far, he had been satiating his ego by boasting about me, about how it was rare to find such a cook who could also write stories. Now that there was no proof to present, there was no fun. He would have loved to show the books, but now there were no books. So, he lost all interest in showing me off.

* * *

I had not met Duttada for a very long time.[1] He sent a word for me to meet him urgently at his place, so I went. I had been to his house, which was on Ajanta Road, a couple of times before. That day it seemed like I received some extra attention. Boudi served me coconut narus and chilled water from the fridge. She said that she had seen me on TV. The daughter-in-law, Mou, was summoned from the other room. 'Come and see who's here.'

The daughter-in-law seemed delighted to see me. She said, 'Madan kaka when did you come? You used to come to our place so often. Now that you have been on TV, you don't come at all. We always remember you.'

'Tell him what you wanted to say,' her mother-in-law hurried her.

'What?'

'Arre, that thing about the TV programme.'

'Oh, right!' The girl continued with a pause, 'Madan kaka, you spoke about so many things on TV. Couldn't you have said something about Babu? Had you said that he had helped you get the job, they would have definitely asked for his picture. Wouldn't that have been so nice? Why didn't you?'

From her face it felt like Duttada was vicariously stating his wishes through Mou. But I had no answer to her question. After some time, Duttada said, 'I am thinking of a project—a big one. You are the only one who can do this. If you manage to do this, your worth will grow in Boro Sahib's eyes, and so will mine.'

'What sort of a project?'

'You have to write a biography.'

'A biography? But I don't have a proper bio at all.'

'Not yours! You have to write Boro Sahib's biography.'

'He has said so? That he will make me write his biography? Has he told you this?'

'Not him. I am telling you.'

'How will I? Do I know anything about his life?'

'I will be able to tell you some of it. When he first had to flee from his neighbourhood, I was with him for a long time. He told me a lot then. The rest you can find out yourself.'

'From where?'

'From Boro Sahib directly. He knows you. He also knows that you write. Go to his house and explain that both you and I want to write his biography. Will you be able to do so? What will you say? Tell him that Duttada and I think that your biography should be published. That he has been part of so many movements, so many struggles. Without him the Left Front government wouldn't have been able to come to power. Yet, people here are not aware of his contributions. People should be told about the actual history, because of which Duttada and I feel—and say it exactly like this—that Duttada and I feel that your biography should be written. You just initiate the conversation. I will take care of the rest. You will see, in no time he will be ready to share his own story without any further prompting.'

'He will share everything? Will he be able to?'

Bangla literature is full of biographies. These narratives based on a single life are usually packed with inspirational stories, motivational episodes wrapped in a distinct literary flavour. Therefore, they do not remain merely as biographies but emerge as a record of time, a part of history .Usually, the author is someone who has a social responsibility as well as immense respect towards the said person. If the respect and devotion exceeds the expected boundary, it reduces into idolatry and shameless flattery. Too much of it is never good, as is too little of it. A person who lacks these skills cannot become a biographer. If he forces himself to write, the writing will have no soul.

Letters, words, sentences, even punctuation—everything has a soul. A lot remains hidden behind that which is said. Everybody is not skilled at this. I dived into my own heart to frantically search for this love and adoration. I was not able to find any that could put some life into the lifeless letters. Instead, some hidden nausea surfaced that was of the opposite meridian of respect, devotion and love. Apart from being a crafty, aggressive, political personality, I did not see any humanitarian qualities in him. This man had once walked all the way back from the Kalighat cremation ground after performing the last rites of his father because he did not have the bus fare. How did the same man, armed with a red flag in his hands and the tenets of workers' rights on his lips, amass a property of crores in the last forty years was something to wonder at.

Despite that, I was unable to say no. I did not want to provoke Duttada. There was already a conspiracy going on at the school to provoke me. The Warden twisted my ears one day, just for fun. I was stopped at the gate and my bag and self searched on another day. In the garb of 'it was a joke', they were trying my patience so that I would end up breaking rules which would be fit for punishment. The Teacher-in-Charge was literally waiting with her paper and pen, to hand me a show cause notice as soon as the opportunity demanded. Having Duttada also turn against me would not be a good option.

People say that the world is full of selfish people. What was Duttada's interest in suddenly wanting to publish Boro Sahib's biography? It was completely pure and untainted. It was as insignificant as the contribution of the squirrels who had helped Rama build the bridge across the ocean. Yet, it was also something that surpassed many big things. Duttada wanted to make me write about the time when he was on the run with Boro Sahib. How, chased by the police and fleeing from one place to another, Duttada had suffered so much on Boro Sahib's account. They had shared food bought with the little money they had. Today, Boro Sahib had reached such heights that even the tallest monuments would look like a small pole in front of him. At such a time, Duttada wanted the world to know how he had always been beside Boro Sahib when the entire world had forsaken him. Now that Boro Sahib had everything, it was Duttada who had been forsaken. In fact, it was wrong to say that he had been forsaken. Duttada merely wanted to request him not to forsake him, by reminding Boro Sahib of the olden days and curry favours for himself as well as his future generations.

I went to Boro Sahib's place one day. These were difficult times. The topmost CPM leaders had been forced to take police protection in order to safeguard themselves from the wrath of the poor people of the state. There was a police camp in front of Boro Sahib's place. An armed policeman stopped me. After a thorough interrogation session, convinced that I had no intention of killing anybody, they let me in. It was a big beautiful house and clearly a lot of money had been spent on it. The house had everything without which life seemed incomplete. The moment I reached, a cup of tea was offered to me, but the tea left a sour taste in my mouth. To remove the taste, I needed some tobacco. I know from experience that it was the same with all tobacco users. Boro Sahib was one of them. Many a time during visiting the school, he would ask me for some tobacco after drinking a cup of tea. Not directly, he would send someone to fetch it from me.

He shared another cup of tea with me and judging by past experiences, his mouth, too, would have gone sour. I started rolling tobacco for two. I did it in front of him, without once realizing that this might be disrespectful for him. I have been mingling with Left workers right from the seventies. They would share my beedis and we would all smoke together. Such insignificant matters did not cause them any disrespect.

Once on my way to Purulia's Lotha festival with Mahasweta Devi in a train, her son, Bappa, and I smoked in front of her: he a cigarette, I a beedi. People who had read my piece on Shankar Guha Neogi in *Pratikkhan* knew that for our first meeting I had offered him a beedi and the matches had been provided by him. Even when I travelled from Nagpur to Raipur in Swami Agniveshji's car, I had smoked beedis all the way. In terms of stature, Boro Sahib was definitely not bigger than them. Hence, I did not think twice about rolling tobacco in his presence. I did not realize that the times had changed. He was not the same person anymore; he had won his first ministerial position on MLA votes. Seeing me roll tobacco in front of him was annoying him. He was looking for an opportunity to tell me off.

He found the opportunity when I extended my right hand with his share of the tobacco. He uttered in great annoyance, 'Is this how you offer tobacco?'

I was shocked, not realizing my fault. I asked, 'How do I offer it then?'

He put his left hand on the elbow of the right hand like making an offering to the gods. 'This is how you offer something to a respectable person.' I knew of this practice. I also knew that this was a custom followed under the traditional brahminical culture. To lie down prostrate on the ground with joined hands or to touch the dust under another's feet with one's head or tongue, these were all practices that had been designed by a barbaric priestly class in order to denigrate another class of people. They were all now part of the old dark ages. Thanks to the modern liberal education, people were now more progressive. For the enlightened, these practices were obsolete.

The Leftists had told me ages back that everybody was equal and deserved the same respect. Why the contradiction today? The respect that he was demanding from me, the way he was asking me to offer him the tobacco, would he do the same for me? Why not? If he was a minister, I was an author. Writing was an art, the author was an artist, the text was a creation and the writer was a creator.

It was true that he had helped me with a job. Providing a job was like social service. But conversely, I was one among the public. The public had voted for him. He was under the compulsion to help the people. All these thoughts crashed like a wave against the shores of my mind in a flash. I saw that the person sitting opposite to me was not a communist but a high-class Brahmin. He was not a Marxist but one in possession of a huge amount of capital and hence would be what the Marxists called such people.

I was a Dalit, I was a labourer. My primary fight was against the priestly traditions and capitalism. It was an ongoing fight. I ended up saying, 'You are a member of the Communist Party, I thought that these traditions don't matter to you.'

Boro Sahib was not happy to hear this. In a hoarse voice he said, 'Put the tobacco in a piece of paper and leave it on the table.'

After a while he wanted to know, 'Why are you here? What work do you have?'

I said, 'Duttada has sent me. He asked me to write your biography. I don't know much about your life. If you tell me, I will write it down.'

He was quiet for some time. Finally, he asked, 'That you are here, who will cook at the school? What will the children have?'

I said, 'It's Puja vacation. The kids have gone back home.'

'The remaining few, what do they eat?'

'They cook on their own.'

'So, you don't have to cook?'

'No.'

'How long are the holidays for?'

'There are still about fifteen days remaining.'

He took some tobacco from the paper I had wrapped it in and put it in his mouth. Closing his eyes, he seemed to be immersed in deep thought. Opening his eyes, he said, 'Come for your duty from tomorrow. The sports ground is full of weeds. Clean them. The ground should be clean in fifteen days.'

My rotten luck! I had come to visit Boro Sahib with the pride of an author. I was returning back with orders to weed the school playground. I did not have any value for a businessman who dealt in votes. He only found those people valuable who knew how to fill up his ballot box.

The entire school was on holiday, only I would not.

* * *

The news that I had gone to Boro Sahib's place spread like wildfire. There was widespread speculation among my colleagues about my visit. Why did I visit him? Did I put in a complaint about somebody? Or did I suck up to him for my own personal gains? Boro Sahib had a lot of vehicles which he rented out. Two of them were reserved for his personal use. He had a lot of vehicles but not enough garage space; hence all of them were parked at the school. One of the drivers, who had seen me at Boro Sahib's place, was responsible for this news leak. This had led to this squall of conjecture and fear.

An atmosphere of mistrust and suspicion was slowly engulfing the school. There was no unity. The person who would be so courteous in front, would be plotting the other's downfall behind him. It was the same within the CPM Party. It only took more than ten cadres to assemble in a place and a similar atmosphere would set in. The same people who had voted for Sujan Chakraborty, the winning councillor of the Jadavpur ward, had caused Boro Sahib's defeat in the previous elections. This heartbreaking occasion which Boro Sahib had already faced would be experienced by all the CPM leaders in 2011. Their own people, who had fleeced off them, would secretly cast their votes on the symbol of the twin flowers in grass. Similar to the downfall of the mighty Roman empire, the CPM would also fall on its face.

A change was seen at the school for the deaf and mute around this time. The kitchen was shifted from the third floor to the south-facing ground floor of a newly constructed building. Spread across a huge area, it was a good space to work in. The purchase of bricks, cement, doors, windows, chairs, tables, lights, fans and various other items that had gone into constructing this building had generated a sense of anger among the influential people of the school. Some of these came to my ears. One of Boro Sahib's closest aides, his 'right-hand man', would look after the construction materials. The Warden was in charge of the food items for the hostel. The Teacher-in-Charge was not responsible for any purchase. Her only job was to sign on cheques. Everybody referred to them as the Pandavas. I didn't know much about the others, but the Teacher-in-Charge had purchased a new car—a big new car.

NOTE

[1] Duttada is discussed in *Interrogating My Chandal Life*. He helped the author get the job at the school.

CHAPTER 16

How Duttada's Intentions Came to Nought

A friend named Raju Das lived at Dum Dum and worked at the airport. In addition, he also wrote plays and was an actor. He had his own theatre group. Raju belonged to the group of people who used to be previously referred to as the Chandals and now as the Namashudras. It was evident that his writing would have a lot of anger against the caste system.

He came up to me with a request, 'You will have to prepare a a piece?'

'What sort of a piece?'

'About your life's struggles. Do you know of such and such Biswas? He publishes a magazine. For this issue he wants a Dalit writer's account in his own words. I have spoken with him and we want you to inaugurate it. You write for this one, I will write for the second one and somebody else can submit for the subsequent edition.'

Was I a Dalit writer? According to Bimal Biswas, the editor of *Adal Badal*, who had been singlehandedly running the magazine for almost twenty years now, 'Any writing by Dalits, for Dalits and about Dalits would alone qualify as Dalit literature.' Even though I was a Dalit by birth, according to Bimal Biswas' undersanding, my writing did not fall under this category. Apart from 'Reewaz' (Tradition), 'Atithi Sewa' (Serving Guests) and my episodic novel *Jiban Chandal* (*The Runaway* vol 1; *Nemesis*, vol 2), nothing else I had written had been to raise my voice against the caste system, even though they were based on lower-class people and their anger, love and resistance. Hence, the major portion of my oeuvre would not qualify as Dalit literature and therefore I couldn't consider myself as a Dalit writer.

Raju said, 'You are a Dalit writer. There is no doubt about that. The people from the lower-class communities whom you write about, who are they? The Leftists would say that they are the working-class people. I will categorize them as Kaora, Bagdi and Namashudra. In the gentleman's language, they are the lower classes. In this country, the working classes are the ones who tirelessly labour to procure their daily rice and get regularly oppressed. These are none but the Kaoras, the Bagdis and the Namas. You write about them. Hence you are a Dalit writer. Forget whatever others say. I am asking you to submit a piece. I have already prepared the questionnaire. You only have to write the answers. It is up to you to decide whether this is an order or a request.'

My father was illiterate but a very knowledgeable man. He once told me, 'If somebody lovingly invites you for a meal, eat it like a delicacy even if it be a night-old fermented rice. If the reverse happens, just leave. A loving plate of fermented rice is thousand times better than a delicacy served with disdain. Even ambrosia can turn into poison if served without love.' My luck was such that the latter had become a regular thing in my life. Concern about my family's future was preventing me from following my father's advice. Even today I remember clearly how it felt to leave Ravi Srivastav's job offer.[1]

I had to write my own story in my own words for this magazine. I had reached a certain juncture in my life, which I am sure everybody goes through at least once in their lives, when unbearable blind rage was beginning to overpower my senses. I was slowly losing control over myself. Any sort of action undertaken under this effect was tantamount to suicide. The inhuman working conditions I faced were so extreme that it had aroused my bitter anger to the extent that I was on the verge of losing my emotional balance. I did not know where to start and where to stop.

And in my writing? My simple maths told me that all those people who had filled my life with suffering were all affiliated to the CPM. This could have only one meaning, that the CPM was a poisonous tree and hence, anything that came from it was poisonous. They had once said that the land belonged to those who held the plough. When the circumstances permitted, they were the ones to go back on their word and kill those who had seized possession of the landlords' properties. Talking of that period I had written, 'It was the time when Naxalbari was burning. The rural poets had broken into songs of 'Tarai is burning, so is my heart. The Naxalbari fields are ablaze, in the seven daughters' blood.' These seven daughters had been pierced with bullets fired from rifles held by the same people who had once raised slogans in favour of the workers. This was the magic of the throne. It turned anybody who sat on it into bloodthirsty hounds.

A large part of my life comprised the Partition, life in a refugee camp, Dandakaranya and Marichjhapi. Recalling these episodes, I had written:

> At that time, some people championing red flags had joined the refugees to play a dirty game of leading a resistance movement. People did not realize that it was merely a political move. This realization dawned years later by when they had already come into power. The hell that was subsequently opened on the poor and destitute people at Marichjhapi was capable of matching up to the Nazi atrocities on the Jews. How fascism and communism could coexist in this fashion, was not known.

The CPM government had removed the subject of English from the primary school educational system. By removing the very essence of the educational system, they had made sure that nobody would be able to become truly 'educated'. Instead, they would turn out to be uncivilized barbarians with overlord tendencies, shallow opportunist people without any conscience. At one point of time, those who were into politics were required to study. The party would hold regular classes. Nothing like this happened anymore. As a result, the CPM members did not have any relation with books. When were books needed? When one wanted to learn something, right? They who were born omniscient, did not have any need for books. Just like a Hindu kid gets to know about God and the Muslim kid about Allah right from their childhood, any child born in the CPM era immediately knew that it was the most powerful party. There was no alternative to supporting the party. If done properly, it opened up various other avenues like opportunities in the real estate sector, and so on.

The editor of *Adal Badal*, however, was different. He was an avid reader, but for some unknown reason did not find the time to go through my writing once before publishing it. Or maybe he did not feel the need to. He must have thought that given I had been employed by Boro Sahib, it was impossible for me to write anything against the CPM. Maybe for this reason, he sent my piece to the press in haste without so much as a proper glance or major edits. The compositor arranged the text, the proofreader went through it and the publisher published it, not finding it necessary to go through my submission themselves. They were convinced that the editor wouldn't have sent it to them in the first place had it been problematic.

A large section of the population whose houses had been burnt and who had been injured, killed and raped at Marichjhapi were Namashudras and they were present in large numbers in North 24-Parganas and South 24-Parganas. Many were followers of the Matua sect. They were also a precious vote bank and had the power of making candidates win or lose in certain Vidhan Sabha or Lok Sabha seats. The CPM leader Anil Biswas, who was like the Chanakya of politics, had realized that the Marichjhapi incident would have left a wound in the hearts of these people and the CPM prospects would be doomed if they did not take precautions to dress this wound.

This was the way in which began the CPM Party's search of minions among the Namashudra community, one who would be referred to as the 'yes-man' by the leaders of the Dalit movement. It was not difficult to find such people. They earned the trust of the party by being of service to them but later on proved that they were in fact not sycophants but very much our people.

When the magazine was published in the 2004 Book Fair, one of 'our people' from the Tripura CPM government, helped it win the Adwaita Mallabarman Award. That the contents page of the magazine boasted of the names of a bunch of CPM leaders was reason enough. Eventually, some other editor saw that a disruptive piece of writing had somehow slipped in unnoticed and found a place among the others in the magazine. Not having much faith in the postal system, he immediately sent one of his men to deliver the magazine to the school as proof of exposing me. As for the other magazines, they removed my piece before releasing it to the market. The scent of a flower was enough to inform that it had bloomed. What could happen was that the scent of a flower might or might not please an onlooker but the smell of a rotting animal was bound to annoy them. It was an odour that would follow them, announcing its unwanted arrival! Similarly, the scent of my existence as an author was coolly disregarded, but the odour of my current action reached them. How could he who had lived off the CPM Party so far write so bitterly against them? 'Summon the sister fucker!'

Duttada's call came. 'Come immediately.'

As soon as I reached, he picked up a magazine from his table and hurled it at me. 'What have you written? How dare you?'

I answered, 'But I have written the truth.'

Duttada was furious. 'You are an arsehole of an author. There were so many like you who have since disappeared off the face of the earth. You fucking have come to speak the truth? You know very well that you will be reduced to ashes.' His whole body was trembling in rage. Sweat drops were forming on his forehead. 'I had taken a fucker like you to Boro Sahib once. He ran away with a few things and then got caught for smuggling them. I was left totally screwed. I thought you would atone for that sin. How wrong I had been! Your actions will royally fuck me in the ass. How am I supposed to go and show my face to him!'

His wife came and asked me, 'Would you like some tea?'

Duttada shouted at her, 'No! Don't serve him any tea. Not even water. Having entered my life like a small needle, this asshole is now about to make his grand exit as a ploughshare.' Looking at me with his eyes almost spewing fire, he said, 'I had caught you once, but you lived. I don't know if I have to drive bullets into you again, after so long. I am a party member. I will have to obey whatever they order me to do. Nobody is as close to me as the party.' I detected a hint of regret in his voice. 'Who else do I have? I have lived my entire life under the party's protection. If I have to pull the trigger on you someday, don't mourn. I had given you an opportunity. You were not able to utilize it. I had asked you to write Boro Sahib's biography. You didn't even do that.'

I said, 'He did not pay any heed to my request but sent me to weed the school playground.'

'Does that mean you will write all this? Weren't you afraid? If the boys now pick you up and crush you, what will you do? Killing somebody like you is akin to killing a mongrel, I hope you know that?'

I don't know what came over me. I had become like those fire-chasing insects who jumped into fire the moment they saw it. I picked up the magazine and said, 'Duttada, this is an issue on Somen Chanda. Many years ago, he was beaten to death for the crime of providing leadership to an anti-fascist rally in Dhaka's Rajpath. Do you know who killed him? Who danced over his dead body? Who squeezed out his eyeballs? People from the RSP and the Forward Bloc. The people he was leading that day and the people who eventually killed him, all of them together comprise the Left Front today. The Communists and their killers have all become an indistinguishable mass. Somen Chanda's death would have been in vain, had it not been for some people who chose to make him immortal in their thoughts, ideas and historical reminiscences. If I die like him, magazines and news channels will be filled with my news. I will be immortal. Who doesn't seek immortality?'

Duttada stared at me for long seconds and then said, 'All right! You may now leave.'

I did not realize then, which I do now, that it is time that immortalizes and glorifies people. It was time which had turned a hated nawab into a patriot. For freedom fighters, Siraj ud-Daulah had become a symbol. Similarly, the drunkard and adulterous soldier

Mangal Pandey had become a hero in the struggle for independence. Everything was simply a question of time. Time had turned Lenin into a great hero in the pages of history. It was time again that caused his statue to crumble into dust.

* * *

There was a power cut all evening. Everybody was feeling restless in the heat. Even when the power came back and the fan started spinning, the air was mildly hot. I had taken leave from work, a CL (a casual leave) which I could take now—a total of fourteen in a year. I used the opportunity to take my wife out in the evening. My desire was to buy her something she really wanted today. I would treat her to the sweet chanar jilipi, which she loved.

Anu considered me to be an angry man without any sense of romance. Seeing my romantic mood after so many years, she was shocked. She said, 'What is the matter tell me? The sun seems to have risen from the west that it is snowing in the desert!'

I said, 'Just like that.'

'Nothing happens like that. There must be some reason.'

I smiled and said, 'I felt that this is important too at times.'

'When there was the need, you did nothing. What is the use doing all this now? Will the lost time be back?'

I said, 'A famous person has said, morning begins when you wake up.'

'Even if the sun is overhead at that time?'

'Even if the sun has set.'

At that moment, I was reminded of the story where a man went to the jungle to pick up flowers for his wife and then lost his way out. After years of searching, when he finally reached home, twenty years had passed. His beautiful wife had become old. I felt like the regretful hero of this story, through whose fingers time had slipped.

Strolling with Anu, we reached Jadavpur. I stood at the place where I had first seen her. The wall near the bus station was no more. It had been broken down to expand the road. I bought some sarees for Anu from the hawkers market and some clothes for my son and daughter. Anu said, 'Buy something for yourself.'

I said, 'I won't buy anything now. I have plenty.'
'How? You just have a pant and a shirt.'
'Let that be. We will see about that later.' In my heart I said, 'Will get to wear clothes only if I live. Otherwise, everything will go to waste.'

After shopping, as we were preparing to leave for home, Anu said, 'Will you get me a pair of conch bangles? See, my hands are empty. It doesn't look good for a married woman to have hands that are so empty. The ones from our marriage—how long will they last? Today you have bought me so many things. Please buy me a pair of those too.'

I said, 'These are nothing but superstitions. You don't need to wear them. It is so fragile; just a tap can break it down. It is a waste of money. Instead, buy something else with that money.'

'Like what?'

'Umm, let's buy a mosquito net? What say? We will be able to sleep in peace.'

We bought a mosquito net and two white bangles for Anu and then finally returned home. Anu and I stayed up till late that night. When the night was thick, I told her, 'A bank employee had come to our school a few days back. They offer loans. Everybody at the school applied for loans through him. I managed to do the same and acquired around sixty-five thousand rupees. The loan has to be paid within five years. I still haven't withdrawn it, but will do so tomorrow or the day after. I am thinking of buying a small plot of land with that money near Khudirabad, Gopal Nagar. A lot of people are doing so. The CPM people are selling each katha of these demesne lands for fifteen to twenty thousand rupees. If we can construct a small house there, we can save on the monthly rent. In case I die, you can live comfortably with the kids.'

She said, 'You want to buy a plot of land, which is good news. Why are you suddenly talking about death?'

I said, 'Human life has no guarantee. I am here today, but who knows about tomorrow. Every day in the newspapers you will hear of people dying because of random reasons like cooking gas cylinders exploding. My job makes me work with two big and two small stoves on a regular basis. Nobody knows what can happen. If by chance something does, you as my family will be left without any means.'

'Will you stop,' Anu scolded me.

However, I really ended up buying a small plot of land with twenty-seven thousand rupees in Khudirabad. I bought it in Anu's name. A guarantor was needed to loan money from the bank. My job was my guarantor. If my job remained, the money would be paid back. If not, I would disappear. The plot was in Anu's name. How would they reclaim the money?

Everybody was of the opinion that as difficult it was to get a government job, it was even more difficult to lose it. At the same time, apart from me, everybody else in the school also knew that the job we had landed was more because of the CPM and less because of the government. If they wanted, the job would remain or else not. If I was made to sign a resignation letter at gunpoint at ten in the night, I wouldn't have much to say or do. Various other things could also happen: five or six boys standing at the gate might refuse to let me enter, the Teacher-in-Charge might refuse to let me sign in the attendance register, I might be suspended on the allegation of being absent for six months. There was nothing much I could do under such circumstances. Even if I went to file a general diary at the police station, I might not be allowed to. The CPM was a very powerful party. There was nothing they were incapable of, just as there was nobody who was not scared of them.

After the house was taken care of, I told Anu, 'I have my own income. If you, too, can start something, we can start saving some money. After a long gap, Anu finally found a job at a reputed shoe factory near Ruby. It was a contractual position, on a monthly salary of around two thousand rupees. I heaved a sigh of relief. Puffing up my chest like Ghatotkacha, I now stood on the battlefield ready to face anything.

Duttada's call came in a couple of days. 'Come to my place. I need to discuss something with you.' I knew the call would come sooner or later and was ready. On meeting him, he said, 'Tuesday is your day off right? You will have to accompany me on that day.'

'Where?'
'Singheshwar.'
I had been to the area with Duttada earlier and knew the locality pretty well. It took around an hour from Jadavpur to reach Taldi by train. From Taldi, it would take another hour or so in a van. Thereafter, another half an hour's walk would take us to Singheshwar. It was a small village surrounded by empty fields on all sides. Around thirty to forty poor Muslim families lived in this village.

Duttada had never had any other job apart from his party work. His party connections had helped him acquire a lot of fisheries around Jadavpur and other areas. He owned a huge fishery at Singheshwar too. The entire stretch of that fishery, from one end to the other, was completely empty. His was, however, not the only fishery there. Around twenty-five other CPM leaders also had their share at this place. If not everybody, at least a great number of people knew that much blood had been shed over the possession of these fisheries. Here, human life was cheaper than fish. The guards at these fisheries were infamous dacoits for whom killing came easy. People who came to steal fish were butchered into small pieces and fed to the fishes.

During my earlier visit to the place, I had not been scared. But this time it was different. Duttada was a dedicated member of the party. There was nothing more important to him than the party's orders. He was not one to ask questions. He would blindly follow orders. Nobody knew what orders he was following. In any case, there were deaths everywhere. The newspapers were red with people's blood. All this relentless death had been reduced to mere news stories; these were no longer painful occurrences with real consequences, but just routine procedures.

Perhaps orders had come from the bigwigs to kill me off. Since I already knew a lot of their inside stories, they must have been afraid of sacking me lest I reveal these intimate secrets to the news media houses. Hence, they decided that the best way forward was to remove me without a trace. The extent of their powers was such that if they had really wanted, they could have easily accomplished their plan in the night when I returned home in the darkness flanked by empty streets on either side. But with new settlements cropping up everywhere, it could have been difficult to hide my body.

A doubt started growing inside me. Perhaps they did not want to take any risk. Why would they? It was not impossible for them to take their prey to a place of their choice. They would get the entire night to slice up my body into tiny pieces and dump it into the ponds. The hybrid catfish were savage. They would rip off a live human being if he were dipped into the water. I would be already dead by then. In a single night, I would disappear, nobody would have any clue. I was able to understand everything; yet I was not in a position to refuse. I got back home with a heavy heart and started counting my days. The forthcoming Tuesday would be a black lettered day in my life.

By now Anu had a fair idea about my attitude towards the CPM Party. She turned sick with worry and said, 'Don't go. Everybody knows that Duttada has brought you back from Dandakaranya and given you a job. He has been your benefactor. You have talked about this yourself on so many platforms. If he kills you today, nobody would ever suspect him. Your own previous declarations will protect him. It will be easiest for him to kill you. You shan't go at all.'

I answered, 'I have no other way but to go. If they have really decided to kill me, they will try every means possible even if this fails. They will not let me go. They don't leave anybody who can harm them.'

'How will they kill you if you don't go?'

'They will definitely send somebody. I am their employee. I will have to do whatever they ask me to do. You know they have a press. What if they print some posters and ask me to deliver it to Boro Sahib's Vidhan Sabha centre? I won't be in a position to refuse. On my way there, a random person could aim a shot at me. My dead body could then be paraded in a rally with them proclaiming, 'Look at the posters. He is our guy. He used to work at the school for the deaf and mute. He has been killed by TMC and SUC.' I am not bothered about dying, but to see CPM gain points over my dead body would give me a lot of pain.'

* * *

It was Monday. Another night and it would be Tuesday. The two of us could not sleep. Come morning, I would have to go to Duttada's house and from there to Singheshwar. We were both worried about what would happen. Just like the clock seems to tick faster for prisoners sentenced to death, we felt like the night was passing away too quickly. I remembered Shankar Guha Neogi at this juncture. On the page of a diary, before his death, he had in detail written down how he would be killed, who would kill him and why. He had also recorded the details in an audio tape in his own voice. As a result, the truth was revealed to the people of the country right after his death.

I, too, had to do the same. I sat down with pen and paper, and wrote down where I was headed to the next day, who was leading me, why he was taking me along and if killed, the reason for it. Handing it over to Anu, I said, 'In case I don't return by tomorrow, make a photocopy of this letter and send it to *Dainik Jagaran*. You will find the address jotted down in the diary. Send the other copy to the human rights activist, Sujato Bhadra. Make sure to give a copy to Mahasweta Devi also.'

After spending the entire night in this fashion, I left for Duttada's house the next morning on my broken bicycle leaving behind a tearful Anu and my two kids on whose cheeks I planted a thousand kisses. I was finally ready to accept my fate. On entering the two-storey house in Ajanta, I was shocked. Duttada was lying on his bed. His eyes were closed and his right hand diagonally placed over his forehead. He was not sleeping, but groaning in pain.

'Dada, what's wrong?'

Whimpering with pain, Duttada replied, 'I slipped in the bathroom last evening and hurt my hip. Now, I am not able to walk or sit. The doctor has asked me to be on complete bed rest. I have no idea if this will ever heal or when.'

This was fantastic news—I didn't know if I should dance in joy! I cycled back home as fast as I could and gave Anu the good news. We both had a good laugh. Two more days later, more good news came knocking at our doors. A CPM leader had been murdered in Boro Sahib's Vidhan Sabha area. This man was known in the area as Boro Sahib's opponent. For this reason, many people were of the view that his murder was a result of the CPM's internal feud. There were also people who were suspicious of Boro Sahib's involvement in the case. This had left Boro Sahib in a precarious position. Given this situation, even if he harboured any anger towards me, there was no time for him to act on it. He became engrossed in tackling his own situation.

Time was supremely powerful. The tide of time left its sediments on the magazine's article for the moment. Consequently, I took Anu to a shop and bought her a pair of conch bangles for eighty rupees. It was not a waste if they broke, but only if they broke before time. That time now seemed far away in the future. Superstition it might be, but what's the harm in letting Anu wear them? At least, it would prove that I was still alive.

NOTE

[1] See *Interrogating My Chandal Life*, Chapter 17.

CHAPTER 17

Mutating Viruses

A woman by the name of Rama—quite brave and confident by nature—joined the hostel with the task of looking after the female lodgers. She did not much care for other people's banter. Mother wanted to subdue her, while all that Rama wanted to be was independent. This kickstarted a cold war between them, Rama armed with her own gumption and Mother backed by the Super and the Warden. Suddenly, a lot of whispers started doing the rounds. What was up? Apparently, Rama did not have a good character. Rama's husband remained in the village and she stayed alone on the first floor of the ladies' hostel. At night, when everybody went off to sleep, she seemingly made trips downstairs. Where to? She went to visit a guard whose wife was in Bihar and who lived alone here. As proof, used contraceptives were found all over the school for some days after the allegations were made. This news was delivered to Boro Sahib by a greatly distressed Mother herself and as expected soon Rama was served an eviction notice. She left in humiliation with her head bowed low.

Another girl by the name of Supti joined around this time. She too had to leave in a similar fashion for not being able to please Mother. Kanan joined after her. The poor soul was unmarried and would perhaps never get married. There was nobody in the whole wide world she could call her own. On getting the job, she had hoped to spend the rest of her life with the other girls. She was of a quiet nature, very calm and soft. One would not hear a single sound from her. Mother decided to bully her too for reasons unknown. She started picking fights with her regularly and heaping the choicest abuses on her. Unable to take any further abuse, she too left the job one day.

Mother was now set loose upon me. Having tasted victory three consecutive times, her confidence was at its highest. She was in any case miffed with me over the fish and milk incidents. Backed by powerful others, she launched her attack on me with a barrage of abuses. One day, before the kids had had their breakfast, she was found happily filling up a small paper bag with batasha or candy-like sweets that were supposed to be served with puffed rice. 'Please do not take so much on your own. I'll have to give it to everybody,' I stopped her. A small altercation followed. She called me names. I answered back in the same language; the torture which the helpless Kanan had been subjected to was still fresh in my mind. I forgot that she was a senior. The matter ended there, for the time being. It was 7 am. When the Warden came after three hours for attendance, Mother came running with her complaints. 'Dear one, ask this son of a bitch not to mess with me.'

Son of a bitch! Just two little words, but something in my head flared up. I forgot where I was and who all were around me. I ran towards her and said, 'You swine, what did you call me again? I will pull out your tongue from that filthy mouth of yours! Have you taken me to be Kanan? I will beat you to pulp so that your jaw will be shattered to bits.'

She had not expected my reaction to be so extreme. She became a bit subdued, but did not stop fuming. She said, 'I will tell Rajat.' Rajat was a convict in the Saibari murder case.[1] I shouted back in the same tone, 'Go and tell anybody you like. What will they do? Kill me? Ask them to come.'

Needless to say, the incident stirred up a storm. A few days after this incident, the Childhood Friend entered the field. It was slowly emerging to be like the battlefield at Kurukshetra in the *Mahabharata*. One fallen commander was being replaced by another. There had been a power cut around eight in the evening. The school had a generator. He commanded, 'He who knows how to operate it, please turn it on.' I did not know how to do this. I was in the kitchen with my helper. Suddenly the lights went out. It had affected only one phase of the building, so even though the kitchen was in darkness there was light in the other building. Prodding my way in the darkness, I reached the Right-Hand man and told him, 'We will need to turn on the generator.' He called up somebody else and barked his orders, 'Turn on the generator.' What would I do in the darkness? I couldn't get back to work until the power was back. So, I sat down on a chair, in the lighted area outside.

Around this time, the Childhood Friend was on his way to the kitchen for some work. Being obstructed by the darkness, he started retracing his steps when his eyes fell on me seated outside. He was Boro Sahib's friend and came from a position of entitlement. That entitlement was now projected on me. 'You are nicely sitting over here while your assistant is sitting in the darkness like a ghost. Do you have no concerns?'

I said, 'I have already informed Dada.'

'What?'

'To turn on the generator.'

'Does he know how to do that?'

'He asked somebody else.'

'Who?'

'I am not too sure.'

He came charging at me. 'Get up. Go and see who is turning on the generator.'

I did not leave my chair. Remaining seated on it, I said, 'I have already done my part. He has ordered somebody else. Let's wait for five-ten minutes.'

'And you think your job here is done? Get up from the chair.'

I still refused to get up. I did not think it necessary to pay any heed to his bullying. This hurt his ego and he pushed me to the floor. He loved beating up people, be it our disabled gardener, the nightguard Saha, or certain school kids. One time he also landed some punches on Master Das. Nobody was interested to hear the victim's side of the story. Armed with this confidence, he also landed some blows on me.

But I was the kind of person, who did not shy away from teaching a good lesson to such people even if they happened to be our 'respected' superiors. In any case there was nobody who fitted the bill here. These people were really powerful. The origin of their strength was a party's flag and its rod. But none of them was respectable. At least not for me. I decided not to let him get away with his antics today. Pulling myself up from the ground, I pushed him. Like a pumpkin which had been severed from its stem, his heavy body fell. After this incident, he refrained from physically assaulting anybody on campus. He turned totally non-violent.

* * *

Around this time, Mamata Banerjee coined a new term, 'harmad', as mentioned earlier, to refer to the CPM army reared by the party, comprising dacoits, goons, rapists, real estate agents, landlords, and so on. Before this, she used to refer to them as the Bhairav Bahini. Bhairav is the other name of Shiva, the protector of the innocent, the brave, the righteous and the selfless. Hence, his army was referred to as the Bhairav Bahini. This name was understandably not at all appropriate for the CPM rogues. It was similar to naming a blind boy as Padmalochan, or the lotus-eyed. Hence, the name was changed to harmad, which was the name of a group of foreign looters.[2] It was the most appropriate name for the CPM.

By this time, the Chhoto Angaria massacre[3] had already happened. Instead of Sitaram Yechury, Prakash Karat, Jyoti Basu, Benoy Choudhury, and other famous and proven leaders, the names of Tapan-Sukur, Majid Master and others began to surface as the party's new assets. From accusing the Tata–Birlas for being oppressors and the enemy of the common man, the CPM took a hundred and eighty degree turn and began fraternizing with the very same industrialists as their comrades with the motto 'We will not let anybody touch a hair of Tata' and if anybody does 'will break his head'. Under the changed circumstances, a CPM leader joined hands with one Salem, who had killed lakhs of communists in Indonesia, and gave him open access to West Bengal through an MoU signed with the declaration 'This is the happiest day of my life!'

Wasn't it strange that this leader's happiest day was not when he became a member of the party for the first time, not when the Left government came to power, nor when he was elected the Chief Minister of the state, but the day when he set forth on the journey of destroying the future of the country's farmers? Finally, it was clear that the party had come under the complete control of the political HIV virus. Instead of fighting for workers' rights, they had started walking on the path set out by the capitalist regime, one that was a favourite with America. It had been said that Marxism was the most powerful ideology and we sincerely believed in it. Slowly, it was becoming apparent that out of all the 'isms', capitalism was the most powerful. Capital had so much power that even certified Marxists could be crushed under its silver boots. This is the reason that the Communist Party which once believed that all the Tatas and Birlas and Goenkas and Dalmias were the country's biggest enemies, had changed their tune to become their fervent supporters. Such were the wonders of the all-powerful capital!

The Communist Party of India (Marxist) and its mass organizations were now firm and strong like steel. Try as you might to create a dent from the outside, it remained unharmed. One of its biggest proofs was the movement that grew up around Naxalbari; the ruling class completely destroyed it by launching a severe attack during the seventies, but was it really destroyed? They reorganized themselves into a new form, their strength growing manifold. What started off as a movement contained within a small region, went on to spread its influence to almost eighteen other states. The Home Minister was compelled to accept the truth. The capitalists were aware too and had to come up with new ways of dealing with it.

When blood comes in contact with infected blood, the small particles of white blood cells flowing through the veins and arteries are alerted to fight any external germs that enter the body. For ordinary health issues, this is how we recover even if we don't take additional medicines. For HIV, the situation is different. This virus changes its shapes within three to four days of entering the body, taking up the form of the white blood cells. As a result, the actual white blood cells get confused. Considering these outsiders to be their own, they refrain from attacking. The virus starts expanding its cells. If the actual white blood cells produce one cell in a minute, they produce almost ten to twenty. Eventually, the actual cells get outnumbered by the duplicate ones. Following this, in the event of other disease germs entering the body, say, of tuberculosis or typhoid or malaria, the counterfeit white blood cells desist from attacking them as the real ones would have. In the absence of resistance of any kind, this new disease does not find it difficult to kill the patient in no time.

The bourgeoisie had started using this technique to destroy the CPM. They had infiltrated the party spaces with a few salary-minded people. By rattling off higher idealistic sermons, much more than the actual communists, and by creating a crowd of fake communists around them, these people had captured the highest powers through majority support. Now they were destroying the organization by eroding it from within. The same technique had been used to break down Soviet Russia into seventeen pieces, turning this huge and powerful country lifeless and powerless. Even the American capitalists—leader of the world capitalists—could not have achieved this by dropping bombs from the sky.

I assume that this slow infiltration into the country's communist groups by the bourgeoisie has been going on since the sixties. Those still involved in the struggle would easily recognize these infiltrators, but what about the rest? The latter were the ones who had turned their faces away from the struggle, brainwashed by the sweet allure of power on their way to parliamentary democracy. There remained no practical method of judging a person's Marxist leaning today, be it through revolutions or struggles. Both the real and the fake leaders—all with their large protruding bellies—were now fulfilling their public service from within the precincts of their air-conditioned rooms.

Naturally enough, the common people were beginning to turn against them. This was exactly what the fake communists had hoped for. Their wish had been to create a situation where people would spit in hatred merely on hearing the party's name or seeing its flag and they had accomplished it quite splendidly in West Bengal. In my opinion, it would be impossible for the Marxist souls to escape from being called harmad, synonymous with all kinds of lowliness. It was my bad luck that I ended up with a group of people exactly like this. Severing ties was not easy mainly because of the worry over food and shelter. And despite these long years of association, I found not a single soul to stand with me. It was unimaginable that these same people were actual human sympathisers at one point of time and had even embraced hardships because of their love for the people. It was a wonder to see the same people change so much.

Presently, the blame fell on the lower-class employees. In actuality, the first cracks started appearing when the higher-class leaders experienced the advantages that came with power after years of enjoying that position and tried prolonging its effect through various despicable means. From here it seeped into the lower sections, spreading from the organization's branches to its roots. Be it a party leader or a member or a sympathizer, nobody was exempt from its reach. As a result, they fell in just thirty-four years, even though the expectation was that they would survive for centuries.

When the people who had lost their lands in Singur organized themselves in a powerful movement, numerous attempts were made to break it by implementing Section 144; by beating up farmers; by murdering Rajkumar Bhul; by raping Tapasi Malik.[4] Having somewhat quietened down Singur through these antics, by 2006, the CPM cadres in police uniform and the police playing the role of CPM cadres, unleashed themselves on the innocent people of Nandigram. Murders and rapes; arson attacks and kidnappings were carried out indiscriminately.

My identity was no longer unknown. Everybody knew that I was a regular at Mahasweta Devi's house. She was fighting injustice with dedication, fire as fierce as the sun's rays raining from her pen. I had also been caught, on one of the numerous TV cameras around, talking to Medha Patkar when she had come to visit Mamata Banerjee during her hunger strike at Dharmatala and I had used the opportunity to meet her. The footage where I am talking to her was not more than a glimpse, but it was enough for those who were monitoring me to know who it was.

Around that time, somebody donated an expensive TV to the school. It was set up in a big room near the door of the new kitchen. After sundown, the Warden along with some hardcore CPM supporters would lounge there and watch television. Every time the screen flashed the news of the Committee against Land Evictions facing a setback because of the NCPM harmad forces of Nandigram, they would shout out in joy as if Saurav Ganguly had hit a sixer. They would make sure that their shouts reached my ears, making my heart burn. My heart would burn. To me, they would appear as embodiments of those brutes who had raped Tapasi Malik, Radharani Ari, Narmada Sheet and I would itch to teach them a lesson.

At night, when the group of outsiders—people unrelated to the school who were being sheltered by the school—arrived for their dinner, the Warden would make sure I heard him telling them, 'They need a good thrashing, a good sound beating. That will immediately settle them down. Once they are surrounded from all sides and taught a lesson—like the people of Marichjhapi—they will not be in a position to lift up their heads anymore.' His mentality disgusted me and whatever he said would inevitably escalate into full-blown fights or arguments between us. On that day, the fight was a bit too extreme—it could have led to murder. It is common knowledge that the range of such fights is dependent on the amount of poison harboured by the two parties against each other. One word usually leads to another till both parties forget the real issue.

This cycle started for us when the Warden said, 'I shouldn't even try to talk politely with people like you.'

I replied, 'You can't even if you try. You don't know anything about politeness.'

He retorted back, 'Don't try my patience. If you mistake my politeness as my weakness, you are wrong.'

I replied, 'Just like politeness is not a sign of weakness, being impolite is also not a sign of strength. I am not afraid of your threats. I am eager to see what happens when you lose your patience.'

He said, 'You used to be a rickshaw-puller, right? You haven't mixed with gentle folks. You don't know how to talk to them. Just having your name appear on TV and newspapers a couple of times doesn't change your origins.'

I replied, 'In any case, you won't be able to mix with the people I mix with, at least in this life. Try and change that in your next life. Just the way a mullah's reach is only till the mosque, your reach is only up till Boro Sahib.

He said, 'You have grown up getting beaten up by people. Apart from that language, you understand no other.'

I said in reply, 'I didn't just get beaten up, I also beat up people. I even razed Kamarpara's Kartik to the ground. Did you know that? I can show you how.'

He answered, 'All right, let's see what you can do.'

I said, 'First show me the extent you can descend to. Only then.'

We had both reached the finishing line, on one side of which lay a sharp chopper. But before the situation could get any worse, everything fizzled out. This harmad, a proud follower of Runu, backed down.

NOTES

1 See Chapter 4, n 2.
2 See Chapter 4, n 1.
3 This was a case of allegedly burning alive of 11 Trinamool Congress supporters on 4 January 2001 by alleged Communist Party of India workers in West Bengal.
4 Among the 14 people who died in 2006 against giving land for the Tata factory at Singur.

CHAPTER 18

More Pilferage and Persecution

*A*duri Gosai, was aware that certain sacrifices were necessary to retain a relaxing government job. She bought herself a couple of small bowls knowing well that the way to the heart is through the stomach. Every day on duty, she would bring something or the other in these bowls. Thereafter, her job was to ensure that the bowls reached the most influential people in the school, ones who had power to inflict harm if wrongly triggered. As a result, the five Pandavas were quite happy with her. Royda and Bordi loved Aduri Gosai, and Aduri in turn worshipped them—every word they spoke was like a word from the Vedas for her.

A few days after my altercation with the Teacher-in-Charge, my assistant slipped on the stairs, injured her hip and was unable to come to work for a few days. It was taking a long time to prepare and serve food to the kids all alone, so Aduri was sent to help me out in the mornings. The kitchen was on the roof of the second-floor building at that time. After the vegetables were cut, the peels would be temporarily stored in a potato sack. Once the sack filled up, I would throw it on the road so that the municipality cleaning staff could take it away.

One day, I threw down the sack as usual. I immediately had the sense that something was not right as the sack seemed heavier. When I ran downstairs and opened the sack, I found a whole stack of potatoes inside. I knew this was Aduri's doing. This was her plan for getting me into trouble. That day, Saha was on duty at the gate. He was Royda and Bordi'strusted aide, who frequently checked my bag on my way out. It must have been decided that as soon as the municipality people would be on their way with the sack, Saha would request to check it. It would thus be proven that I collaborated with them to smuggle out vegetables and grains in this fashion. The plan failed because I caught it on time. In order to hush up the whole thing, excuses were made about Aduri's age. 'Aduri-di is old. Maybe she did not understand that the sack had potatoes, mistaking them to be peels.' That was indeed a possibility. But my suspicion was not wrong; I knew it was a conspiracy against me.

The five Pandavas from the *Mahabharata* were brothers, but they had two mothers. Step-siblings would always have some differences with each other. Here too the case was similar. The Teacher-in-Charge and clerk Roy were on one side and the remaining three on the other side. One group always aimed at putting the other at a disadvantage. Once the Teacher-in-Charge had a huge fight with the Super. With me, it was a daily occurrence. In an attempt to extract her vengeance, Bordi called me over to give me some well-meaning advice. 'Cook a pot of rice and vegetables and dispose it off into the cleaner's drum. The Super rarely stays at the hostel or looks after the children. It will help me tighten the leash on him. I will give him a good earful. Will you be able to do it?'

I wasn't able to do it. For me, wasting food was a social crime. I even scolded the kids for wasting food. Because of this habit, I once even scolded a guest at a banquet thrown by Ganesh, who was like a brother to me, on the occasion of his daughter's wedding for leaving around thirty rosogollas untouched on his plate. I gave him a piece of my mind with, 'He is a rickshaw-puller and has arranged for these celebrations with great pain. Has he committed a sin by inviting you? Why are you making him suffer such a huge loss? Eat those and only then can you leave.'

It was my gut feeling that it was the Teacher-in-Charge who had asked Aduri to stealthily put some potatoes in the disposable sack to get back at me for this act of disobedience. I now decided to wait for an opportune time to retaliate.

It was Saraswati Puja and a donation of one-hundred-and-fifty rupees was demanded from me. I was yet to receive my salary and was totally broke. Out of their 'kindness', the school paid the amount for me—to be deducted from my salary later. I was an atheist, but more than that, I did not like any of the celebrations at the school be it a puja or any other occasion. For me, it was a hassle as it increased my workload. On the occasion of Saraswati Puja, the numbers to feed increased from the regular one hundred and fifty to around four hundred as the staff's family members and Boro Sahib's special invitees also joined the crowd. While everyone enjoyed the holiday mood by lazing around idly, I toiled away relentlessly —this was my biggest problem!

As part of the festivities, the responsibility of cutting the fruit offering had fallen on Aduri Gosai and Mother Killer, as usual. Like every year, this year too, they were smuggling off some fruits into their bags in between cutting them. This would be shared by them after the ritual ceremonies were over. Apart from this, whatever could be extracted from the collection of sweets, cashew nuts, chips, and biscuits brought in to welcome Boro Sahib's special guests, whatever rosogollas were left after serving everyone two pieces each, a bucket of khichuri and half a bucket of payesh were also stealthily removed. But with everything put together the bundle grew so big that it was impossible for Aduri Gosai to carry it alone. There was more! The dal, salt, spices and potatoes left after cooking would also have to be taken care of. Up till the khichuri and payesh were taken, I was able to exercise my patience. After that, my patience ran out. A lot of money had gone into buying the grains and spices, which included my own hard-earned income. My ten-year-old son had once been abused for having a bit of this very khichuri. What right did Aduri have to take away all these raw items?

So I pressed the brakes on the rickshaw handle as it was about to leave and said, 'The rice and dal won't leave the school.' The Teacher-in-Charge and clerk Roy tried to save Aduri and placated me, 'Let her go. We will extract a monetary sum from her for this. We will add that sum to the puja account next year.'

I said, 'Then let there be an auction. It will go to the highest bidder.' But my suggestion was not to anybody's liking. As a result, all the extra rice and dal was sent back to storage. Later, it was used to make khichuri for the kids.

* * *

It was those terrible times when the forceful land acquisition in Singur stirred up ripples in the pages of history. Tata built walls around the land and occupied it. Nandigram was left burning. A barbaric government was out to evict the masses from their homesteads. There was a blast on the road to be taken by the Chief Minister's car, allegedly for his part in the conspiracy to trade off Jangal Mahal to Jindal, a multinational corporation. No deaths or injuries were recorded, save for the noise that too a whole ten minutes after the Chief Minister had passed. But treating this incident as a reference point, the CPM police created a havoc. All of this started breeding a sense of protest among the affected masses. Many people, who were previously associated with the CPM, joined in this protest. Many others, despite not physically switching over, were now covertly against the CPM's decisions and actions. In the darkness of the night, these people were killed by unknown assailants. A poster was left behind with these mutilated bodies, saying *Maobad Zindabad*.

In this regard, a story I heard comes to my mind. Since it came to me second hand, there may be some factual errors in my narration. Apparently, there was a time when Hitler wa suddenly taken in by the idea of ending the rise of leaders of the communist movements in his country. To this end, his men were sent to a prison. Some of the most infamous criminals housed there were told, 'You will have to accomplish a task. If you do it, you will be released from the jail and also rewarded with some money. With that, you will be able to spend the rest of your lives in luxury. There is just one condition: you can't breathe a word about it to anyone.' What was this work? They would have to set the Reichstag on fire. The criminals agreed; they were then trained accordingly and sent to

Reichstag in the Red Guard's uniform. Meanwhile, a lot of police officers in white were deployed at the place with orders to fire anybody engaged in destructive activities without sparing a single soul.

The criminals did not realize the politics behind this. Considering themselves to be assisting the government, they ended up setting both the government and the non-governmental buildings on fire. Bullets were rained on them, causing their deaths. Using their bodies as a ruse, Hitler put the blame for the incident on the communists doing, thus finding an excuse for throwing them in jail. There was no telling if the Buddhadeb blast episode was because of a similar conspiracy or not. Otherwise, how was it possible that a month-long search of the area with thousands of police, detectives and dogs prior to his visit did not yield to anybody's eye the three-mile long wire which had been dragged across the paddy fields and connected to the explosive device?

Jindal required thousands of acres of land. For this, the Adivasis needed to be evicted from their lands. A situation had to be created so that the people would be forced to give up their houses on their own—sell off their lands cheaply and just be happy to escape. Under the pretext of the blast, the administration cracked down on the area claiming it to be infested with Maoists, holding them responsible for the incident. A new wave of killings and rapes began. This time, however, the other side also retaliated.

These incidents stirred up the whole country in agitation. From students, teachers, writers, singers, actors, film directors, only one sound of indignation could be heard '*Chii* Chief Minister, *chii*!' The whole country was burning, and dead bodies were piling up. In their long thirty-two years of rule, the CPM Party had never faced such a backlash before. The thought of losing their powers and beloved empire was driving them desperate and insane. Any small sign of protest was being stamped down severely. Nobody was spared: Trinamool Congress, the SUC or even the Forward Bloc. And Jangal Mahal? It was quickly turning into a cremation ground. There were around thirty-five staff at my school, all of them associated with the CPM in some way or the other. The fire raging outside was also driving them to a boiling point. Such was their attitude that if they had a gun in their hands they would have immediately gone and killed a Trinamool member or a Maoist. In me they found a representative of both the groups. Their attacks became more vicious. The five Pandavas were already pretty pissed with me. The Childhood Friend, Mother and Aduri Gosai also joined in.

The five Pandavas wanted to teach me a lesson by using their official powers. The other three, with the support of a few more people sheltered by the school, would defile the food cooked by me by adding salt or sand to it, whenever the opportunity presented thereby provoking the kids against me. Someone else was sent to sabotage the gas cylinder so that I would die in some accident.

Of course, I had no direct proof that it was their doing, but his nature strengthened my suspicions. It could be him, it could be somebody else, I was not sure. The connecting screw between the stove and the gas pipe was found neatly separated one day. Usually, when I turned on the stove, I always had a torch made of a cloth dipped in kerosene wrapped at the end of a stick in my right hand. It was my habit to turn on the cylinder knob with my left hand while pressing down the torch on the stove.

The whole thing had been planned in a way that the dislodged screw would obstruct the path of the gas. Instead of reaching the oven, it would ooze out of the open end of the pipe which usually lay just a foot away from my body. Any slight contact with the torch in my hand, would immediately cause a fire. My clothes could catch fire, I could be burnt me to death. It didn't seem like a coincidence but a well-hatched plan. It was my good luck that this happened in the afternoon, when I was back home and the kitchen empty. For some reason, I was unable to go to work in the evening. My assistant, who went to work in my stead, had to face the brunt of it. The fire did light up, but she somehow managed to escape it.

Just a couple of days after the cylinder incident, it happened again in the afternoon in my absence. Everything was in place in the morning when I had used the stove to cook. In the evening, when I tried to turn it on, I found that somebody had removed the circular plate between the stove and the regulator, which regulated the amount of gas emitted. The moment I would turn on the knob, with the amount of gas oozing out from it and the smaller stove on the side with dal boiling on it, there was a possibility of the cylinder catching fire. This might lead the gas-filled cylinder to explode. If that happened, I would not die alone; others might also die, like my assistant cook. However, my enemies did not have the good sense to think of all that. This time too I got out unscathed by foiling their plans. Before it caught fire, I was able to turn off the gas, albeit putting myself under a lot of risk.

The gas stove was targeted a third time. The thin copper wire right at the base of the stove was flattened with a pair of pliers. The pressure of the gas in a full cylinder was immense. That pressure could have led the pipe, softened in the heat, to burst anytime. It was done in the hope of getting me into an accident and the stove mechanic Babu Das, who had a stove repairing shop, was of the opinion that anybody could have done it. Following this, I wrote a letter to the school managing committee, explaining the situation at my workplace. I knew nothing would come of it, but I still wanted to try. As expected, nothing happened.

As mentioned earlier, I had a mobile phone for staying connected with my family and friends, since my house was far away and the roads difficult. A foot of rain could lead to muddy sludge up to one's knees. Big potholes would develop in the rainy season under the weight of the trucks that were a frequent sight on these roads. It was difficult for my friends to reach me when in need. If they came to meet me at the school, I was rarely informed; if they called at the school, they were told that I was at work and wouldn't be able to receive the call. Not knowing any better, I distributed my number to everybody in the school. I didn't realize then that I was, in reality, digging my own grave. I didn't anticipate that my phone would make my life hell. I started receiving missed calls, threats and abuses from thirty to thirty-two mobile numbers and landline connections. They did not even spare my mother from their filthy rape threats!

Having made a bit of a name for myself, people would invite me for different events. These calls didn't stop even during the duration of these events. I would request them to spare me; that I was on the stage for an event. The voice from the other end would say, 'What bloody event, you fucker?' Once, just as I had boarded a train in order to join a conference at Delhi University, I received a call, 'Going, are you? Go! This will be your last journey. I will make a trip to your place.' As expected, I reached Delhi in a bitter mood. I was there for four days—the whole time nursing the rage in my heart.

As a result, when *Kathadesh*, a reputed magazine from Delhi with readership spread across the country, came to interview me, I couldn't say a single positive thing about the CPM. I vented out all the poison on its pages. In September and October of 2008, they published my views in the issues of their magazine. A Hindi translation of my story 'Reewaz' was also included.

Later, I found out that all the numbers from which I was receiving calls were somehow or the other linked to the school. Interestingly, among them were also a couple of teachers who had joined the school in 2008, many of whom did not even know my name—yet, what a wonderful understanding these people had! They were all on one side of this ugly battle of powerful muscle-flexing. One of the teachers would take turns calling me from a random phone booth, starting from early evening till late in the night, hurling abuses at me whenever I picked up.

None of my complaints ever worked. Yet, I wrote a letter to the Teacher-in-Charge being of the belief that there should be at least one written complaint.

CHAPTER 19

To Eat or Not to Eat?

This multihued world is inhabited by so many different kinds of people, all of whom strive to find the reason for survival and the ingredients for happiness. To attain this happiness, many have taken up the cause of the people; others have rotted away in jail or braved bullets. There have also been others who have taken a vow to harm human society, to destroy lives and derive a demonic pleasure out of it.

As I was saying—happiness. There is a group of people who likes donating rice to the needy and poor at regular intervals for their own happiness or to relieve themselves of sin. I had seen this while in the jail too. On certain special occasions, they would land up at the jail with a basket filled with luchi and halwa, and satisfy themselves by feeding the prisoners. This was a normal occurrence at my school too. People threw banquets for their mother's shradh, or their son's birthday, or for other special occasions. Twice or thrice, the mime artist Jogesh Dutta had also organized such events.

One time, I don't remember exactly when, somebody bore the expenses for organizing such an event at the school. Was it a land broker, a promoter, or a contractor? Whoever it was, this person must have earned great profits because of Boro Sahib's benevolence. In exchange, Boro Sahib must have ordered, 'Everything else can happen later, but first treat the kids to a good meal one day.' There was a leader by the name of Jay or Bijay who lived in the area and was in a position that was a rung lower than Boro Sahib's. He was part of the CPM, a role that he assumed with utmost sincerity. He had amassed a great quantity of wealth just by dealing in land and would sometimes treat the deaf-and-mute children, partly to earn a name for himself and partly in the hopes of reducing his worldly sins.

Once a variety of dishes was being cooked at the school thanks to a benefactor's grant. Apart from the kids, others were also invited to be a part of this feast. The total headcount stood at four hundred. The shopping was already done; we started cooking from the morning. As it was a Sunday, there were also some of the kids helping us. It was a joyous occasion; people were laughing and singing, when suddenly there was terrible news. The Warden's eldest brother had suffered a heart attack (he would later die). The family had no dearth of money given that all the brothers were bringing in wealth. He was, therefore, admitted to Shetty's hospital, one of the most luxurious hospitals in Asia. It took three hours, from eight to eleven in the day, to carry out the required tests. A bypass surgery was to follow, which would take anywhere between six to eight hours. After sending his brother to the operation theatre, the Warden must have felt guilty with the thought, 'There is an event at the school, so many delicacies are being cooked, so many guests will come. And here I am at the hospital!' Despite being a big eater, he vowed not to touch food for shame of what people would say if they saw him munching on mutton while his brother lay in the hospital? As Kamini Roy's poem goes, 'I cannot do my chore/ Constant fear and shame galore/Doubt renders my will wobbling/ What if they say something?' It was this fear that had deprived him of so many delicacies so many times before.

Just as happiness always increases by sharing one's things with ten other people, one can reduce the burden of one's sadness by engulfing ten others in it. If everybody accompanied a person to sit under the open skies or to get burnt in the sun or freeze in the cold or to get wet in the rain, then everyone would be equals and nobody would get the opportunity to laugh at the other. This logic made the Warden rush back to the school for half an hour after getting his brother admitted to the hospital. He scrutinized everything, informed everybody about his brother's situation, adding that he was admitted at the Shetty's Hospital, because of which he wouldn't be able to stay for long.

Right before leaving, he turned around and beckoned me in his own characteristic style. In a low yet nonchalant tone, he said, 'Make sure you don't eat.' I sensed a murderous look in his eyes, just like fire hidden under a pile of ashes. He continued, 'Maybe you won't understand this protocol and sit down to eat. The reason I am clearly forbidding you is because you are not an invitee here. All these arrangements are for those who have been invited and those who eat here regularly.' Having doled out these precious words, he rushed out. He did not have the time to linger, his brother was dying. The fact that he had not lost his sense of duty or religion even in these dire times impressed me.

* * *

Culture, courtesy and civility do not have distinct criteria but are instead determined according to place, time and the individual. In the community that I come from, I have seen a large section of the poor Namashudras residing in the Dandakaranya region. Even though they left Barishal, Faridpur or Khulna in East Bengal, they weren't able to relinquish its customs, traditions, practices and folklore and continued to preserve it like an oyster protects a pearl in its bosom; things that many people would regard as superstitions.

If there was a wedding, or a shradh, or a rice ceremony at somebody's house, the master of the house was expected to go to the house of his guests after the food had been cooked and invite him, 'Please come. The food is done. Come and taste some rice.' Just because the invitations had been sent out days before, it did not imply that the guests would arrive on their own and sit down to eat. That was seen as an insult. According to the holy scriptures, god resides in our guests. It was natural for the guests to feel that, 'I am god. Pay me due respect. Or else we will not grace your house with our presence. Let your food rot in your utensils. We will not eat it.'

I was reared in the womb of this culture. As mentioned earlier, my father had told me that if someone served simple fermented rice with love, you must treat it like a delicacy. But if they serve a delicacy without love, reject it flatly. I treated the food served at the school in a similar fashion. It disgusted me to bring it near my mouth. Even the little that I had to bring in contact with my tongue while cooking to taste if the quantity of salt or sugar was all right, seemed like a curse. On some days, however, I was forced to eat that shit.

One day, the Teacher-in-Charge arranged for a feast at the school in honour of her daughter's marriage, for those who hadn't been able to join the festivities. As usual, I returned home after feeding everybody. Somebody informed her the very next day that Ranjanda did not partake of the feast. She called me over and gave me a thorough scolding. 'Why did you not eat? This is an insult to me.'

I said, 'But I was not invited.'

'What do you mean? Everybody was invited. I did not inform them individually. But I had asked the Super to make sure that everybody attended the event.'

'He did not inform me anything about it. How am I supposed to know! Like every day, I left for home as soon as my work was over.'

'Which means you never eat here?'

I nodded my head. 'No.'

'Why?'

'Boro Sahib instructed me not to.'

She thought of something for a while. Finally, for reasons unknown, she added in the most humane way I had ever seen, 'It is all right that you do not eat on other days, but if there is any event, do not leave without eating. This is my order. How can this be that everybody will eat except for the one who cooked the food? That is not possible.' For this reason, on days when there weren't any strict orders, I had to eat before leaving. Everything depended on the person throwing the feast. It was entirely up to him to decide whom he wanted to spend his money on. The time that Boro Sahib's eldest son got married, almost thousands of people were invited except for me, although, the feast had been cooked by other cooks and not me.

If the organizer followed in Boro Sahib's footsteps, they would obviously not favour me. The Warden had set a benchmark in this regard by madly rushing to the school to make sure this order was implemented even when his brother lay dying in the hospital. I had never seen anyone as aware of his responsibilities as the Warden.

Previously, the Warden and company would have tea brewed at the hostel. Given that I prepared it for them, I would also treat myself to some. It was black tea, without any milk and very little sugar. The cost would have been barely anything. The Warden was still greatly concerned that I was cutting in a share. To this end, he lent his well-meaning advice to the Super and stopped the purchase of tea leaves and sugar —it was not entirely stopped, but it was decided that the stuff would now remain in the custody of Mother Killer. Preparing tea was added to her list of responsibilities. The Super, the Warden and Mother were the only three people who had claim over that tea. This was an extremely insignificant matter. Nonetheless, it was a good way to judge the real nature of a person. These were not scattered incidents, but little sparks of animosity which they harboured in their hearts against me.

I was also a human being. I too felt sad, hurt and angry. But what choice did I have? There was nothing I could possibly do, apart writing a few lines. At that time, I did not have any other alternative save for my writing. I would pour out the stories of my aggrieved heart on paper for the people who were yet to be born and hoped that it would generate a wave of change among thousands one day. Their hearts would puke up a dollop of spit in disgust towards my perpetrators. It was around this time that I wrote a short story titled 'Ei Samay' (The Present Time), describing this unbearable mental torture.

PART II

The Right to Write

CHAPTER 20

Jogenda, Ashokji and *Podokkhyep*

*W*as this even possible? A man from Uttar Pradesh goes to Madhya Pradesh, meets another man and they become friends. The man from Uttar Pradesh then returns back to his state. After ten long years, the man from Madhya Pradesh comes to West Bengal and lo and behold! There he meets the man from Uttar Pradesh again. Doesn't this sound impossible? When the impossible becomes real, one has to realize that there is some hidden power behind it.

Ten years back I bumped into Delhi's Jogenda in Dalli. I chanced upon him again in Kolkata. Having sold off his house in Delhi, he had shifted back to Kolkata to live with his mother in Sodepur where he had bought a house. In Delhi, he used to live in the Chittaranjan Park area. His father had been a high-ranking government officer and his mother, a superintendent at a hospital.

The only son of such an illustrious family, Jogenda was educated at some of Delhi's renowned institutions. All his friends belonged to well-to-do families. However, they all shared a special quality. They were not merely concerned about their own careers but put in an equal amount of thought for the upliftment of the poor and the downtrodden of the country. Their dream was to eradicate inequality from India and see everybody get equal opportunities with regard to food, clothing, education, shelter, medical facilities and employment. It could be said that, in their own heads, they followed ideals which were very close to Naxal ideology.

Jogenda's father wanted to see his son climb up the ladder of education and acquire the highest degree. Perhaps, he wished for his son to build up his career abroad. When the same son started showing Naxal tendencies by putting aside his education and getting involved in anti-state activities, his enraged father had disowned and disinherited him. None of this seemed to affect Jogenda, who continued with his life as before.

Finally, the turbulent seventies ended and the revolutionary ideas that were slowly raising their heads simmered down again. Disheartened with this unexpected turn, Jogenda's friends started settling into a new life by getting married and taking up big positions inside the country and abroad. Their hopes for the country's poor, however, did not die down completely. They decided to spend a portion of their salaries for the country's betterment. To this effect, a shared fund was created where all the responsibilities were put on Jogenda's able shoulders. Still a bachelor and leading a saintly life, he had continued his association with almost every people's movements of the country. Therefore, it was decided that Jogenda would have full freedom in deciding how to spend the money from the fund.

There was not an iota of doubt that Jogenda was the perfect person for this job. He handled this responsibility for years. When the Bhopal Gas Tragedy happened, the first truck to reach with relief items would have Jogenda in it. Be it the Narmada Bachao Andolan or the fishermen's movement at Mongra Dam or any other movement, Jogenda would reach out with help in whatever capacity possible. But he would do all of this silently, not caring about speechifying from a stage or giving interviews to magazines or appearing on TV during news-hour. His true aim was to help the people.

During one of his philanthropic pursuits, he came to Dalli to deliver medicines to the Shaheed Hospital, set up by the Chattisgarh Mukti Morcha. The electoral battles were on. Jogenda managed to hitch a ride from Dalli to Bastar, on a jeep out for campaigning. His wish was to observe in person the Adivasi movement of the region, which was being run by the organization, Chetana Mandal.

I happened to meet him at a village in Paralkot, where refugees from East Pakistan had been rehabilitated. Thereafter, Jogenda would often come and meet me. He would eat whatever little I could offer and sleep beside me on my tattered mat. Our connection severed after he returned to Delhi but he would occasionally write to me, from which I figured that he hadn't been able to forget me.

After the death of his father, his mother re-established their broken ties and welcomed him back into the family. In her old age, her only desire was to breathe her last in her own homeland, Bengal, and not in faraway Delhi. To respect her wishes, Jogenda moved back to Kolkata which turned out to be a boon for me. Had he not returned, there would have been no chance of our reunion. I looked upon this as a strange connection that was supposed to push me further towards my predestined aim. For lack of a better word, one could call it destiny. Otherwise, why would I suddenly meet that person who was never supposed to come back to Bengal or even to Bastar, right here in Kolkata!

After rekindling my old connection with Jogenda, we started meeting often. On one such occasion, he took me to Lord Sinha Road. Here lived a very learned man by the name of Ashok Seksaria. He was the son of Padma Shri awardee Sitaram Seksaria, the founder of Bharatiya Bhasha Parishad. The Marwari community is often criticized for being money-minded. Ashokji was one of those rare individuals who had broken all these myths through his work. Although he hardly wrote anything, he was extremely enthusiastic about getting others to write. There were hardly any Hindi writers in the city who had not come to him for guidance. It was under his inspiration that Alka Saraogi, a Marwari woman who wrote in Hindi, entered the world of literature. Going forward, her debut novel *Kalikatha via Bypass* won the Sahitya Akademi Prize for Hindi in 2001.

My first meeting with Ashokji was a revelation for me. I did not once feel like it was my first time at his place. It was as if I had always known this saint-like literature aficionado. Despite being the jewel of the Marwari community of Kolkata, Ashokji had no fascination for wealth. He loved to be surrounded with books and book lovers. This was the reason he had moved away from the hub of the business community to this palatial house in Lord Sinha Road, where he occupied a solitary room on one side just like a saint who had found refuge in a small cave in the heart of a huge mountain. Out of the family income, he put aside only thirty thousand for his own expenditure. Ashokji was extremely happy to meet me. The morning sunlight sitting bright on his face, he asked me in Hindi, 'So you are Manoranjan Byapari?'

'Yes, I am Manoranjan Byapari.'

'He who never tires out? Who has never learnt how to fail?'

'Who says so?'

'I do.'

'That is entirely untrue. It is only through failures that I have reached where I am today. My life is nothing but a series of failures.'

'To each his own,' he replied. 'Everybody has their own perspective. A glass can appear either half-full or half-empty, depending on the person seeing it. Of course, you might feel that you have failed in life. But the fact that you have lived numerous lives within this one life is what makes you a winner for me. Do you know who fails? One who accepts defeat. If you can stay strong in your heart, there is no power in the world that can defeat you. I would say your life is an example of the spirit of never giving up. It is the life fit for a novel. Somebody should write about your life.' On my departure, he told his goddaughter Alka Saraogi about me, about my life's story. He encouraged her to write about me, about my 'undying spirit'.

On the same day, through Jogenda, I met a few people from CESC (Calcutta Electric Supply Corporation). None of them were poets or writers or politicians. They were simply good people, something that was rare to find nowadays. Devoid of any artificiality, these people were open minded, kind and genuinely helpful souls. Whenever I was depressed, I would run to their office in Dharmatala and my heart would be immediately rejuvenated in the company of Kajalda, Amarda, and Debashishda.

Sekhar was Kajalda's brother and he published a magazine named *Podokkhyep*. Since my return to Kolkata, my second innings with the literary world began with this magazine. I wrote a story entitled 'Khanchar Pakhirao Gaan Gaay' (Caged Birds Also Sing') based on an incident from my time in jail.

* * *

The phrase *Brittyer Sesh Parba* (*The Final Turn of the Circle*) is incorrect. A circle has no first or final. Despite many intellectuals explaining this to me, I still chose this name as the title of my book, as I believed that the journey from birth to death is like a circle. For every birth, death is the grand finale. But is it really the finale? Maybe life does not end with death. After all, a person's work continues to exist even when the person is gone. The same is true about his reputation. At least the body remains. After cremation, the ashes remain. The funerary ceremonies remain. There lies another turn, the final turn of the circle. My life which started as an illiterate child born to illiterate parents completed one turn as soon as I became a man of letters. To guide this in the right direction is, in my belief, taking it to the next level, to the final turn of the circle.

The final turn of the circle is also in a way the story of disrupting the circle, by transgressing beyond the ambit of the traditional circle guided by a raging hungry man's pen. So far, the privileged classes have written about the lower classes. Its beginning can be traced to Sailajananda Mukhopadhya's 'Koila Kuthi' (The Coal Factory). Other writers have carried forward the legacy with this newly awakened consciousness. The writer of *Brittyer Sesh Parba* has emerged from this flowing stream like a wave. There is, however, a significant difference. This writer's attempt has been to use his writing as a means to see and be seen by the privileged classes from his lower-class position.

Brittyer Sesh Parba was published with a total of twenty-two stories. Once the verdict of the book was out, some found it heartwrenching; others cynically called it the ballad of the starving folks.

Many people praised the author's dexterity. Book critic Sandip Bandyopadhyay wrote in the 2000 June edition of the magazine *Anik*,

> Manoranjan has woven fiction, but in reality, has poured his own life into it. Manoranjan's life—his sweat and blood—are enmeshed in every piece of this anthology. Each of his stories has one narrative, the struggle to survive. With a compassion-filled heart, he has not written about somebody else's struggles but the one through which his own life has progressed having been punctured at each point. Being able to read these stories is thus a rare opportunity, one we have not encountered before. Manoranjan reverses the gaze of the same narrative that we are more used to.

Despite the positive reviews, the main purpose was not achieved. The books hardly sold. Not that my book came with a cover or content attractive enough to deserve being displayed on the shelf! This was the year 2000. The book fair was due to begin in a few days. I did not have the financial capacity to open my own book stall or put out a newspaper advertisement. How then could I use the book fair? I did not want to lose such a golden opportunity. My mind started looking for ways, but without much success. It was the age of publicity, and proper publicity could help sell even those with no real value and the contrary could kill actual talents. I was convinced that good publicity could help me greatly.

There was a worm inside my head and there was no telling how it would react once it started wiggling. At that moment, words like 'impossible' vanished from my dictionary. That worm had started acting up again in my brain, trying to make the impossible possible. Come what may, I decided to put myself out in the market! Otherwise, there was no chance of getting my books sold. My money worth fifteen thousand rupees was stuck; this was my only chance of retrieving it. I had not been able to pay the whole amount of credit at my grocery shop. On failure to pay back my debt, I would no longer be eligible for such benevolence. My family would die of starvation.

At that point, *Khas Khobor* was one of the most popular TV shows. Roads emptied out at six every evening when it was broadcasted. People would rush to their TV sets, leaving everything else behind. I found out that their office was on the second floor of Navina Cinema theatre. After that, I just directly launched an attack on their office. I had done a similar thing at the *Anandabazar Patrika*'s office way back in 1988. Nikhil Sarkar, who was otherwise known as Sripantho, was in charge of the Kolkata division of the newspaper at that time. Gulping down a mouthful of cholai,[1] I straightaway approached him, put down the newspaper in front of him and asked, 'It mentions the story of a bus conductor who can play the flute, a vegetable-seller who can play the tabla, a driver who can act. Why does it not have my story?'

Sripantho was a highly respectable man and had perhaps never expected someone to talk to him in this fashion. Shocked out of his wits, he hurled back 'Who are you?' at me. At this, I upturned my jute bag in front of him. All my literary works from the past seven years was there. I told him, 'I am a rickshaw-puller. These are my writings. This qualification is my very own. But *Anandabazar* has never published anything on me. Why so?' On 28 March, the same year, my story was published in Bengal's most circulated newspaper. The truth is the well never comes to the thirsty. The person dying of thirst has to go to the well himself. The same was true for an alcoholic, who could find a seller even in the pitch dark. While for the milkman, it was he who had to go to people's houses.

Jogenda, who always shied away from any kind of publicity, was averse to braggarts. He would say, 'People have this ugly tendency to beat their own drums.' But he had not lived a life like me. I, too, was not like him. Then how could I embrace his life's philosophy? I knew I had a small drum and a broken one at that. Nobody would be interested in giving up their big drums to beat mine. So, the onus was on me to beat my own little drum. The saying goes that god himself plays the drum of the more fortunate. The less fortunate must not only carry their own drums but also beat them. Forget my case, even Bernard Shaw had to resort to so many tricks for selling his books once upon a time. Compared to him, I was just ordinary Madan.

Dibyojyoti Basu of the *Khoj Khobar* fame was then the head of *Khas Khobor*. After three or four days of persistent effort, I was finally able to reach his desk. But wonder of wonders! The moment I opened my mouth, he stopped me, saying, 'Come back some other day. Make sure not to be drunk. I will listen to whatever you have to say.'

I cursed my bad luck. I was drunk on the day of the *Anandabazar* 'attack'. But this time I had drunk nothing but water. Then why would he presume I was drunk? Perhaps my appearance was such that nobody could take me to be a sober person.

It was nothing new! At the *Khas Khobor* office, however, I decided to protest. I said, 'I have not touched liquor. There was a time I used to drink. Not anymore.' I had really given up drinking. The day I went to cremate Neogiji, Vishnu Prasad Chakrabarty, the Bengali advocate from Kanker was with me. He told me how our dear leader had been killed by drunk goons. Neogiji was someone who had made around twenty thousand people give up liquor in one day. If we were his true followers, we too must stop drinking. That would be our way to pay homage to him. From that day onwards, I gave it up.

But Dibyojyoti Basuwas unconvinced. He said, 'I can smell liquor on you!' Smell! For my lunch I had had some chutney made of coriander, green chilly, tomato and garlic. The smell of the damned garlic in my mouth was the main culprit. Only after explaining the truth was I able to get his attention. Thereafter, he listened to the stories of my life and my literary pursuits in all earnestness. He sent a reporter and a cameraman to my place. Two days later a feature was aired on *Brittyer Sesh Parba* and its author. Although it failed to bring about any significant change in the author's daily life, it did manage to sell a lot of books at the book fair. For lack of a proper stall, I spread out my books on the ground and in three days managed to sell around two hundred copies!

So far, I had managed to keep my real identity hidden at my workplace. After this media coverage, everybody came to know exactly who I was and what I could do. They realized I was a writer. What did I write about, was I a competent writer, and why did I write—these questions were not so important. The bigger thing was that I had appeared on TV and had been addressed as a writer. If man was the most intelligent of beasts on the planet, the opposite was equally applicable to him. The idiot box had turned him even more idiotic. The influence of the television set on contemporary life was deadly. People were more taken in by the visuals than the audio. They had the power of changing governments, of making the unknown known and the known unknown.

Till yesterday, I was just an ordinary man. Thanks to the television set, about 200,000 people now knew me by my name and face. Many people came to meet me at my workplace. This caused my co-workers to seethe in anger and envy. People say fame can also bring a lot of flak. This was exactly what happened to me. The backlash began and I started being ridiculed.

* * *

Pranab Chakraborty was a resident of Bardhhaman. He had settled down there permanently with a job and didn't travel much to Kolkata. Also, he no longer had any ties with the RSP (the Revolutionary Socialist Party of India). He was visiting his ill mother at his former address, where I went to meet him. During our conversation, he informed me that the leaders of RSP, the party which had broken away from the Left and become a stooge of the capitalists, were kowtowing to the party only for power. Hence, he had severed all links with them. Currently, he was in charge of two magazines, *Haate Bazare* and *Atul Batul*. He was busy with these and wanted to keep it that way.

Haate Bazare was a four-page weekly magazine, which ran all year. Its Puja edition was especially spectacular, a sparkling jewel amidst the crowd of many other celebrated journals.

After our meeting, I pulled out a copy of *Brittyer Sesh Parba* from my bag and gifted it to him. This was the first time he got to know that I could now read and write, and had gained some reputation as a writer in the literary circuit. He had only known me as the illiterate Madan. Even today many people were not aware that Manoranjan and Madan were the same people. It was beyond his imagination that the illiterate Madan would end up writing an entire book.

He left for Bardhhaman with my book. There was no news from him for some months. Suddenly one day, I received a call at my workplace. From the other end, I heard Pranabda's voice, 'Send me an article for *Haate Bazare.*' My innings with the magazine began with a short story. I had already come across the weekly edition of the magazine, but was yet to see the Puja edition, not having an idea about its grand proportions. On realizing its bulk, I decided to send a novel for the next edition.

Bangla literature has more poets than prose writers. In any case, writing poetry requires less effort. Weaving together a couple of obscure words culled out from the thesaurus and giving it the shape of poetry doesn't seem too difficult. The editors, too, are kinder towards poets. They can easily fit in four poets in one page. Hence, poetry is published like hot cakes. Nobody is actually bothered about the quality of the poem or has any curiosity regarding the sequential pattern that gives words the shape of poetry. Next in line are short stories. If a narrative is short in length and like a story, it will definitely find a place in the pages of some magazine since most magazines are desperate for 'good writing'.

But the situation is completely different in the case of novels. Even if there happens to be a good piece of writing which magazines would love to publish, it is not feasible for them to do so. The ones who are capable, do not care for a lesser-known author's work.

Hence, *Haate Bazare* seemed like a mine of treasure to me. My entire novel was published here. It seemed like *my* magazine, I felt like I was Pranab Chakraborty, the publisher, and Mita Chakraborty, the editor. The publisher 'me' had only one word of advice for the author 'me'—the writing should be excellent; otherwise, it deserved to be dumped into the Ganga instead of being sent to Bardhhaman on a train. The other option was for me to go to the river Damodar to dump it.

For the entire next year, I wrote a page or two each day and finished two entire novels: *Channachara* (Homeless) and *Batashe Baruder Gondho* (English transaltion available as *There's Gunpowder in the Air*). The first was based on the struggles of a group of homeless people who had taken shelter at a railway station. Its protagonist, Naba, was one with no past or future but only a present, where survival itself was an everyday struggle. For me *Channachara* was a tribute to these people from the margins, chronicling their dreams, love and vengeance. *Batashe Baruder Gondho*, the other novel, was about a group of prisoners among whom were a large number of Naxalites. My attempt was to foreground their ideological struggles, fearlessness and sacrifices. Its prime character was a thief, who would rather embrace death in a jailbreak expedition with the Naxalites in the hope that his son would be called a revolutionary's son and not the child of a thief. I selected the first one for *Haate Bazare* and thankfully even Pranabda approved of it. As he began the process of publication, I told him of the second novel, lamenting, 'I don't know where to send it and who will publish it.'

He said, 'Just send it.'
'Where?'
'To me.'
'What will you do?'
'There are so many newspapers in Bardhhaman. Will send it to somebody. You just send it.'

As a result, I sent the second novel too. Thereafter, every time I called him to ask about the status of the novel, he would say, 'It is being published.'
'Where?'
'You will see.'

I did see. In the 1411 (2004) Puja edition of *Haate Bazare*, both the novels were published. *Channachara* written by Manoranjan Byapari and *Batashe Baruder Gondho* by Madan Dutta. My heart leaped with joy. But why so? Pranabda said, 'Had I got *Batashe Baruder Gondho* first, I would have published that. But by the time I received it, I had already finished composing *Channachara*, so I couldn't leave it out. At the same time, I did not want to lose a novel like *Batashe Baruder Gondho* to some other magazine. I had no option but to publish both of them.' I had no clue that Pranabda would do something like this. He had not given me a single whiff of it. We established a new bond between us. He became my editor and I his regular author.

The following year, *Amanushik* (Inhuman), another of my novels, was published in his magazine. It was about an innocent man who was unjustly hanged because of a wrong sentence passed under the blind legal system. The story revolved around why he was killed and who benefited from his death. This was my first attempt at channelling my personal rage into a collective one through my writing. As a fuming author, tormented by a handful of CPM followers at his school, I tried lashing at the entire administrative system. Like a drain infested with dengue-ridden mosquitoes needs to be sprayed with medicine, I targeted my arrows towards the Writers' Building via Alimuddin[2] by probing how they could have launched a full-blown attack to suck the life out of a distressed wretched man, turning his death into a grand festival—an episode that had filled my entire being with hatred. My biggest regret was that these same people were our rulers. The bearded poet has said, 'When the punisher cries with the punished, it is the greatest judgement.' So far, that's how I had known them. But gradually they were showing their true colours and emerging to be merely theatre actors playing the role of a butcher in the guise of a yogi. That is why I needed to bare the facts in my novel,

> A brutal state murder has happened. Yet, there has been not a single protest from the socially conscious section of the society, no word from the poets and artists. What is the guarantee that our rulers will not pass off another such murder as a grand festival in the future? By now they know well that human beings have turned into spineless reptilian beasts with no power to resist. This will prove to be harmful for the future of the country.

This novel was published in *Haate Bazare* in the 2006 Puja edition. There was no need to tell how accurate my prediction was, especially after the Netai massacre case in the Singur-Nandigram incident.[3] Had people been more aware and resisted as a collective, many lives could have been saved. I was not able to sleep the night Dhananjay was hanged. My friends had taken out a candle light vigil, while I had written all night placing myself in the shoes of the unfortunate man. That is what had later taken the shape of this novel.

In 2007, *Janajuddha* (People's War) was published. It was a dialogue-heavy novel. The Singur-Nandigram incidents had still not unfolded. In my own way, I wrote about the eviction of the common man from his habitat, the mushrooming of industrial projects in different places and its ill-effects on human life. It was the story of the common man's fight against industrialization. This was followed by my novel *Bibarno Shabdera* (Colourless Words). It was based on a group of people living in Dandakaranya, whose state of existence evoked more laughter than pain. In 2008 and 2009, *Chandal Jibon* (*My Chandala Life*) was published.

Apart from these novels being published in *Haate Bazare* annually, I was also regularly publishing my short stories every month with Pranabda's *Atul Batul*. This was the reason I had more readers in Bardhhaman, rather than Kolkata. Simultaneously, I was also writing for a number of Kolkata-based publications, like *Bartika, Bhasabandhan, Adal Badal, Chaturtho Duniya, Jwalabhumi* and *Dwipbangla*. In the meantime, I won a certificate and some ready cash as first prize for winning the 2003 Umapada Duttaroy and Niharbala Devi story writing contest organized by *Atul Batul*. Before this, I had won a second prize at another contest arranged by them. Despite winning the second position, the prize money was immense. I had received money for my writing only twice before this; once from *Manorama*, an amount of four hundred and fifty rupees, and another time from *Pratikkhan*, an amount of one hundred and fifty rupees.

When I went to *Pratikkhan's* office in order to collect an article, I found them guarding the writer's remuneration of one hundred and fifty rupees for eight years just like a dragon would protect its treasure. In the meantime, Pranabda collected all the short stories I had written during the time period of 2000 to 2005 and published a second anthology *Jijibisha-r Golpo* (The Stories of Jijibisha). Thereafter, a place was fixed for me in the annual *Haate Bazare* magazine to publish my novel. From 1411 (2004) to 1419 (2012) in the Bengali calendar, ten of my novels were published with them.

When *Chandal Jibon* was first published with *Haate Bazare*, the tremendously enthusiastic reaction from the audience enthralled me. As a result, I was greatly inspired to publish the novel as a proper book at the 2009 Kolkata Book Fair, albeit after incurring some debts. There, the novel was finally released in the book format.

Notes

[1] Country liquor.
[2] Writers' Building was the seat of the government from the days of the British Raj; it is being repaired and the government offices are at Nabanna, Howrah; Alimuddin refers to Alimuddin St where the CPM Party has its headquarters.
[3] In a horrific massacre in Netai village, Lalgarh, at least 7 people including 2 women had been shot dead by the CPM's private armed brigade (*harmad vahini*) while they were protesting against the CPM's attempt to force young men to join the armed brigade. From http://www.archive.cpiml.org/liberation/year_2011/feb_11/commentary4.html

CHAPTER 21

More Literary Expeditions

I happened to come in touch with Manoj Bandyopadhyay, who ran *Priyoshilpo* magazine and publishing house. His wife was the poet Nandita Bandyopadhyay, under whose editorial guidance *Kabiman Patrika* was published. It was not that I did not write poetry. Actually, I could not write poetry. One such poem, which I could-not-write, was published with *Kabiman*. That's how I was introduced to the couple. I had told Manojda during a meeting that my world of starvation was filled with prose; I was not a verse-person at all. I submitted one of my manuscripts to him for review. This was a novel I had composed based on my experiences of living in Chhattisgarh, where I had the opportunity of observing the life and culture of a small tribal group from close quarters. My handwriting, however, did not inspire him to read the manuscript. It was left unread even after six months had passed. Dust started piling up on its pages. I was firmly convinced that if he read it once, he would definitely want to publish it, but I did not know how to make him read it. I would ask him every few months, if he had read it. The answer would always be, 'Not yet! Very busy.'

Finally, I said to him in great rage, ' Give it to me, I will take it back. It's useless to keep the manuscript hanging here. Let me try elsewhere.' Manojda returned the manuscript. He expressed regret for not being able to read it. When he could have said, 'Sir, how do you expect me to fathom this handwriting?' he had said instead, 'Have some tea.'

While sipping tea, I told him, 'If you give me some time, I can read you two pages of my novel.'

The gentleman was unable to say no to my face. He gave permission and said, 'Please do.'

I started reading. Being no gentleman myself, I ended up reading ten pages instead of the promised two. Then I paused. The moment I paused he said, 'Why did you stop? Read a bit more.' I read ten to twelve more pages. Then I packed the manuscript and put it in my bag. I said, 'I will now leave. 'By that time, Manojda's facial expression had totally changed. He said, 'Manoranjanda, if you don't mind, please leave your manuscript behind. I promise to publish it in the forthcoming Book Fair.' He did keep his word. It did not come out in the forthcoming year, but in the following one. In the 2006 book fair, *Anya Bhuvan (Another* World) was published—my first novel as a book.

Both my publishers were financially not that solvent. It was much more than a business venture for them. Their voluntary act of draining money on me was their way of motivating an author, who was hardly known but had a lot of potential. Nonetheless, I was well aware of my own responsibilities. If my publishers weren't able to retrieve the amount they had spent on me, they would not be interested in publishing any of my works in the future. With this thought in mind, I started making trips to different schools and colleges during my afternoon breaks, armed with my books. Owing to *Khas Khobor* and other factors, many people were already familiar with my name because of which one or two copies always got sold. But compared to the labour put in or the travel cost, it was hardly anything. During *Brittyer Sesh Parba*, Dibyojyoti Basu's support had brought in a tide. I was able to sell around thirty to thirty-five copies at Jadavpur University within hours. This time, however, it did not even cross five. That worm in my head started wiggling again. It was time to bring in a high tidal wave. I was in no position to promote my books. All that I could do was create such a situation that would act as the publicity stunt for the book.

I remember a man who had climbed up the highest point of the Howrah Bridge and garnered a lot of publicity. What if do the same with my book? Another man had garlanded a tiger. He, too, had attracted a lot of attention. Unfortunately, he had also died because of his antics. What if I don't die? With various such possibilities squirming in my head, I could not help but laugh at my own foolishness. There was another place, higher than Howrah Bridge and required more courage than going to a tiger. If I reached that place, nothing else would be required. All the publicity would come crawling to me. So, one afternoon, armed with my broken drum, I left for the *Anandabazar Patrika* office. It was the only newspaper in Bengal which sold almost 2,000,000 copies and was read by around 20 million people. The newspaper was such that one may love it or hate it, but one could not ignore it. There were many other newspapers, but even after reading them the public was always interested to know 'Let's see what *Anandabazar* has written!'

A beautiful woman was at the reception desk at their office. I approached her. In my gruff voice I asked, 'I have a news item with me. Whom should I meet to make sure that it finds a proper place in the newspaper?' The woman was extremely gentle and helpful. She said, 'Talk to reporter Riju Basu.'

'How?'

'Call him.'

'Can you give me his number?'

She gave me his number without expressing any annoyance. As soon as I dialled the number, I found Riju Basu on the other end. 'Hello, can I take two minutes of your time?'

'For what?'

'I am an author. I have brought two of my books with me. I wanted to give them to you.'

'Submit it at the reception, I will pick it up.'

'That will not serve the purpose. This book has a history of its own. I want to tell you about that.'

My voice reflected my obstinacy, courage and intensity. This compelled him to leave his air-conditioned room and meet me outside. He said, 'Wait, I'll come.' He came downstairs in some time. He must have taken around only ten-to-twenty steps, but I felt like I was in seventh heaven. In a short span, my name and life's struggles reached the Bengalis, not just in Bengal but all over the country:

something that so many wretched souls like me must have only dreamt of.

In the scorching heat of the afternoon son, Riju Basu himself travelled to my little hut. With him was cameraman Rajen Bose. They stayed for almost two hours. I spoke nonstop during that time. Instead of feeling conscious in the presence of such a big personality, I narrated my story right from my childhood to the present date. Finally, on 3 April 2006, occupying almost a quarter of the page, Riju Basu's report on me was published with my picture in *Anandabazar Patrika* under the title, 'Not a Tree, but the Sapling of a Fighter Banyan Is His Inspiration'.

* * *

My debut article was with *Bartika* magazine, published in 1981. I was not satisfied writing mere surveys. I wanted to write stories, to become an author. In that hope, I ended up writing a couple of stories. But *Bartika* did not publish fiction at that point of time. I decided to send my fiction pieces to some other magazine. I also knew that almost everybody who was associated with the world of magazines knew of Madan Dutta, a rickshaw-puller who also wrote, whom Mahasweta Devi was very fond of. They would perhaps publish his writings just to please Mahasweta Devi. How then was I to test whether I could actually write? As an experiment, I sent four stories to four publications: *Ranar*, *Hatiyar*, *Sisrikkha* and *Lok Bigyan* under the pseudonym of Jijibisha. Later, I sent another story to *Banga Barta*. At that time, Naren Bhattacharya, a former neighbour with a cultural bent of mind who had introduced me to Manojda, had started publishing a magazine by the name of *Udaharon*. I contributed a story entitled 'Runner-er Nupur' ('The Runner's Anklets') to this magazine and a poem for its next issue. The poem was never published. The magazine went out of circulation. Naren entered the world of acting. He formed his own theatre group, which too he named 'Udaharon'.

I had not kept any second copy of the poem which I submitted to Naren. I didn't know at that time that it was mandatory to always preserve at least one copy of any submitted piece. This sense came to me much later when Afif Fuad, the editor of the little magazine *Dibaratri-r Kabya* lost the manuscript of a 300-page novel of mine named 'Path Hara Pothik' (A Lost Traveller). It was based on my wonderful travel experiences from the year 1977, when I ran away from home to reach Lucknow via Farakka, New Jalpaiguri, Darjeeling and Guwahati, without spending a single paisa. A part of this travel narrative was later used in my novel *Chandal Jibon*.

I met Naren again after almost twenty years. It was he who recognized me. He had seen me in *Khas Khobor*. He had got to know that the pen that I had picked up so many years ago, was still intact in my hand despite the many storms I had weathered. He reminded me of his little magazine *Udaharon* and wanted to know if I had submitted the poem to any other newspaper. I had completely forgotten about the poem. But Naren still remembered a line from that never published poem. 'If you could laugh, I could kill myself.'

We went to the Jadavpur Coffee House. There, much to my surprise, I discovered that all the young authors, poets, actors hanging out knew about this yet-to-be-published poem's poet and the story of his ever strange diverse life. It was Naren's doing. I realized, even though I was not physically present, I was there as a metaphor, as a myth. This very same Naren one day felicitated me with an address of honour at Bijoygarh's Niranjan Sadan as part of Udaharon's 2007 Theatre Festival.

Later, I met a young boy from the village of Ranabhutiya-Katipota by the name of Uttam Panja. Their colony, each year, celebrated Jagaddharti Puja with great pomp and show, holding a fair for the occasion, where a theatre contest would be held for twenty days. They also published a magazine named *Jwalabhumi*. Uttam would physically drag me every year, make me sit on the stage and honour me with a garland, an address of honour and a memento. It was on this stage that I had the fortune of sitting alongside famous writers like Pabitra Mukhopadhyay, Ajit Pandey, Soumitra Chattopadhyay, who was also an actor, Nabarun Bhattacharya, Ardhendu Chakraborty and Nabaneeta Dev Sen.

Around this time, I met by chance an extraordinary writer by the name of Manik Mandal on the road. He had a heart like the wandering Bauls. He wouldn't bathe for days, or eat or sleep, wandering on the roads in such a way that one could easily mistake him for a crazy person from his unkempt beard and hair. But the man was extremely talented. He knew everybody, right from the king to the pauper. The day, I went to his place with him, he heard my stories and said, 'Wait, let me get you a TV programme.' He immediately called someone and within half an hour, one of his friends arrived. His name was Amit Ghosh. He spoke with me and reached my house some days later with a full unit of light and camera. The shoot went on for three to four days. Some things were narrated by me, the others by the actor playing my role. There were around ten to twelve people, playing different roles. That's how the docu-film *Sadharon-Asadharon* (Ordinary Extraordinary) came into being.

This 30-minute long programme was then aired on Akash Bangla three consecutive times. After this, a crowd of TV reporters started lining up at my door. Tara TV created a half-hour-long programme *Tara-r Najar*, narrated by somebody called Ananya. From Akash Barta came a reporter named Adhir, Dipannita came from the cable channel Dishari and Manirul from ETV. After a few days, Dibyojyoti Basu came again, but not in person, he sent his minions. He was in charge of a new programme called *Khoj Khabar* for Akash Bangla. As more and more people were getting curious and excited about me, the folks at my workplace, the school—colleagues and others of more influential ilk—were growing more incensed. It seemed like the people around me were wild animals like cheetahs and hyenas. They would tear me apart as soon as they found the opportunity. How could I gain so much fame? How could I appear on TV this frequently? This was the reason behind their rising rage.

One day, a letter signed by Ramkumar Mukhopadhyay, the regional secretary of Sahitya Akademi, reached the school. It said: 'Sahitya Akademi is arranging a programme in the hall room of Jiban Tara Bhavan. We will be highly obliged if you read one of your short stories or poems at this event. This programme has been arranged to hear those people who continue writing amidst so much adversity and whose writings have a sense of originality. We would hope that you would accept our invitation to join the event .... Please confirm your presence through post or a call.'

There was no way I would refuse such an event! But I could have conveyed my acceptance, only if I had received the invitation, right? After the courier package bearing the letter reached my school's address, the 'Sahitya Akademi' tag on the cover was enough to explain the situation to the school's responsible administrator. The letter was sent back with a stamp and a sign. I was home for the afternoon break, so the letter was sent back unopened. How could Sahitya Akademi address a letter to an ordinary cook? Was there nobody else? Wasn't this a slap on the faces of the more literate people? Amarda, an employee at the CESC office whom I regarded as an elder brother, was quite close to Ramkumar Babu. He had acquired my address from him. It is through Amarda that I got to know that the letter had been back.

Procuring Ramkumar Babu's number, I called him and informed why I had not received the letter. I told him that I would definitely come! Through *Anandabazar Patrika* I got to know that poet Binod Bera, prose writer Abdul Jabbar and story writer Ansaruddin would all be there. My imminent presence remained undisclosed, as the advertisement had already been sent to the newspaper office before my confirmation.

The event was on the very next day. I informed the school in the afternoon that I was sick and took leave from work. Thereafter, I left in the direction of Jibontola Bhavan at Taratola. As soon as I reached the bus stand, however, I was informed that the Bus Owner's Union had gone on strike the same day with the demands of raising the bus fare. Taxis were running of course, but I did not have enough money at the time to take one. Suddenly, out of the blue, a motorbike came and stopped in front of me. I didn't know the boy much, but it seemed he knew me. They had a TV shop, where he had seen me on screen many times before. Upon hearing of my plight, he offered to let me ride pillion on his bike towards Taratola. When I reached the Jibon Tara Bhavan, the programme was just about to begin. Amarda, worried, was waiting for me. He breathed a sigh of relief on seeing me.

Sahitya Akademi had named the event as 'Asmita'. Giving examples of how the invited authors continued their literary pursuits despite such hardships, the host of the event Ramkumar Mukhopadhyay narrated my story with a lot of anger. He stressed on the difficult conditions in which I had to write and added why I hadn't received the invitation letter to the event.

I didn't know my exact age. It could be fifty or above, but I had not let my heart age. It was still stuck in the early hours of a person's life, at the age, when the heart is filled with courage and rebellion and the self refuses to accept injustice. In the words of the bearded bard, 'He who sins and he who lets him sin, are both deserving of the same hatred from all quarters of life.' This saying kept poking my heart and charging it up. It was natural for a person who followed this saying to become the target of organized attack by opponents. This was not the case in West Bengal alone; this would have been true in Rama's kingdom too.

I had moved around quite a bit in life. Life had taken me to hundreds of places and made me go through a whole host of experiences. In knowing thousands of people and in experiencing so many things, my life had been able to come out of its pit of ignorance and find such a priceless gem. He who had the capacity to embrace life's overabundance with intense passion, would always find his baskets filled to the brim.

Somebody had once said that consider the earth with its mountains, rivers, forests, deserts, its towns, cities, ports, its living world, to be a grazing ground filled with weeds. He who wanted to be an author, would graze on this land like a cow and carefully pluck out the greenest of grass. He would eat it, digest it and excrete the waste material as dung. The main substance would stay in his possession, soon to be converted into milk. This milk would be donated for the well-being of humans. The writer was indeed nothing but a cow. He would eat the most inferior quality grass and give back the most superior quality milk.

As for me, it felt like the place on which I was grazing was not a ground or a field or a forest. Within its grassy surface was hidden a couple of leeches, snakes and scorpions. This was the ground where tigers, bears and human skull hunters wandered about. Life was the name of a terrible experience; moving forward in spite of pain was another name of life. In this life that I had led and was leading, it felt like I was being burnt alive on a funeral pyre. There was darkness everywhere and no direction. There was no one whose hand I could hold and move two steps ahead. There was no one to pick me up if I fell or to push me ahead.

* * *

One afternoon I went to Mahasweta Devi's house. At that time, she lived in Golf Green. I took my recently published novel, *Chandal Jibon*. She had written the Introduction for the book. Handing over the book to her, I knelt and asked for her blessings. Two teardrops from my eyes fell on her feet. It was as if the secret history behind those years of humiliation, poverty, complaints and torture were hidden in these teardrops that seemed to be saying, 'Look, look at me. I have kept aglow the little lamp that you lit in my heart one day, despite all storms. I have protected it like my life, like my breath, shielding it within my two weak hands. And I have carried it like a flag.' I have never bowed down to any fear, nor sold myself to greed. With my head held high and my spine straight, I have only spoken the bitter truth with all my courage every time. This book was its biggest evidence.

Mahasweta Devi did not utter a single word. She just held me tight and planted three affectionate kisses on my forehead. Her eyes welled up. There was no visible sign outside, but it felt like a round of rain had washed away the desert of her heart. Patting my head with her hands, she said, her voice choked with emotions, 'I did not realize that you were a dark horse made for a long race. I really wasn't able to recognize you that day.'

She taught at the Jogesh Chandra Chaudhuri Law College in 1980 and lived at a rented flat in the house of Jyotirmoy Bose at Ballygunge. She travelled daily on a bus or a rickshaw. In that short trip, she would usually forget about the rickshaw-puller as the rickshaw-puller would forget about her. That day, things happened differently. This rickshaw-puller was different from the others. He read books and kept himself abreast of the happenings around the country. She was editing a journal by the name of *Bartika* at that point of time. One of its founding editors was Manish Ghatak, who was Mahasweta Devi's father and which she now edited. As the new editor, she was trying to give a different shape to the magazine by focusing more on providing the actual picture of the lives of the common man living in the villages instead of delving into short stories, novels or poems. The magazine had already received writings by people who worked as labourers on farms; cultivators; small vendors; bricklayers; hands in shoe factories, but not yet from a rickshaw-puller. She had a sudden idea of publishing an article by a rickshaw-puller. The lives of these people working in Kolkata were filled with a lot of issues that she wanted to bring to the forefront.

So, she had made this rickshaw-wallah write for *Bartika*. It was published in its January 1981 issue. A few days later, she had forgotten about this person. She boarded one rickshaw or the other every day. It was impossible to remember so many faces. So many people wrote for *Bartika*, how could she remember all her contributors?

Once, Prime Minister Indira Gandhi went to Basanti in the Sunderbans. Something must have stirred up inside her on seeing a child labourer at a tea shop for she called him near and petted him. Soon after, she left for Delhi. Everybody back in Basanti expected the boy's fate would change. But in reality, nothing happened. Returning to Delhi and burdened with work, Indira completely forgot about him. The kid continued with the same work, but somewhere within the depths of his heart the memory must still be burning bright. In an almost similar incident, an MLA from Chhattisgarh got the opportunity to shake hands with Bill Clinton. For a month, he did not use that hand for any work. In fact, he did not even wash it. And Clinton? He must have washed his hands with an antibacterial soap to cleanse it of that poor person's touch!

For Mahasweta Devi it couldn't have been such a big event, but in the life of the rickshaw-puller it was astounding, the beginning of a new era in his life. Her small touch had given rise to a small seedling of hope in the rickshaw-puller's heart: 'I will be a writer someday!' Armed with that hope in his heart, he had spent twenty-eight years of his life making a place of his own in the crowd of thousands of writers. This was nothing less than a story or a novel. Did she feel guilty? That she should have done something more for the young man? Humans were for humans, life for life. Had she extended a hand of help and support, he could have gone much further in life. Had that been the case, history would have remembered her not as Eklavya's Guru Drona, but as that of the victorious Kurukshetra hero Sabyasachi's guru Dronacharya, all depicted in the *Mahabharata,* and given her the same respect. Was that the reason that I sensed some regret in her voice? 'I really did not understand that day. I have published so many people's work in *Bartika*, nobody could become like you.'

My father had a silver coin. He used to call it his 'sholo ana' (16 annas that made a rupee then). He had picked it up on the way some day. Despite severe scarcity he never exchanged it for money but protected it like a dragon. Later on, however, the money found on the street was lost to the street. My own sholo ana was still intact. I couldn't ever lose it. With this determination, I had held on to my two-rupee worth pen with my life. This was my pride and my arrogance—the sholo ana of my life was the fact that I was an artist, I was a creator, I was as great as any god!

A king had once playfully declared on a bitterly cold winter night that he would give one thousand rupees to anyone who stayed submerged up to his neck in the water of a pond. One man did so. When the king asked him how he had managed to do this, the man said, 'See that window far away? A ray of dim light was emanating from it. I spent my night staring at it. The night passed away quickly.' There was such a ray of dim light in front of me too: hope that this grave darkness would pass away one day. A bright sun would be up soon and its light would wash over everything. In that hope against hope, I had been able to cross over those calamitous days. I had been able to cross mountains, oceans, forests and the deserts of danger and obstacles in life.

Handing over the book to Mahasweta Devi and seeking her blessings once again, I descended the stairs of her house, down to the streets where rickshaws were running, a poor boy was picking up paper, and a homeless mother was sitting with an infant in her lap and groaning for some stale roti. That was my road too! I would have to walk down this road to reach my destination, with no companion who could show me the right way or pick me up if I fell. To stop would be to reach the end, to stop for death. And I was not ready to die yet.

CHAPTER 22

Ananta Acharya, Khokon Majumdar and Dalit Writings of Bengal

They say it is not completely impossible to find a lost needle in a haystack, but who would spend their energies searching for something that is so readily available for a rupee? If a person still decides to do this, he is nothing but crazy! Such a crazy person existed, who had been looking for me since 1981 ever since coming across my writing in *Bartika*. He wanted to establish contact with me. His first stop was at the *Bartika* office but I had already given up frequenting that place! Besides, people like me did not have a stable address, so nobody could help him much. But they knew that I was a rickshaw-puller near Jadavpur and could be found somewhere in that area. He reached Jadavpur only to find that I was not there either; and that I now lived somewhere near Narendrapur. On reaching Narendrapur he found that my life, which was like a dry leaf being tossed about in the storms, hadn't been able to grow roots there. I had been pushed far away in Chhattisgarh by that time and joined the legendary labour leader Shankar Guha Neogi at Dalli to work with his organization.

He came to Chhattisgarh, not for the rickshaw-puller but to meet Shankar Guha Neogi. He, however, did harbour a small hope that maybe he would finally be able to meet me. After asking around, he found out that I lived 200 miles away from Dalli in Paralkot of the Bastar district, but often came to Dalli. As luck would have it, I had been in Dalli just the previous week, stayed for four-five days and then returned to the deep forests of Bastar. He stayed in Dalli for a week, but I did not make a trip during that time and he was once again unable to meet me. Many years passed in this fashion. Neogiji passed away and I returned to West Bengal.

Suddenly one day, he chanced upon a news item that the person, whose bore the same name as that of the rickshaw-puller he was looking for was to inaugurate a programme arranged by the Bangla Dalit Sahitya Sanstha at the Poundra Kshatriya Bhavan in Garia. To find out if this was the same person, he reached the event and once the preliminary introductions were done pulled me into a warm embrace, 'Mashai, you are such an elusive person! I have searched high and low for you, but you have been here all this while!'

This man's name was Ananta Acharya and, like his name, he was infinite. He was akin to a tube well, two-and-a-half feet outside while the rest of its hundred feet underneath. I had no measure of the depth to which Anantada's roots had been spread out in society's welfare. He was of infinite wonder to me.

Before 1911, higher-caste people would insult us by referring to us as Chandals, spew hatred against us and avoid us. The land we stood on had to be purified by sprinkling dung water and our touch had to be cleansed off with a bath. A group of barbaric people found great pleasure in calling innocent humans criminals, just on the basis of their caste at birth, and used that allegation to humiliate, ignore and torture this targeted group. This inhuman ill-practice still exists, although in Bengal it is not practised as nakedly as in Bihar or Uttar Pradesh. There, if a Dalit dying of thirst happens to drink water from a well owned by an upper-caste person, he would be beaten to death for his crime. In West Bengal, this was not the case. From the time when the Communist movement picked up steam here, caste hatred has been encased within the airy envelope of class hatred—just like bitter medicine encased in a sweet capsule.

Now, a group of caste lords were trading the theory of castes coexisting together, as a result of which the poisonous tree of caste hatred was slowly branching out again. Despite the long drawn Left rule in Bengal, the so-called upper-caste people were refusing to let small children eat the midday meal cooked at the schools by these so-called lower-caste people. Take me, for instance. Was caste difference the sole reason why people were constantly trying to stir trouble for me at the school where I worked? Not really. The heart of a large section was burning merely because of my caste identity. Had I carried the surname of Banerjee, instead of a Byapari, the attack wouldn't have been all-pervasive. Somebody would have surely taken my side. Caste had stamped its presence in the consciousness of the people of Bengal in such a way, that even the perpetrator did not understand the reason sometimes. People who used words like 'Chamar', 'Muchi' or 'Kaora' loosely in stereotypical utterances, hardly realized the actual import of what they are saying.

Over the ages, some higher-caste people have also joined hands with the lower castes to protest against the caste system. This list included intellectuals like Shibram Chakraborty, Sukumari Bhattacharji, Shibnath Shastri, Ranajit Guha, Goutam Roy, Hirendranath Mukhopadhyay, Sekhar Bandyopadhyay, with Rabindranath Tagore right at their apex who strove to terminate this practice. They took their protests right from the streets to the domain of literature.

Out of these socially conscious higher-caste people I have known, the one I believe is at the forefront currently, is Ananta Acharya. To be honest, when I met him for the first time, his hair was dishevelled, his beard overgrown and his clothes unwashed. I did not see his torn shoes or the bag on his shoulder filled with books, but only his two worn-out feet. Unless one had walked thousands of miles, it was impossible to have such feet. I also listened to him. There was no attempt to polish it with intellectual jargon, theoretical embellishments, or the arrogance that came with knowledge. From whatever he told me in his simple language, I was convinced that there was no corruption in the work that he had made into his religion. There was no self-interest and there was no attempt to assume leadership. His only desire was to have a caste-free world. He immediately took a liking towards me, and thus our association began. We started meeting more often, exchanging ideas and getting solid work done.

The organization with which Anantada was associated was called DAFODWAM (Democratic Action Forum of Dalits and Women). Like APDR, PUCL, Jan Chetana Manch, Bharat Jan Andolan, this was a social organization. Their only slogan was 'Struggle is our answer to every forceful torture.' *Chetona Lahar* was the mouthpiece of DAFODWAM, for which I became a regular writer. I already had *Haate Bazare*, now I found another magazine where I could write freely and where there was no fear of the editorial scissors.

Anantada came to meet me one day, as he often did, this time accompanied by another person who was eager to meet me. The numbers of such individuals were growing by the day. They came not just to meet me, but to examine me and to impale me with their overabundance of questions. Some said, 'You never went to a school for real? I hope you are not making it up!' Others said, 'You don't exactly look like an author. Are you sure you have written all this?' Anantada had told me of this new trend abroad where apparently authors hid their names to write books as killers, burglars as well as hustlers and the readers lapped it up.

The person who came with Anantada was exactly like him. He couldn't be placed within the conventional category of a gentleman, in the sense of the outer appearance. He must have been fair once but the sun had burnt his skin into a shade of copper. He was thin and quite old and couldn't walk properly. When he spoke, his throat made a raspy noise that was difficult to decode, because of which Anantada had to 'translate' whatever he was saying.

This man, originally from North Bengal, had come to Kolkata for two compelling purposes: one, for his medical check-up; and two, to meet Manoranjan Byapari! We sat at a tea shop near the road—he asking questions and I answering them. Time passed in the blink of an eye and suddenly an hour-and-a-half had passed. It was time for him to go back. I then turned to Anantada and asked him, 'We discussed so many things, but I still haven't asked the most important question yet. What is his name?'

Anantada said, 'His name is Khokon Majumdar.'

Binayak Sen, author and Ananta Acharya.

In 1977, when I was in Siliguri, I did hear this name a countless number of times. Khokon Majumdar's name was one out of the five or six names of leaders cited when giving the credit for organizing the farmer uprisings in Naxalbari, Khoribari and Phansidewa. Was he the same Khokon Majumdar? It was impossible. He was of a much higher league. It was not possible that he would come to meet an ordinary writer—it had to be somebody else!

Author with Khokon Majumdar.

I told Anantada, 'I have heard this name many times.'

'It could be possible,' responded Anantada. 'There are so many people by the same name. He, however, is not anybody famous. He is just an ordinary person like you and me.'

Our conversation came to an end. They had to leave. As I waited for him to board the bus, Khokon babu shook hands with me. He said, 'We will meet again.' He then fished out a packet from his bag.

'What's in here?'

He said, 'A book. I brought it for you. I, too, like you have never been to a school. Do read it and tell me how you like it.'

I didn't open the packet immediately but put it in my bag for the time. Soon they were off on their bus. On returning home, I tore open the packet and took out the book. An electric shock of a thousand volts seemed to hit me hard. Wonder of wonders! He came, stayed for so long, spoke about so many things and I wasn't able to recognize him? He was *the* Khokon Majumdar.

The whole of India knew him by that name. In the seventies, a group of people who believed in armed revolution had gone to China and met Mao Zedong. Khokon Majumdar was one of them. He was the first person from India to shake hands with the great leader on behalf of the revolutionary masses. Despite holding that hand, I had not been able to recognize him. This book was based on his experiences in China—how they reached the capital of China by either avoiding the eyes of the border security forces or taking the more arduous roads, and the warm welcome they received from the Chinese people. The book was *Basanter Bajra Nirghosh*. He was now eighty. The frenzied revolutionary movement of the seventies was no more. Yet, he was still walking ahead with the hope in his heart that revolution never ends, it never stops; it was and would always stay alive.

* * *

It was 13 December 2004. My eyes were glued to the reports in *Anandabazar Patrika*. There was a book launch of the Bengali and Italian translations of Alka Saraogi's novel *Sesh Kadambari* at the Oxford Bookstore at 6 o'clock. Sunil Gangopadhyay was to launch the book at the event which would be attended by Antonio Silvi from Italy. I was unable to contain my excitement. My eyes started to well up because this book had a character by my name! I ran to the Teacher-in-Charge's desk almost in tears and said dramatically, 'Bordi. A disaster has happened. I will have to take a leave in the second half of the day. My mother-in-law is in a critical state in Taldi. I have to go there!'

As soon as my leave was sanctioned, I ran down to the Oxford Bookstore at Park Street. The place where the book launch was being held was a stone's throw away from the American embassy. Just about seventy days back, Islamic terrorists had launched an attack on the building like bloodthirsty hyenas. At that time, any Osama Bin Laden follower had only one task, to kill all the Americans. Italy and America were allied countries. A few days back, America, Italy and Britain had attacked Iraq. Some people from the Italian embassy were supposed to be present at the event today. Somebody could target a human bomb on them, who knows! As a result, the security was rather tight in the area.

Under such circumstances, my heart beating with excitement, I went and stood in front of the bookstore's main entrance. Two muscled guards were positioned at the gates. One of them asked in English, 'What do you want?' I did not understand it and like a stupid person nodded my head. In my mother tongue, I answered, 'I have come for the event.'

'Card please,' he said asking for the invitation letter. Out of all the people entering, nobody had been asked to show the card. I was the only one to receive this royal treatment. Neither my appearance nor my clothes were appropriate for the venue. I replied in Bengali, 'I don't have one.'

He pointed his fingers and said, 'Go away!' To my ears it sounded as 'Get out!'

What could be done! My heart heavy with disappointment, I went and stood on the footpath. I looked around me to see if I could spot someone familiar. Luck was in my favour. Soon Alkadidi alighted from her car right in front of me. She asked, 'When did you come?'

I said, 'Just now.'

'Let's go inside.'

The guard knew Alkadidi. Seeing me with her, the guard no longer stopped me. It was intimidating to enter the hall room. It was filled with people in expensive clothes speaking in fluent English. There was not a single other person like me. No, I was wrong. There was one person whose skin colour was like mine. He was the centre of attention for today's event. His presence on the stage made it look brighter. What shine the colour of black had! He was none other than the poet-litterateur Sunil Gangopadhyay. The Bengali translation of *Sesh Kadambari* was being launched by him.

After the event ended, Alkadidi introduced me to a good-looking elderly woman. She lived in Hyderabad and her name was Meenakshi Mukherjee. She was the one to translate

Sesh Kadambari from Hindi to Bengali. Alkadi introduced me to her, 'This is Manoranjan Byapari.'

Meenakshidi had seen this name a number of times on the pages of the book while translating. She was surprised to see a real person of the same name in flesh and blood. She said, 'I was of the impression that the character was fictitious. This is a huge surprise!'

I said, 'Alkadi has named a character in her book after me. Now I will create a character in my book by her name.' Meenakshidi was even more surprised on hearing this. Because, even though the book mentioned a lot of things about Manoranjan Byapari, there was no indication that he could write. In a voice filled with wonder, she asked in an informal tone, 'Do you write?' I nodded my head, 'I have been writing since 1981. My writing has also been translated into Hindi and English.' Then I handed her two of my novels: *Channachara* and *Batashe Baruder Gondho* to read. After some time, she asked, 'Is there anything called Dalit Literature in Bengal?'

Dalit. In Bengali, this word does not have a wide circulation. To explain Dalit or Untouchable one generally uses the word 'chotolok' or persons of the lower class. Some people give it a gentle English touch and refer to them as scheduled castes or scheduled tribes, people who have been deprived of social respect and are eternally oppressed. There is, of course, a group of intellectuals in Bengal, ones who occupy the higher echelons of the caste system, who believe that whatever is literary should also be universally beneficial and that literature has no divisions like Dalit or non-Dalit. On the other hand, many other intellectuals with the surnames of Biswas, Mandal, Bag, are of the opposite view, believing that literature also has caste and class divisions. Similar to the genres of Vaishnav literature, Muslim literature, Marxist literature, Progressive literature, which steers clear of the mainstream while providing an alternative dimension to it, the literature about the love, anger, resistance and revenge of people once denounced as criminals just on the basis of birth could definitely be referred to as Dalit literature.

There is another condition: just by writing about Dalit life did not turn a piece of writing into Dalit literature. The writer has to be a Dalit by birth and would have to write about the trials and tribulations, the hunger and humiliation of Dalit life. For this reason, Manik Bandyopadhyay's *Padma Nadir Majhi* is not considered as Dalit literature and the Rabindra Prize awardee Binoy Majumdar is a non-Dalit poet. His poems do not have anything about the pains of Dalit life, while the depiction of the Dalit life in the former does nothing to restore the dignity of the Dalits.

It could be said in favour of the Dalit intellectuals that there hasn't been enough written about the lower-class and lower-caste people. In many ways, this has been a blessing in disguise as the portrayal of Dalits by upper-caste writers when observed from the Dalit lens might seem to possess much error and deviation. Instead of being an exact replica, it might appear as a stark contrast. Even in *Padma Nadir Majhi*, Manik Bandyopadhyay wasn't able to build up a single character in a grand manner. Was it a conscious decision? Or was it because of the years of caste conditioning that had created a bias in his heart? It was natural for a non-Dalit writer to make such mistakes.

For instance, take this reputable magazine I read. It frequently uses the word 'Chamar' in relation to thieving and in a negative sense. Everybody knows that stealing is not a good thing, but how does that equate to a 'Chamar'? Is it a crime that a person has to tan leather to fill his stomach? How could it be equated directly with thieving? This could easily come out of the pen of a non-Dalit writer but never from a Dalit writer. His Dalit consciousness would prevent him from making fun of an entire community.

One could also talk about Munshi Premchand in this respect. Perhaps no other Indian author can compete at the level at which he has written about the Dalit community. His 'Kafan' is truly an extraordinary story, yet writing from his Kayastha non-Dalit position could be the reason why his creation of Ghisu and Madhav— the father-son duo—comes across as bordering on caricature. In the story, the money they accumulate with great pain in order to buy the shroud of a close relative is ultimately wasted on alcohol. Were

Dalits really this cruel, inhuman, heartless and wretched? If a Dalit writer is ever asked to rewrite the story, they would never be able to end it in this fashion—their hand would tremble from knowing the actual experience of life as a Dalit. They would instead write about Ghisu and Madhav getting overwhelmed by the smell of boiling rice at the hotel on their way to buy the shroud, remembering how they have not eaten rice for so long. One of them would perhaps say to the other, 'He who is gone is gone. Let us live for another day. Let's have some rice.'

This is the reason that Dalit writers usually refer to the writings of non-Dalit writers about Dalit life as sympathy literature. It's not the same as Dalit literature. Meenakshidi's question was aimed at this kind of literature, which was composed by Dalits and was based on the sadness, pain, society and culture of the Dalit community.

I told her, 'There is definitely Dalit Literature in Bengal. This marginal literature, far removed from the mainstream, has been in gradual motion. After Adwaita Mallabarman, there hasn't been that powerful a writer from this community whose writing could create a special place for itself within Bengali literature based on its qualitative excellence. Had that been the case, you wouldn't have been asking me this question. But that does not mean that there is no Dalit Literature in Bengal.'

She asked, 'Can you write on this? I will send it to a good publication. Please do write if you can.'

I had never composed an essay before this! I had written an autobiography, short stories, and novels, and even published a poem or two with different newspapers and magazines but never an essay. The reason was mainly because I thought essays did not have anything radically fundamental in them but was a patchwork from different sources. Somehow, it felt like plagiarism to me, almost as if I was benefiting from someone else's hard labour. An inferiority complex grasped me when I sat down to write an essay. So, I replied, 'I will try.' Following this, I got in touch with a few Dalit intellectuals and requested them to submit an article on the topic, informing them that it would be published by a big newspaper. But none of them had faith in me.

My relationship with these Dalit poets and intellectuals was fairly new. Actually, I had never worked in this field. Save for my short story 'Reewaz' and my novel *Chandal Jibon*, none of my other writings could be categorized as Dalit literature. That which I had so far been involved with was a dark continent for them. They hardly had any knowledge of it. Their world was surrounded by Ambedkar, Jyotiba Phule, and Periyar down to Kashiram and Mayawati. They only knew of me as a poor rickshaw-puller who also wrote a bit on the side. If I told them that Swami Agnivesh—thrice elected as the Chairperson of the UN Trust Fund on Contemporary Forms of Slavery—was known to me, they would take me to be the world's biggest liar. They had no inkling about my past; hence, they did not believe me.

A word here might not be irrelevant that just as there is class within caste, there is also caste within class. If I was hated by one section for being a Chandal or a Namashudra, another section hated and ignored me for being an uneducated poor rickshaw-puller. Hence, I was equally an outcaste for both sections, loved by only those who were not limited within the boundaries of any single caste or class group. When none of them heeded my request, I had to take the task upon myself. After relentless labour for eight to nine months, I prepared a fifty-sixty pager write-up, having consulting a lot of Dalit writers and sources. Thereafter I sent it to Meenakshidi's address in Hyderabad, whereby she added a small introduction to it, brought down my article to around ten to fifteen pages, translated it into English and sent it to the well-known journal *Economic and Political Weekly (EPW)*.

On 13 October 2007 it was finally published. This was the second time that my writing was published in English. Eventually, the whole article was published in the festival edition of *Bartika* in 2010. Despite Meenakshidi having promised some money, I did not get remunerated for this writing. I don't know if *EPW* paid her anything; now that she is no more, it won't be easy to know. What I know is, as soon as the writing was published by *EPW*, Manoranjan Byapari's name came into the focal point of attention all over India. I started receiving invitations from intellectuals to attend events at various places like Delhi, Hyderabad, Maharashtra.

Sitting in faraway Canada, the article was read online by Kalpana Bardhan. When she came to Kolkata, she spent all her energies tracking me down. This was the same person who had translated one of Bengal's best writers Adwaita Mallabarman's topmost creation *Titas Ekti Nadir Nam* (A River Called Titas) into English and helped it reach readers from around the world. She informed me that she had been given the responsibility of compiling an anthology of Bengali literature by Oxford University Press where she wanted to include my piece 'Is There Dalit Writing in Bangla?' She wanted my permission. Her question made me feel like a starved person being offered pilaf. I did not hesitate for a moment and handed her my written permission, and, thus, the writing was duly published.

* * *

A milky white car stopped in front of my house. It reminded me of the episode from the *Mahabharata* when a chariot had been sent to the earth to take Yudhisthira to heaven. What must it been like? I had no clue. But it felt like a chariot had been sent for me and just like I had once journeyed from the dense forests of Bastar zilla towards Dalli in a car in order to be a part of a game-changing, turbulent period in Indian politics, this white car had arrived to pick me up from the soil and take me to what seemed like outer space.

Out of the car came Dr. Sayantan Dasgupta, professor at the Comparative Literature Department of Jadavpur University. He came bearing an important message from the head of the Comparative Literature Department of Hyderabad University, Tutun Mukherjee. She later wrote, informing me that it was through my writing that she discovered that there was indeed something called Dalit Literature in Bengal. She was at that time entrusted with the initiative to compile an anthology of Dalit literature, which would be translated into English and published by Oxford University Press. It was understood, without her having to mention it separately, that the collection would reach people all over the world. In this regard, she requested my assistance.

Everybody must die someday. This includes me. But my deeds will keep me alive even years after my death. That's what immortality is like—I was unable to give up this temptation—so, I told her that I would be more than happy to assist her with this. It would in fact be nectar for my soul. Subsequently, she included me as a coordinator in this work. A person like me, who had never even stepped inside the boundary of a school, who was unsurprisingly dumb, was given a dignified position in a committee that had been set up by four professors from the Comparative Literature Departments of four universities, namely, Jadavpur, Delhi, Assam-Silchar and Hyderabad. I was given the responsibility of the anthology on Dalit Literature. I was an insignificant, ordinary person. Never in my life had I thought that I would attain such huge prestige in my lifetime. This respect and prestige were, according to me, the best reward in my life. And if ever there was anything bigger than this, I was not aware of it!

CHAPTER 23

The Story of Jibon Das

*I*am reminded of a short episode from the *Mahabharata*. The Ashvamedha horse sent by the Pandavas was captured by the boy Babruvahana. Subsequently, a huge fight broke out between him and Arjuna with the Pandava aiming his arrows towards Babruvahana's chariot. The force of the arrow sent the boy flying 320 miles (40 jojon) away. Finding no other option, Babruvahana slowly returned to the battlefield and released an arrow in the direction of Arjuna. His chariot now was pushed back three steps by the force of this collision. At this Sri Krishna applauded and encouraged the boy, 'Bravo!'

Disappointed at this, Arjuna asked Sri Krishna, 'When I sent his chariot flying miles away in the air, you did not congratulate me, but now that his arrow has shoved my chariot by mere three steps you are raising him to the skies?'

Sri Krishna replied, 'Is there anybody or anyone significant occupying his chariot? Leave alone 320 miles, it will not be difficult to send it flying for even 3,200 miles away. But moving the chariot, where I am seated with the entire weight of the universe, even by a hair's gap is close to impossible. But here the boy has moved it back by three steps. I applaud his military training.'

Scholars have a lot of time to acquire knowledge. It is but natural that they would compose high standard work in large quantities. Rather, it would be rather unusual for them not to do so. But doesn't a person like me, who has never been formally educated, who has had to write braving not only the blistering heat of the summer but also an unsympathetic workplace, deserve applause for whatever little he has achieved? For me, this applause was invaluable.

The novel which had given me the greatest fame and name was *Chandal Jibon*. Initially, a part of it had been published in the *Bahujan Nayak* magazine under the name of 'Jibon Chandal'. The magazine went out of print because of which the rest of the novel remained unpublished for a long time. Finally, I went to the person I always ran to under such circumstances. He was my Pranabda, the editor of *Haate Bazare*. Pranabda was deeply anguished on reading about the ugly, troublesome and accident-prone life of a Chandal, who was only in his mid-twenties. If he published my work, there would be no space for him to publish the work of other writers, but it was equally impossible for him to refuse my request or should I say my demands. He was very fond of me. He advised: 'Break it into smaller parts. End each part in a way that gives it a befitting ending. It should keep the suspense alive. Readers should be curious to know more, but by no means should any part look incomplete.'

I did exactly what he asked me to, breaking it into four separate volumes. For the next four years, the four parts were published in the Puja edition of the magazine, under the headings of 'Chandal Jibon' (My Chandal Life); 'Abar Chandal Jibon' (The Story of My Chandal Life Once More); 'Ei Jibon, Shei Jibon' (This Life, That Life) and 'Noroker Ek Nam Jibon' (Another Name of Hell Is Life).

There was nothing more left to write about the Chandal's life story after that as he would move from his hell of a life towards the heavens, from the lived surroundings of free people to the walled life in the gaol. He would no longer remain a Chandal after stepping out of the prison. Here the word 'Chandal' was used for anger—after this it was only life for him; his life which was like the birth of Valmiki from Ratnakar's dead body, every detail of which I had poured into my story. That might have been a novel, but this is an autobiography. Even if the contents of both documents match, there is a basic difference in their premise and description. The bit of orchestration required to turn my life into a novel had been done to the fictional account without any attention to chronology. What was true of both the texts was that despite questions about their literary merit there was no denying that they were all based on bare unadulterated facts.

After seeing the enthusiastic responses from the readers on publishing *Chandal Jibon* in *Haate Bazaar*, it felt like it would be good to publish it as a book. But who would take care of the expenses? That's when I remembered Manoj Bandyopadhyay, the head of *Priyoshilpo Prakashan*, who had published my novel *Anya Bhuvan*. Gathering a meagre amount, I went to him with the request of publishing the first part of the novel. I gave him the little I had, with the promise to pay back the rest after the books were sold. He accepted my terms. The Introduction was written by Mahasweta Devi, whose stature in the literary world was as great as the Himalayas! A few others also pitched in with their endorsements for the book. These included Ashrukumar Sikdar, professor at North Bengal University and also an essayist, Salam Azad, the controversial Bangladeshi writer, and Achintya Biswas, critic and professor at Jadavpur University.

Chandal was the name given to the people occupying the lowest rungs within the Indian caste system, whom society had demarcated as untouchable, hateful, inhuman creatures. The word 'Chandal' had another meaning. It meant 'extreme anger': 'raag-chandal'. In that sense, 'Chandal Jibon' would then depict the lived life of an untouchable or the way of life of a person consumed with rage. Both were characters in the novel *Chandal Jibon*. The protagonist, Jibon Das, was an untouchable by birth and extremely resentful by nature, the reason behind his resentment being the inhuman behaviour meted out to him by the society. It would be the thoughtful reader's responsibility to identify these causes. Maybe it would also lead to a social consciousness towards eradicating such behaviour.

Jibon Das was just not any fictional hero, but a person moulded in the very flesh and blood of this country, society, and these times! I am speaking in the past tense, because he has already passed away; at least, the person I knew. Nobody knew him as well as I. Hence, it was a claim only I can make. If I did not present him properly in the readers' court of judgement, the blame would fall on my own weak writing.

Having heard a lot about 'Jibon Das' from me, Alka Saraogi, a Sahitya Akademi Award winning author, had painted a partial image of Jibon from 'Jibon Chandal' in her famous novel *Koi Baat Nahi*. My wish was to write an unabridged biography on the strange life of this peculiar person, who spent his life harbouring a death wish in his heart and died with the undying, intense desire to live still alive in his heart.

* * *

On 27 November 2011, I found Manohar Mouli Biswas on the other end of the phone. He was asking, 'Manoranjan, have you received the invitation letter for the All India Dalit Sahitya Sammelan to be held at the Indumati Sabha Griha of Jadavpur University on the 29th and 30th?'

I said, 'No. I had no idea that something like this is happening.'

'Sayantan Babu didn't inform you of anything! He will be reading a paper on your writing which will be discussed at the Sammelan.'

After a moment's thought, I said, 'Maybe he will inform. There is still time, right?'

He said, 'The Sammelan is being organized by the English Department of Jogesh Chandra College in collaboration with the West Bengal Dalit Sahitya Sanstha. It is being funded by the University Grants Commission. Honestly speaking, it's a huge event. There has been no such programme on Dalit literature in West Bengal before this. Will you be able to come on the day? If you can, I have an invitation letter. I will be able to send you one or two extra ones. The programme starts at nine-thirty in the morning. Just call me once you reach the gate. I will deliver the invitation letter to you because you won't be able to enter without the gate pass, and the letter will function as one for you.'

It was a Sunday, which meant that the 29th would be a Tuesday. It was my weekly day off. I don't know if I would have been able to attend it had it been on some other day, but since it was my off day in any case, I decided why not. It was just next door and would cost me barely five rupees to travel by bus. I decided to talk to Sayantan Dasgupta, who taught at the Comparative Literature department of Jadavpur University. I told him what Manoharda had conveyed to me.

In a calm voice he asked, 'Will you be attending it?'

'I was thinking of attending. I heard you are reading a paper.'

'Yes, I will be reading one.'

'I will go to listen to your paper. Had it been on any other day but Tuesday, I wouldn't have been able to attend.'

He said, 'I would have informed you, but I didn't because the whole programme will be in English. Since you ... you would have been bored.'

I said, 'Whether I understand or not, I would definitely like to attend. At least I will be able to assess what people think of my work from the listeners' response when you read your paper!'

As decided, on 29 November morning after taking a proper bath and shaving my beard, I reached the Sabha Griha. I had no invitation letter and I was feeling a bit hesitant to go up to the gate. I was also a little scared. This was not new; approaching educated scholars always caused my hands, legs, throat and heart to tremble. Especially people who knew an excess of English, I feared them more than a tiger.

I called Manohar Mouli Biswas, 'Dada, I have come. I am standing in front of the gate. Please come and help me enter.'

He said, 'I don't have to come. You can come straight on your own.'

'What if they stop me at the gate?'

'They will not. Just tell them that you are headed for this event and that you are a member of the Dalit Sahitya Sanstha.'

'What if they still do not let me enter?'

'Then give me a call.'

They did not stop me, but they did ask, 'Where will you go?' I was in any case quite afraid of such crisp English and did not understand anything. But I understood what he was trying to ask and replied in pure unadulterated Bangla, 'I am here to attend the programme.'

From the gate, a young girl—perhaps a student—ushered me towards the final destination, showed me my seat and left. I hid myself in the crowd in the way I used to travel ticketless in the train so many years ago, occupying a seat in great embarrassment.

The hall room was completely packed. The inaugural candles were lit, the Rabindrasangeet sung and the guests felicitated, after which the main programme finally began. Jaydeep Sarangi, a professor at the English department of Jogesh Chandra College and one of the organizers, rose to speak first. I knew I wouldn't understand a single syllable. My state here was like a fly sitting on a honey-filled jar. Nonetheless, my eyes were focused on the stage, my ears attentive to see if any familiar favourite word came my way.

It did. It came right at the beginning of the programme, something I could not have imagined even in my wildest dreams. For me it was like the coming together of the sound of gunpowder and flute creating an electric shock of the kind that would send shivers through my entire body. Professor Sarangi said, 'None of us knew before this that Dalit literature existed in Bengal. We knew of its presence in Maharashtra and Gujarat, but not in Bengal. On the 13 of October 2007, an article by Manoranjan Byapari was published in *EPW*, translated by Professor Meenakshi Mukherjee. It was only after reading the article that I came to know that Dalit literature indeed existed in Bengal, as a result of which the idea of organizing a conference on Dalit literature—of Bengal and the other Indian states—first came to the mind. This conference is a culmination of that idea.'

Did he really say this? I don't exactly know, as the entire speech was in English, a language more incomprehensible to me than Gondi. Yet, there was no mistaking at least three words from whatever he said: Manoranjan, Meenakshi Mukherjee and *EPW*. From these three words it was not difficult to infer the rest.

When Jaydeep Sarangi descended from the stage, I went and stood in front of him. 'Dada, this is me. Manoranjan Byapari.'

The wonder was clear on his face, 'You are Manoranjan Byapari?'
'I am.'
'You and Meenakshi Mukherjee worked on the essay together?'
'Yes. We did.'
Before I had the chance to extend my hands for a handshake, he pulled me to his chest for a warm embrace. He hugged me and said, 'I will be in touch with you. We will have to do so much work together. The journey has just begun.'

I went back to my place again. From far away, I could see Jaydeep Sarangi pointing towards me and telling everybody, 'That is Manoranjan Byapari.'

After the first half of the programme was over, a soft melodious voice from behind hesitantly asked me, 'Are you Manoranjan Byapari?'

I came to know later that the voice was of Angana Dutta. I nodded my head, 'Yes, it's me'

She said, 'We were talking about you just this morning. Sir was mentioning you.'

A male voice from the side now asked me the same question, 'You are Manoranjan Byapari?'

I nodded my head again, 'Yes, I am. I am that person.'

He said, 'My name is Sanjay Kumar. I have come from Delhi.' After pausing a bit, he continued, 'I translated your story 'Reewaz' into Hindi. It was published in *Kathadesh* magazine.'

I replied, 'Oh, yes, now I remember. We have spoken over the phone once or twice before, but this is the first time I am meeting you in person.'

He said, 'I want to translate your *Chandal Jibon* into Hindi. Where can I find the book? Can I find it here?'

I said, 'I will get you a copy.'

Four papers were scheduled for the next session. Sayantan Dasgupta's paper was right at the end. Surprisingly, he would be discussing my story 'Reewaz' and two other works.

He had translated 'Reewaz' into English for the Dalit literature anthology to be published by Oxford University Press.

What he read and what he said was beyond my understanding, but Sanjay Kumar seemed to understand it quite well, given that he had read the story a number of times. When the discussion session started after the paper was read out, Sanjay Kumar and Sayantan Dasgupta had a long conversation. There were a lot of ideas thrown around. The funniest thing, however, was that even though I occupied a large part of the entire programme, I was not there somehow. I was not supposed to be there. I had no invitation. I was like an alien.

At the end of the programme, I received a conference file stuffed with some printed papers. The other guests had already received their files before me. My uninvited self received it at the end. I was letter-blind and did not understand a word on the papers. The people who could, found my name mentioned many times on them.

After this, I walked towards Jadavpur University's gate, where I used to be a rickshaw-puller once upon a time. The rickshaw line was still there, but I was on the other side. The wheels of my rickshaw which started its journey here had rolled over to the Indumati Sabha Griha today. The journey had just begun and a lot more was left to be covered.

CHAPTER 24

A Tumultuous End to a Decade

The stretch from the middle of 2010 to the middle of 2011 turned out to be a really difficult time. I am not talking about the tumultuous time in Bengal but of my own life. Things in West Bengal were crazy enough with the state undergoing a ruthless bloodbath in preparation for birthing a new future. The pangs of labour were inevitable.

The situation in the state was proof that one should never underestimate the power of the masses. If this group of 'trinadapi'—as meek as grass, getting trampled on but never complaining—with no food in their bellies, no slippers on their feet, no clothes on their bodies and no oil on their heads turn around fearlessly and stand united, they can upturn world history. Their combined power was enough to drag arrogant autocrats from their high throne and reduce them to dust. The red flag bearers seemed to have forgotten this truth after being invincible for so long. They had become like the foolish proud giraffe, believing the entire stretch between the northern mountains to the southern seas to be under their domination and the freedom to boss around people as their birthright. Nobody knew this better than the people of rural Bengal, the primary victims of their entitled existence and unreasonable demands of 'Give me your land, your temples, your mosques, your open fields, your schools, hospitals and ponds, your civility and culture, your safe lives. Don't shed tears. Instead, paste a smile on your faces and say, "Hirak Raja is god and all his actions are for our own good."

If you don't do this, you very well know what will happen to your daughters, your wives, and your mothers. Do you understand that? Our powerful brigade does not spare anybody anywhere between the ages of eight to eighty.'

When the same people conquered their fear and stood up against their oppressors, it brought about the downfall of these rulers whose thirty-four year's rule was chequered with instances of misgovernance. The rest of the history is known to all. What remains to be known is whether this new group which replaced the old would be able to live up to the expectations of the masses who put their faith in them. One must, however, keep in mind the fact that it doesn't take long for newly elected heads to turn corrupt if they are left unsupervised and unaccountable. It could very well happen that everybody would wake up one fine day to realize that the ones who had promised the welfare of *ma, mati, manush* had also turned into demons.[2]

But that story is for another time. To come back to my own story, in the span of twelve months from the middle of 2010 to the middle of 2011, I fell ill three times. The first time I had to get a cataract operation on my eye. The second time I suffered from the waterborne disease, jaundice. Finally, I slipped at my workplace and got burnt badly. Boiling water scalded my chest and stomach. Almost thirty years ago, I had burnt my right side. This time it was my left. People reading my autobiography would definitely know by now that in my life every ugly period has culminated into a beautiful time in the future. I had successfully squeezed out the appropriate value of whatever life had to offer me, be it sadness, pain, hurt, humiliation or torture which had turned my life into a living hell once. I harboured no regrets in my heart towards my present or my past. The life I had led and the sadness, disgrace and indignity I had been forced to tolerate had left my bag of experiences so rich in flavours without which I could perhaps never even dream to become a writer.

I don't have a single relative in West Bengal, but that didn't mean that I had nobody to call my own. There were numerous people who felt like my own kin, with whom I had the connection of the soul which was stronger than any blood ties. Their protective presence in my life had prevented the opposition camp or my enemies to cause me any grave harm. These honest, brave and socially conscious people had voluntarily extended their hand of friendship towards me and engulfed me in a warm hug. As compared to them my ideas, social consciousness, education, financial and social status, and rank, were hardly any match. Yet these people cared for me. For me, this was a huge achievement in itself.

Author with Jayanta Ghoshal, journalist, *Anandabazar Patrika*, and Jaideep Ghosh, film director, Delhi.

Jayanta Ghoshal was such a friend. He lived in Barrackpore, edited the magazine *Sunyadashak* and was also a writer. One fine day, he began to pester me with a preposterous demand that I write my autobiography. Jayantada was an extremely emotional man. The surname 'Biswas' which also meant 'trust' in Bengali had somehow made him believe that this extremely reputed publisher with the said surname, one who was very well-known to him, would publish my autobiography. He had apparently given the publisher his word. Jayantada fell into the same trap I had once fallen into by believing a Biswas. He started bombarding me with constant requests of, 'Please write. Finish your autobiography as soon as you can.'

I have been on this planet for quite some time now. I remember this one time when it was feared that an imminent planetary disruption would destroy the earth. But proving all assumptions wrong, this wondrous earth has continued to exist. I too have managed to live with it, an unnecessary long life. Thanks to this extended longevity, my life was now rich with numerous stories, anecdotes, incidents and accidents. It was impossible to pen them down in a jiffy. Could I bare them all in all honesty? What if the words written by me came back later like a viper's sting? Would I even have time enough to document everything elaborately?

It is often said that if you sincerely wish for something from the heart, the entire universe conspires to give it to you. I don't know how much sincerity there was in my wish for some writing time, but the universe was definitely working hard to bring it within my reach. I fell ill with a sudden bout of jaundice. Such was my fate. So far, I had eaten so many edible, inedible, rotting and stale things in my life, nothing had ever happened. A mere glass of water left me bedridden. Jaundice was not an ordinary disease. In my childhood I had seen the shaman at the camp put a garland around people with jaundice and make them lie down, and they would strangely recover within days. This was the first time that I learnt that there was no respite once this disease gripped somebody.

I usually considered myself to be quite brave. But the fear on the face, body language, conversations and activities of my near and dear ones, who loved me and wanted to see me alive, started corroding the core of my own courage. It felt like my time on this earth was nearing its end. One morning, a call came on my mobile. It was from Jayantada. 'What's happened Manoranjanda? Have you progressed on the autobiography I asked you to write?'

I replied, 'Dada, I still haven't been able to start work on that. I have not been well. I will take up the work as soon as I recover.'

'What's happened?'

'Nothing, I am down with just a bit of jaundice.'

He was shocked, 'What did you say? Just "a bit" of jaundice? How can jaundice be "just a bit"? Be very careful, don't take it lightly! It is a deadly disease.'

The rest cannot be articulated in words. From Jayantada to Madhumoy Paul, from Madumoy Paul to Bablada, from Bablada to Sandipda, from Sandipda to Jogenda, from Jogenda to Alkadi to Ashokji, to Kajal Das' whole team, the word spread like wildfire that Manoranjan was suffering from a deadly disease. Everybody started traversing perilous roads to reach my house in Khudirabad with financial help. I was more in pain because of their pain rather than my own health. Ashokji, who was around eighty-six then, also come to pay me a visit. My heart was full with gratitude.

We did not have a good doctor in our area. Most of them were quacks. My well-wishers were worried that this would further aggravate my case. They wanted to get me admitted to a hospital, as otherwise a lot of money was getting wasted for nothing. I don't know who, but somebody informed Mahasweta Devi about my condition. She gave me a call, 'What, you are down with jaundice? Call Debapriya Mallick. Get admitted to a hospital. 'On calling up Dr. Debapriya Mallick, he said, 'Reach PG Hospital. I will then see what can be done.'

I reached PG Hospital the next day and gave Dr. Mallick a call. 'I have reached,' I informed him. He gave me the name of another doctor and asked me to meet him. I asked somebody, where to find this doctor.

The person replied, 'He has not come. Why do you need to see him?'

I said, 'Dr. Debapriya Mallick has asked me to meet him.'

This stranger, I am guessing he was a doctor too, took me to another doctor, who I later came to know was Jayanta Dasgupta. The stranger told Dr. Jayanta Dasgupta, 'Dr. Debapriya Mallick has sent him. See what you can do.'

'Who is this Debapriya Mallick?'
'Jyotipriyo Mallick's brother.'
'Do I know him?'
'You know him very well.'

Now Dr. Jayanta Dasgupta asked me, 'How do you know him?'

I said, 'I don't know him. He is known to Mahasweta Devi and Mahasweta Devi is known to me.'

Dr. Dasgupta was totally puzzled by now. He wasn't able to ward off his surprise from his face as to why his colleague was showing such a personal interest in a boorish looking person like me. Mahasweta Devi's name left him even more puzzled.

He said, 'You know Mahasweta Devi? How?'

I said, 'I used to write for her magazine, *Bartika*.'

'You are a writer?'

'You could say so, I guess. I write a bit on the side.'

'What do you write?'

'Stories and novels.'

'Do you write only for *Bartika* or also for ...'

'My initiation was with *Bartika*, but my work has also been published with a lot of other magazines and newspapers. I also have four books to my credit.'

After this, he carefully examined me and then handed a slip of paper to my wife suggesting a blood test. He then asked me, 'Will you get admitted? It is best if you get admitted.'

Debapriya babu had also advised the same. I agreed. The formalities did not take much time. What happened after that is a blurry haze in my memories, even though it was simply a blood test! The five other blood tests I had taken before this had left a hole in my pocket. Now that I was to take another blood test, I knew that I would have to shell out some more. We were not prepared for this and were not carrying enough cash. Dr. Jayanta Dasgupta saw the helplessness of a poor author. The doctor whom I had barely met, instead of taking fees from his patient as was the rule, paid me back five hundred rupees.

I tried paying back the amount later but when he refused to accept it, I gifted him with some of my own books. I didn't want to downplay his greatness with a frail thank you. It is because of people like him that people like us are able to survive in this otherwise merciless society. Or else, we would have become a thing of the past long back. I was bound to the bed for almost two and half months because of this disease. Fortunately, I was able to progress with my writing during this period. It was a huge job accomplished.

A few days later, a problem cropped up in my right eye. I had already been prescribed glasses ten years ago and felt that getting my eyes tested again and upgrading my lenses would be enough. My wife, Anu, was a contractual worker at Shankar Netralaya in Sector V, then known as Shankar Narayan Netralaya. Later on Narayan stayed back at the exact location, while Shankar shifted to Mukundapur. Anu asked me to get my eyes tested at Shankar Netralaya. She was to accompany me both ways, as it would allow her to tend to both my eye check up and her job. So, I went with her.

It was Anu's workplace. She was aware of the reputation of each doctor. She advised me to get my eyes checked up by Vinit sir. Almost ten of his older patients, and not just one or two, attested that he was not a doctor but a god in the guise of a doctor! His touch had the power to give sight to the blind. There were not many doctors like him in the world.

I had been to many pilgrimage sites and also to temples, but never had I ever seen a god. No wonder I didn't find him as he was sitting at Shankar Narayan Netralaya all this time. I got my eyes checked by this god, whereupon I was told that I have cataract and that it was best to get it operated as soon as possible. He said, 'I will leave for California next month, so get it operated either tomorrow or day after.'

On asking around, Anu was told that for an outsider the minimum expenses would have been for thirty thousand rupees. For her it could be lessened to fifteen thousand rupees but nothing less than that. Two days passed. On the third day, Dr. Vinit sent his people to fetch my wife. He asked, 'What happened beta? Why isn't he getting the operation done? His eye health is not so good.'

Anu said, 'What to do sir, the hospital is demanding money.'

'They have asked you for money?'

'Yes sir.'

'How much?'

'Fifteen thousand rupees. Where will we find so much cash.'

He thought for some time, then pulled out a thousand rupee note from his pocket and extended it towards Anu. He said , 'Go and submit it at the counter. Tell them you cannot give any more. Come and let me know what they say.'

Anu hesitantly said, 'I won't take your money sir. Why should you give it? If you can, just ask them to reduce the amount a bit.'

After a moment's silence he said, 'Bring the patient tomorrow and get him admitted. I will see to the rest.'

I was admitted at Shankar Narayan Netralaya the next day. My surgery happened at around two in the afternoon. The ayahs who worked in the OT, were known to us. They said, 'The care with which Vinit sir operated on you is beyond description.' I was told that the lens used for my eye was for twelve thousand rupees. But for some reason, we were not charged a single paisa. After a few days, my bandages were removed and my eye checked once again. Vinit sir examined me and said the eye was fine. Then he sent me to another doctor, who examined my eyes and prescribed new power for my glasses. Vinit sir asked for the paper and told Anu, 'I will keep the glasses. You take it from me, beti.'

Anu brought the spectacles for me after some days. The operation, the medicines, the spectacles—everything was done free of cost, thanks to a god. The name of this god was Vinit sir.

After the eye operation, I got a lot of free time to recuperate at home, which lasted a little over a month. My right eye was bandaged, but my left eye was perfectly fine. Putting on my old pair of glasses, I started writing my autobiography, picking it up from where I had left it. Anu would shout at me, 'Your eye is still very sensitive. The way you are writing with your shoulders slouched, blood will shoot up to your eyes and you will go blind. You have been writing your whole life. What good has come of all that nonsense? A husking pedal is fated to grind paddy even in heaven. Nothing will happen in your life apart from twirling your ladle. If you lose your eyes, that, too, will go. We will then have no other choice than to starve!'

I too was well aware that nothing would come of it. A tree grew as tall as its seed permitted, it was impossible to turn a brinjal seedling into a banyan tree. Yet, I wasn't able to explain it to my heart. My crazy heart would listen to no one. It only wanted to turn its legs into wings and fly off just like a caterpillar transformed into a butterfly. I thought to myself that I wouldn't be able to keep doing my work any longer. Not because of my enemy camp, but because my body would soon give up on its own. I would be left with the only option of begging. In that case, becoming blind would perhaps be an advantage as a blind beggar was definitely worth more than an ordinary one!

I wanted to finish writing as quickly as possible, especially because I already had a ready publisher at hand. Today, he was showing interest in my work. What if tomorrow, he changed his mind? This was basic human nature. So, I wanted to finish writing before the publisher lost interest so that I could at least see my own book before I turned blind!

As the monsoons of June 2011 approached, a timely shower brought relief from the hot furnace of the earth. On that very day, I slipped and fell. The three sides of the kitchen at my workplace were open. If a bit of cool breeze accompanied the rain, the whole place would be soaking wet in no time. I accidentally lost my balance on that slippery floor and as luck would have it fell right next to the stove. The force of the collision toppled the kadhai, where almost a hundred eggs had been put to boil. The entire kadhai upturned on my body and the hot scalding water fell on my stomach, peeling off a large layer of my skin. I had to be admitted to the Medica Superspeciality Hospital in Mukundapur.

The nature of the people at my workplace was such that they wouldn't have brought me to such an expensive healthcare facility. From what I knew about them, they would have dumped me at some government hospital. But at that time, the situation in West Bengal was quite dangerous. Parivartan was being observed everywhere.[3] The change-makers had already won a huge victory in the Lok Sabha elections. A lot of intellectuals and mass organizations supporting the change-makers were well known to me. Many among them were also aware of how the people from my opposition camp were already conspiring against me. Under such circumstances, my death could stir up a huge storm which would be difficult to control. My opponents were not foolish. The one thing they knew about me was that my roots were quite strong and this gave them reason enough to be unable to disregard me. From that fear, they got me admitted at Medica, where a day's expense ran up to ten thousand rupees. I had to stay for around nine days at the hospital.

NOTES

[1] The king in Satyajit Ray's iconic movie *Hirak Rajar Deshe*, a powerful satire against state oppression, where the king emerges as a symbolic representation of the state.
[2] '*Ma, mati, manush*', the Trinamul Congress' slogan, stands for 'mother, earth and people'.
[3] 'Parivartan; or change, i.e., changing the system, another slogan of the Trinamul Congress that proved to be successful.

CHAPTER 25

The Publication of *Itibritte Chandal Jivan*

This was followed by another one-and-a-half months of rest at home. I used that time judiciously and finally finished work on the autobiography, which came to around 700–800 pages. I called up the publisher to inform him, 'Dada, I have finished the work.' I had assumed that the news would turn him mad with excitement, but in reality, the opposite happened. He answered back in a disinterested and indifferent voice, 'Let me see what can be done. Send me the manuscript when I tell you to. I will read it and let you know my views.'

Days and months passed away. He did not seem interested any longer. Every time we spoke, he made the same excuse. I had written the autobiography on Jayantada's insistence. I called him up and said, 'Dada, what will happen? Will it not be published?' In a frustrated voice he answered, 'He is no longer that eager. I don't think he will publish it.'

All my hopes and desires seemed to vanish at Jayantada's words.

Five or six months passed. There was no response from the 'trust'-worthy publisher. My heart seemed to break up into tiny little pieces. In any case, I didn't have too much faith towards such people, having experienced non-cooperation at every bend of life. This incident only strengthened my conviction that if not a crime, trusting people was indeed an act of foolishness. If people did not cooperate with me, did not help me move further, what could I do?

Would I sit and shed tears? Should I rip off my own hair? This would only mean accepting defeat. My fight was against this non-cooperative unhelpful society. I was not yet ready to surrender! I swore to myself that I would somehow get *Itibritte Chandal Jivan* published by the next book fair. It was my autobiography. This was my fight. My *only* fight. There were about thirty to forty days left. I would have to finish everything within this time.

I spoke with Manojda whose *Priyoshilpo Prakashana* publishing house had already published three of my books. He said, 'I can and I will. This will definitely be released at the Book Fair. But financially, I am not doing too well, so you will have to bear the expenses.' Given the size of my manuscript, the cost would come to around sixty-thousand rupees. It was difficult for me to whip up that amount. So, I divided the book into two parts.

The first part would begin with my birth, trace my long journey through various incidents and accidents right up till the beginning of 2000 after my last visit to Chhattisgarh, and end at the point where I was just about to join the school for the deaf and mute. This was the main part, but a small portion from the end was also summarized and added to it. My biggest fear was about the fate of the second part. What if, after putting in so much effort to publish the first part, the second part remained eternally unpublished? Life was uncertain; nobody knew what would happen next. What if something happened to me?

Itibritte Chandal Jivan was my own life story, but it did not remain so after being published. Its responsibility was assumed by Jaydeep Sarangi, now the principal of New Alipore College, Ananta Acharya, the editor of the magazine *Chetana Lahar,* and my friend Bappaditya Bhattacharya. They divided all the post-publication tasks amongst themselves. Jaydeep babu took up the responsibility of publicizing the work. It was because of his initiative that the *Statesman, Times of India*, and the Hindi magazine *Prabhat Khabar* published massive articles on the autobiography and its author. He also took me to the studio of the TV channel NE and facilitated a half-an-hour-long programme. Ananta Acharya loaded with the books in his bag, started distributing it from one end of India to the other. He delivered the book to Goutam Roy of *Anandabazar Patrika*, because of which a feature titled 'The Life of a Chandal as Seen through the Eyes of a Chandal' was published by him. Through his efforts, the autobiography spread far and wide in the country. My friend Bappa took on the responsibility of the city of Kolkata. He was a regular at College Street or the book neighbourhood of Kolkata. With the help of the Dey Book Store, he tirelessly worked to reach out to the readers in Kolkata.

Even though Manojda always said that 'Publishers never disclose the total number of books published', had he chosen to disclose the real numbers it would have surely proven without doubt that the sale of the book far exceeded that of many other bestsellers too! That the book would be so well received among the readers was something that Manojda had not anticipated. He realized it within a few days of publication when all the three hundred copies of the first edition had sold out. If he had he known this before, he would have surely printed a thousand copies at one go. It would have cost less and the profits would have been more. For this first edition, I somehow managed to pay him about twenty thousand rupees by incurring a debt. The agreement had been to pay back the remaining amount with the money earned from the sale of the book. In this regard, publishers have no responsibility. The loss or profit is all the author's share. He would only get the remuneration for printing and binding the book, and the paper and cover expenses.

Manojda was a thorough gentleman who never lost his temper and spoke softly, after putting a lot of thought behind his words. He was an honest person with another big quality: he never hid his own honesty from others. To ward off any naysayer, he had pasted in big bold letters on the wall outside his publication house, 'It might be possible to earn money through unfair means, but not respect or honour.' This was akin to the signs of 'Honesty Is Valuable' as put up by most businessmen in their shops so that nobody doubted their intentions.

Manojda would perhaps have retained his integrity for life, but humans were ultimately mere humans. When even the heavenly gods deviated from the righteous path, what was a petty human to do? It was impossible to bracket people into the categories of talented or non-talented, honest or dishonest, good or bad. Circumstances played a huge role in one's character development. Because of circumstances, yesterday's Ratnakar was today's Valmiki, yesterday's benevolent Sudipto was today's petty thief Sarada Prasad.[1] Such circumstances were also behind Manojda's transformation. The main culprit in this regard was Goutam Roy. Had he not published the feature with *Anandabazar Patrika*, this day wouldn't have come! The first one to publish almost a half-pager on the book along with a big picture of mine was the *Statesman,* followed by *Times of India.* But the Bengali readers were not much moved by it. They were moved only after the feature in *Anandabazar Patrika* was published. The spark soon took the shape of a forest fire. I started receiving calls from all over the place, with people requesting copies. These were not only from readers but also booksellers.

I had always been careful to provide my name, address and telephone number in the books published before this, hoping that my readers would write back or call me in order to share their feedback. However, so far, I had received neither letters nor calls. This time, out of sheer anger, I provided none of my personal details. Surprisingly, this time I was showered with countless calls. I had no clue how they dug up my number but calls started pouring by the hundreds. Just as smoke reveals that there is a fire somewhere, the publisher fathomed that the high tide had come from the avalanche of calls.

The book was released in the 2012 Book Fair. Channel Ten arranged a little programme with the book and its author towards the end of the fair, which alone led to the sale of around forty books. I was not aware if Priyoshilpo had a stall at the Book Fair. They did not inform me, blaming it quite conveniently on their trade secret. A few days after the Book Fair, Goutam Roy dropped the last bomb with his article, hiking up the sales even further. I had a couple of books with me. When all of them were sold off, I ran to the publisher asking for the rest of the books. Having already had a sense of the magnitude of the whirlwind by then, he was not going to be easily obliging anymore. Smiling sweetly, he said with utmost politeness, 'I only have twenty more copies left. The rest have not been bound yet. Come back again in seven days, you'll get them.'

Within these seven days, my friend Bappa and I made a trip to College Street to deliver books to the Dey Book Stall as they kept asking for more copies. Almost thirty to forty books were regularly being sold on a daily basis from their shop; Bappa and I were going crazy just meeting their demands for which they were even paying in advance. Order requests also came from the outlet called Bookmark.

After Dey Book Stall, we decided to pay a visit to Dey's Publishing and Booksellers nearby. Bappa had to buy some books of his own. As soon as we entered the shop, our eyes literally popped out at seeing a huge pile of *Itibritte Chandal Jivan* there. It seemed like there would be around five hundred copies or more. So many books! Where did they come from? I went to Priyoshilpo again after seven days and was greeted again with a cordial smile and some sweet tea and salty biscuits. I received around forty books, along with complaints of a lazy employee, 'They are so careless, I can't even begin to tell you. They will come to work one day and then bunk for three days. Three or four more books are lying unbound, forcing me to go back on my promise.'

I said, 'I saw a lot of books at Dey's Publishing.'

Manojda added in haste, 'They urgently requested, so I had to deliver some books to them. Books travel far and wide from their store as libraries purchase from them.' He added, 'In a couple more days, you will get your book.'

I went back again in a few days. He gave me some more books. I calculated that I had received a total of 132 books from him. Around ten out of them had been distributed free. As for the others, not only had I paid back my dues of ₹20,000 but also made a small profit. Both Bookmark and Dey Book Stall were given a 30 percent discount. Bappa, Anantada and I sold each book for ₹200. That's how we made the money. Assuming that there was no other pile of books at the Dey's Publishing and Booksellers and also assuming that no further copies of the book had been printed, what had happened to the remaining 168 copies of the book of which 300 had been printed according to the agreement and I had received only around 132.

Manojda meticulously explained how, according to the law, certain books had to be sent to the Bhavani Bhawan, the National Library and other public libraries known as depositories. Around 30 books had gone in this fashion. The rest of the books were sold off to pay off my debts to the publisher. In short, the profit and the losses had been sorted out neatly. Thus he did not owe me anything, nor did I owe him anything. The accounts were settled.

There was still a huge demand for the book at College Street. I was, by now, drowning in phone calls. I asked Manojda to quickly start work on printing the second edition. There were a lot of spelling mistakes in the first edition along with some factual errors which could be corrected in the reprint. But he said, 'The plates and the cover are all ready, so just let the errors slide! Let us print some more copies and take care of the immediate demand. The second edition with all the revisions can be scheduled for the next Book Fair.'

'All right, let's do that.'

The books had already been printed; they were also being sold off; the profits were pouring in. I was amazed that so many people were reading my book! I was receiving calls from Siliguri, Indore, Delhi. Newspapers and magazines were writing about me. A number of television programmes were being telecast about my life and work. I should have been happy with it! Trusting my publisher with the matter of printing the extra copies, I should have just devoted my attention to writing. Instead of doing that, I was more concerned with the second edition. At this time Manojda said, 'I don't have the money for a second edition as I just drained a lot of my money on a flat and there were expenses for my mother-in-law's operation too. What do I say! My hands are totally empty. If you give me some money, I can still try. Otherwise, it will be ...'

My friend Bappa's big heart was written off for his friends. He said, 'How much do you need? I will give you the money. How many copies of the book will you print?'

After some calculations Manojda said that 350 copies could be printed for ₹20,000. Knowing that it would not be difficult to sell off these books through the combined efforts of the Dey Book Stall, Bappa and me, Bappa wrote a cheque for him and wanted to know when the books would be delivered and Manojda said it would take another seven days. After this, Bappa and my daily parade to his office began. The following week we were told that the books were not ready since the binding room was being renovated from scratch. Till the renovations were done, nothing else could be done, and so, we were asked to go back the next week. This continued, day after day, for a long time. I literally pleaded with him, 'What should I do? People are going crazy for the book!' Manojda gave me his honest advice, 'Ask them to collect it from Dey's Publishing and Booksellers. They already have a lot of books.'

'Dey's Publishing has books? How?' I feigned ignorance.

Manojda said, 'I had sent them some books, remember?'

What weird magic did Manojda possess that the hundred books that he had sent around two months back were still there? And here some unknown obscure bookseller at the Bagula railway station had apparently sold off some fifty books himself, all of which had been purchased from Dey's Publishing. One day, Bappa and I went to Dey's Publishing and Booksellers and were astonished to see the mountain of books still lying there. What was happening? More books were being bound and directly sent off to their shop. From here it was being distributed to other places. Anantada informed me that even Siliguri's biggest store had around forty copies of the book. After two months of such frantic running around, Manojda finally called me to pick up the books, 'All your books are ready.'

Politics, religion and society, everything has its own cycle. The craziness which say a Salman Rushdie or Taslima Nasrin book receives on its release, settle down with time. People have short-term memories and their tastes keep changing. The waves created by my book were now subsiding, sales were also now in low tide. All the mangoes shed in the storms which raged for the last two and a half months had been swept up by Manojda in his own basket alone. Now that the storm was in its last dregs, there was no problem in sharing some copies of the book with me.

He counted and handed over 350 copies to me. 'Are these the lot?' Manojda answered, 'There are ten to twelve more. Every publisher does this. You have received your 350 copies, right? How does it matter how many I have, right?'

He was right. The landlord lets the cowherd graze his cattle against the promise of a monthly salary. If the cowherd dares to milk the cow before returning the cattle to the shed after grazing them all day, he is nothing but a criminal. So what if the cow is returned intact! Milking the cow without permission is an audacious act and would make any landlord want to replace his cowherd.

Bappa and I went to College Street. From the stack of the books at Dey's Publishing and Booksellers, and countless phone calls from readers, we found out how the lion's share of the books was being purchased from Dey's. It was being kept a secret from us so that Manojda could gather all the honey for himself. We now tried to think of a way out of this situation. To snatch back the opportunity from his hands, we decided to bring out a beautiful, decent-looking, inexpensive and error-free second edition. This would stall the sale of the first edition. Now that the book had created so much rave reviews, it wouldn't be too difficult to find a publisher. We wouldn't even have to pay any money this time. It would all go from the publisher's pocket, who would also collect the profits. I would get royalties.

An agreement was drawn up accordingly and Kolkata Prakashan was given the charge of the second edition. They published the book and also spread the word in many newspapers and magazines including *Desh* and *Anandabazar Patrika*. As a result, the sale of the book which was going downhill picked up some pace again. Book orders started pouring in from Bangladesh. Dey's Publishing, which had a cordial relationship with Manojda, called Manik Fakir of Kolkata Prakashan to place their book orders.

Around this time, I received a call from Nanditadi, Manojda's wife, the same person about whom I had already gushed so much about in my autobiography and who also had been mentioned in my acknowledgements. In an angry tone she enquired, 'Did you do the right thing, Manoranjanda?'

'What did I do?' I answered, totally flabbergasted.

'Giving the book rights to someone else?'

I said, 'I never wanted this. Manojda refused to publish it, thus compelling me to go to another publisher.'

'Did he ever say that he "won't" publish?'

'No, not exactly. He asked for money in return. If the author still has to pay cash to publish a book which has had such massive sales, he would rather go to somebody else who is willing to do it for free. I had no other way. Why would I incur debts again?'

Her voice seemed pained. Nanditadi said, 'All your name and fame today is because of us. You gave us only ₹20,000. You very well know how much else was due. Had we not published the book, who would have known you? We have sold around a thousand copies of your book and you conveniently chose to forget all that.'

I was highly amused. Extreme emotions made people lose all their restraint. They end up saying things that were supposed to be kept within wraps, just like Nanditadi now.

I told her, 'Not 20. I have paid ₹40,000 in two instalments. Also, not a thousand copies; you people have sold only a little over a hundred copies and a little less than one hundred and fifty.'

'What are you saying? Only one hundred and fifty?'

'That is what Manojda's calculations say. Out of the 300 copies that were published the first time, I was given only 132. We received all the copies out of the second lot of 350 copies. Calculations say that he should have around 168 copies now. If a few out of them are distributed for free, how many remain?'

There is something called a trade secret, which businessmen don't even reveal to their spouses. Maybe for this reason, Nanditadi was not aware of the entire truth. It would have been better for Manojda to have warned her in advance. The truth she blurted out was enough to ruin their business reputation.

Manojda was right next to her. Snatching the phone from Nanditadi's hands he said, 'Had you really taken all the copies from the next set? I feel like there were some left.'

'How many were left?'

'I will be able to tell you that after calculating.'

I said, 'You keep your own calculations, I will keep mine. They will never match. The whole world reels under the effects of such unmatched accounts. My work is an ode to such accounting mishaps.'

The line got disconnected.

Note

[1] Chit fund scamster who ruined many ordinary and poor people who became part of his ponzi loan scheme.

CHAPTER 26

A Job Offer Gone Wrong and Returning to Chhattisgarh

A good-looking young man turned up at my workplace in Mukundapur one evening in his expensive car. I had spoken to him over the phone and was already aware of his impending visit. In order to be on time, I had made sure to reach the school on my broken bicycle by four in the afternoon, two hours before scheduled time. He was apparently in charge of a publication and wanted me to contribute. This had become a frequent occurrence. As far as I was concerned, it was another person demanding another piece and they could as well come and take one. What I didn't know then was that the person coming would come in such a grandiose car and in such a regal fashion. That Lakshmi's godson would be goddess Saraswati's devotee was something I had not imagined in my wildest dreams.

Seeing him before me now, I was extremely embarrassed, not knowing where to make him sit. There were of course proper arrangements to welcome such honourable guests at my workplace. Cushioned chairs, fast-moving fans, cold water, tea—everything. But they were reserved for 'honourable guests' alone and *my* guest did not fall under that category. Ambedkar might have had a doctorate degree, but he was still a Mahar. It was just obvious that his guest would also be from a lower caste by association. There had been no change to this casteist mentality in the country. I know from my own life experiences that literature was not enough to change this attitude. One needed to launch a Maoist kick to break this casteist mould. Yet, was there anybody who could shoulder this responsibility? Where Brahminism had appropriated anti-caste thinkers like Buddha and Sri Chaitanya, there was no great hope apart from shedding tears, heaving deep sighs and harbouring one's penmanship in silence.

When the great scholar Ambedkar himself did not find relief from hatred, ridicule and opposition, who was I to find any? Surely, I had some literary works to my credit, but by caste I was a Chanral—as Chandals were called—or a Namo. Keeping with my caste identity, my work was also that of cooking and washing utensils. People like us were hardly considered to be humans. I was unable to decide what to do with my guest and where to find him a seat appropriate to his stature.

From my previous experiences I knew that the moment I would pick out a quiet corner to sit down with my guest and finish some important conversation, somebody would definitely try to disrupt the flow by standing nearby or speaking on the phone at the top of his voice. My presence would be completely ignored and this person would hurl the choicest of invectives at his listener. Whether there was an actual person on the other end of the line was debatable, its effects would still be jarring. It would rattle my ears and make it difficult to concentrate on the discussion. I would be left embarrassed in front of my guest.

I am not alleging that these things were pre-planned; these happened in such an uninterrupted fashion that it was impossible not to doubt. To this I could add so many others. I would find my bicycle tires slashed with a sharp object or pierced with a pin. My bottle of water would develop limbs and walk away. My civil clothes, safely hung up while I changed into my work clothes, would be found soiled in turmeric powder and oil.

I turned towards the well-dressed fellow and asked him, 'Where will I make you sit, brother? Let us sit in your car and talk.'

He said, 'How far is your home from here? Can we go there? I also wanted to see where you live.'

Leaving my bicycle behind, I climbed into his motorcar. My house was about three miles from Mukundapur. The roads were full of potholes which got flooded during the rains. On so many occasions I had slipped while returning back from work at ten in the night. Sometimes, however, I even got lucky by discovering fish which had floated in from the nearby canal.

On that particular day, the car finally reached my home, bumping over the dry potholes. I offered a seat to the suit clad young and fit editor. His name was Ratul as I had gathered on the way here. He was from Bardhhaman. He said, 'Have you heard about Moloy Chowdhury? He lives in Delhi and runs a technical college. There are 18 branches of the institution in different Indian states. The one in Kolkata is at Salt Lake. Recently, he has brought out a magazine which is being freely distributed in the two Midnapore districts. In a way, it is a magazine for rural areas, pasted like a poster on the walls. You will have to write for this magazine, for which you will also receive some remuneration.'

Among many other things, he shared how Moloy Chowdhury was a lover of literature, and had awarded Ramapada Chowdhury, an eminent award-winning Bengali novelist and short story writer, prize money worth ten million rupees for his contribution to literature! Similarly, he had donated ₹2,600,000 rupees to a writer from Afghanistan and ₹5,100,000 to the Iron Lady of Manipur, Sharmila Chanu. Ratul also informed me of Moloy Chowdhury's son Arindam Chowdhury, the editor of the English magazine *Sunday Times*. After some time, he wanted to know what I did for a living. I told him that it was mentioned in *Itibritte Chandal Jivan*.

He said in a somewhat embarrassed voice, 'I have still not read the book. Sir has. He has sent me to contact you. I hastily travelled back from Delhi, because he said this was urgent.'

'Who is sir? Moloy Chowdhury or his son, Arindam Chowdhury?'

'The father and the son have their own separate businesses. I am Moloy Chowdhury's personal secretary. I oversee all his work. He is also my uncle.'

'How did the book manage to reach him?'

'I am not sure about that, but what I can tell you is that he loved it. He wants you to collaborate with us.'

I said, 'I am employed as a cook at a residential school for the deaf and mute. I go to work at six in the morning and sometimes it is already two by the time I return. I go again at six in the evening. My return time varies, ten on some days and eleven on others.'

He expressed great shock and disbelief, 'Then when do you write?'

In a jocular fashion, I said, 'Once a reporter asked the same question to Sibram Chakraborty. Seeing him eat rice at nine in the morning immediately after waking up, he inquired, 'You are eating so early?' Shibram said in his response, 'A whole night of sleeping has made me hungry.' The reporter wanted to know, 'What will you do after eating?' Shibram said, 'I will get tired after eating, so I will go back to sleep again.' The reporter asked, 'If you eat right after waking up and sleep right after eating, when do you write?' Shibram answered in his characteristic manner, 'Why! The next day.' My answer is the same: I write the next day.'

My intention was to make him laugh, but there was no change to Ratul's poker face. These people are barred from laughing. I hear that in the English-medium schools, where they are educated, they are taught everything from ways of walking, laughing, talking, to dressing and the correct manner of combing one's hair. People are programmed to lead a disciplined life: they do not eat without a proper set-up and cutlery; they sip on tea noiselessly; care is taken to hide their teeth while laughing and tears when crying.

He said, 'You must write. How much salary do you get? Leave the job. Join our magazine. We will pay you the same salary you are getting now. Are you interested?'

I said, 'My salary is about fifteen thousand.'

'Fifteen thousand only?' Ratul went silent for a while and then said, 'Fine! We will pay you the same amount. We can also increase it later. Come to our office from tomorrow. We will deposit a security amount of one lakh rupees on your name tomorrow itself. If you leave our job, you will have to return that money. Conversely, if we are the one to terminate your services, we will serve the notice at least six months in advance and will also pay you one more lakh. What do you say?'

It felt like my thumping heart would jump out of my mouth any moment. I had been waiting for an opportunity like this for so long! I didn't want anything else, just two square meals a day, a bare minimum of affordable clothes and some money for medical treatment in case of any illness. My present job served this purpose, but my body was beginning to complain at being exposed to so much heat and work twice a day. My job forced me to be on my feet for almost eight to ten hours a day. A slight tremor was developing on my legs and they would be sore all night.

The biggest torture was that I did not find any time to write. No time at all. An hour in the afternoon and an hour at night. Maybe the words of a new piece were squirming in my head, crying to be born on paper. During such a time I would be forced to leave my pen and rush to mind my chains. Then, after having spent the whole day standing in front of a blazing fire, becoming exhausted with backbreaking labour, warding off the boss' taunts, and suffering the hurtful jibes by jealous colleagues, when I returned home and hunted for words, I would find them dead already. With my emotions lost, it was difficult to give any sort of life to my writing.

But my fortune seemed to have opened up now abruptly! The goddesses of knowledge and wealth, Saraswati and Lakshmi, respectively, both the sisters, had come to pay me a visit as if to beckon me, 'Come, dear son! We are adopting you. Forget all your worries! It will all be ours from now. You just carry your pen in peace.'

Keeping my excitement in check, I asked Ratul, 'Give me some time to sleep over it, brother. I will let you know in a few days' time.'

I went to see their office the next day. They had one near Ruby Hospital. This was the smaller one from where all the magazine related work was carried out. He showed me a room on the first floor and said, 'Whenever you come to the office, you can sit here. This will be your room.'

'What do you mean by whenever I come? Won't I need to come every day?'

Ratul added in an indifferent tone, 'There is no need for you to come every day. You will be writing. You can do that even from your home. Just come and submit it once you are done. If you can't come, just give us a call. The driver will pick it up.'

I asked in fear, 'How much do I have to write every month?'

Ratul said, 'It is a monthly magazine. You have to contribute one article per month. You will decide the topic. But the word limit should not exceed five hundred to six hundred.'

I felt like dancing with joy—only five hundred words a month? Could it be true? ₹30 per word? T-h-i-r-t-y rupees? What maddening joy! I felt like shouting out in joy, so loudly that all the failures, ridicule and disdain I had received in life would go numb in the ears.

Ratul drove me in his car to Sector V where their IIPM college was situated. He showed me around the eleven-story building spread out over a large area. I was about to become an employee at this reputed institution. A wave of pride gushed through my heart. Today, I was an ordinary cook. People did not feel like showing me even a little bit of courtesy. From tomorrow, my life would change. I would also become a respectable individual. I pinched myself to see if I were dreaming.

On my way back home, I was literally brimming with excitement. It felt as if my heart would burst with joy. No! I decided not to look back. Goodbye to my school job, pension, and meagre gratuity money! I was convinced about handing in my resignation within seven days.

The next day, I shared everything with Shankar Roy, who was like a big brother to me. After hearing everything, he said, 'Wait, let me call Chandrasekhar. Moloy Chowdhury loves him like his own son. He will be able to provide us with more clarity.'

My friend Bappa had gifted the book to Chandrasekhar, who in turn had delivered it to Molloy Chowdhury. According to him, Moloy Chowdhury was a sensitive reader. If he decided to give the writer some small amount of prize money, it would change his arduous life. The smallest that could be offered by a person of his stature was big enough for the puny person. Chandrasekhar had not imagined that instead of a reward, the person would directly offer a job to the author.

Chandrasekhar said, 'Moloy Chowdhury called me just yesterday. He said, 'Chandrasekhar, I will be eternally grateful to you that you made me read such an amazing book. My man has already left for Kolkata yesterday. He will get in touch with Manoranjan Byapari. Let's see what happens after that.'

However, at the end, Chandrasekhar added, 'I don't think it might be the best decision to take up the job offer. Moloy Chowdhury is known as an extremely moody person. There is no saying what he will do next. He who is his closest today might become a stranger tomorrow. I, myself, was unable to work with him. Say, if you join the place now and you lose the job after six months, what will you do then? How many days can you survive on two lakh rupees?'

For an old woman living all alone in a shanty in the middle of a field and making money by selling dried cow dung cakes, the biggest fear would not be that of ghosts but the sound of rains. Living in a house whose roof was not protected with straw, made such fear seem real. Similarly, I was also not easily frightened by Osama, Al Qaeda, ghosts or god. My only fear was hunger. Only I knew how painful it could be. One whose gut wrenched like a dead python, was bound to forget all boundaries of morality. To him poems, literature or sermons, would all seem meaningless.

Therefore, I informed Ratul the next day, 'Sorry, brother, I have decided not to take up the job just yet. Let us both observe each other for six months. At the end of it, if we still think we can work together, I will leave my current job and formally join you people. If you want, I can keep writing for you but will not take any money for it.'

Ratul said, 'All right. Let us do that. But give us an article.'

The next edition of the wall magazine was to be published on the occasion of Vivekananda's birth centenary. Vivekananda had delivered sermons his whole life, lovely sermons on Hindu gods and goddesses, saints and wise women. He had taken Hinduism's greatness to its heights in a faraway foreign land. I remembered none of that, but the stomach wrenching dead python. Immediately I wrote down a quote from his Jnana Yoga, where he had said that the starving people say to those who lived a happy well-fed life: we are unfed, at unease, so we will make sure to suck away your happiness too, to drag you down and make you like us. Keeping this at the core of my article, I wrote an advisory for the rich to be more compassionate.

Upon submitting the article to Ratul, he read it and then mailed it to Delhi for his sir to read. He informed me after a few days that sir had loved it but it would not be published. I realized that I had miserably failed the test—and so wouldn't be allowed to sit for the finals anymore. But I was not at fault; instead it was my fate that was at fault! It had forced me to live such a bitter life with so much accumulated poison in my heart that whenever I sat down to write only poison would flow from the tip of my pen! The 'malicious intent' of destroying capitalism did not stay hidden any longer.

Moloy Chowdhury was a wealthy gentleman. He had earned the position of goddess Lakshmi's godson, in terms of riches, by trading in Saraswati's wealth. Surprisingly, he had managed all this without deviating from the right path. Otherwise, by now the income tax department and the CBI would have surely launched raids on him. Amassing wealth was not a crime in this country, whatever be the means. In his defence, he was at least spending a portion of that money for the welfare of the people. It was heard that he had also donated some expensive machines to hospitals. Everything was fine as long as he did not have to pay a salary to a person like me who would unhesitantly strike his axe upon the very tree that provided him with shade. So Ratul never called me back, nor did I go to him again, out of my own volition.

* * *

The reporter Goutam Roy had once written in *Anandabazar Patrika* that Manoranjan Byapari is no longer a person but has turned into a subject. I read the article but did not understand the meaning then. I understood it much later.

I had become a subject—such a strange subject that stories and novels could be written on me, newspaper and magazine features could be composed on me. I was a subject that the audience lapped up with enthusiasm! Financiers were readily available to make a documentary on me as if it would guarantee them solid financial profit.

The way TV and newspaper journalists were making much ado about me had me thinking that perhaps they had all come forward in solidarity against my fight for inequality. Gradually consciousness dawned on me and I saw that just as we would pick out amlaki, haritaki and bahera[1] and mahua flowers from the forest for some quick money, these people were using me in a similar fashion. I was just a commodity that would bring money for their next meal! If they found the right value, they would gladly level up by buying apple wine with it.

Perhaps everybody did not come for the apple wine. Some came on their boss' orders, others because they loved their jobs. The sincerity with which they heard my story and took my pictures was the same sincerity with which they clicked pictures of snakes, tigers, elephants or horses, or recorded their sounds. Some of them wove words with great dexterity and composed their articles.

In today's age, one that people referred to as the Vaishya age, the salesman who knew how to trade things could sell about everything for a decent price—be it laughter, tears, anger, sadness, or poverty! I remember this when I and a photographer friend of mine were standing at the railway station. A beggar was asking around for alms with her baby in her lap, 'I have not eaten the whole day, babu, give me ten paisa.' Nobody seemed to pay any attention to her cries. Having tired herself out, she sat down against the wall near the public toilets, bared her breast and thrust it into her infant's starving mouth. Right at that moment, my friend's camera shutter went 'click!' The beggar mother became a piece of art in an instant, something that could be traded off for a good sum of money. The best kind of poverty porn! A few days later, my friend sent this impeccable artwork to a magazine and received a rather hefty sum for it, an amount that this beggar would never even have had the courage to imagine.

I too had turned my soul into a commodity of a similar nature. Hence, people wrote stories about me, featured me in newspapers and journals, photographed me, and spoke about me at places. After their work was done, they did not even bother to keep in touch. Instead, they went in pursuit of their next subject.

Amit Ghosh, the film director, who had shot a 30-minute documentary film featuring me titled *Sadharon-Asadharon* and which was telecast in Akash Bangla, gave me a call. He wanted to shoot another documentary with me. This time, the duration would be for two hours and the end product would be screened at a proper festival. When the previous docu-film was shot, it had taken us four days: two days of outdoor shooting and two days at my place, requiring me to be absent from work. Huge floodlights and the camera were set up, which had run on my electricity. They had matter-of-factly assured me that the electricity bill would exceed by not more than two to three hundred rupees. In addition to this, I had singlehandedly borne the cost of the frequent cups of tea and biscuits that were served for twelve people of the crew. At that point of time, I had been extremely happy at the entire prospect of my story being rendered to film and did not let myself bother about these petty things.

After the shoot was over, I had put in a simple request, 'I don't want anything more, if you could just send me a CD of the programme.' They had given me their word. 'Let the programme be telecast first, then visit the office in two to three days. We will give you the CD.' I had made a trip to their office somewhere in central Kolkata, a couple of days after the programme was aired. They had asked me to come again the next day. This carried on for a long time, with days turning into weeks and weeks into a month. After a month I was finally informed, 'The channel has no rule for sharing videos. We won't be able to give it to you.'

People said you can be fooled once. But if it happens again, you are not a fool but a grand fool. The same was true for me. I had not learnt my lessons despite being fooled so many times.

I was once again unable to say no to Amit Ghosh's proposal. First off, they asked for the file where I had collected all the articles ever published on me, neatly arranged for the future. I was not able to trust them with the originals, fearing they might lose it—if that happened, the loss would all be mine—therefore, I sent them a photocopied set, which in retrospect I realize was a wise decision as they never returned it to me. I wasted around seventy-five rupees on that. In addition, they asked for two copies of *Itibritte Chandal Jivan* with the assurance of reimbursing me later. As expected, I lost that amount as well. Apart from that, for the duration of the shoot, the crew had tea and biscuits at my expense and also an entire meal one afternoon comprising rice, moong dal with fish head, posto with ridge gourd and rohu. After that they left and totally disappeared. There was no news, no phone calls. Whenever I called, I found their phones to be switched off.

As a result, I was no longer as excited to hear about documentaries. Enough was enough. But as I have already said, I never learn. This time round, another person named Ghosh entered the scene. One Ghosh had already squeezed me half-dry, now this Ghosh would squeeze out his share and leave me completely desiccated. His name was Jaydeep Ghosh who had made the film *Maya Bazar*, funded by the NFDC (National Film Development Corporation of India), a film which didn't do great business. The opportunity to work with such a big name seemed so lucrative that I completely forgot that I might be taken advantage of again and that all the profits would go to his pocket.

The same cycle started again: my house resonating with shouts of 'Silence!', 'Light!', 'Sound!' and 'Action!'—a farce whose other name was shooting. The shoot went on for almost a month at my place, at my workplace, at Joydeep Ghosh's house, at the Sealdah Railway Station, at various places in Jadavpur, at the river's ghats, inside Presidency Jail, so on and so forth. It seemed to be a combat zone with around fifty actors, supporting actors and the rest of the crew working together. At the end of all this, we headed towards Chhattisgarh, where we shot for three more days at Bhilai, Dalli-Rajhara and Kanker.

When everything was over, I sat down to calculate how much I had spent and how much was I given in return. I had spent my entire yearly quota of CLs and medical leaves. Besides this, the expenses of serving the entire crew with tea and biscuits for two days and Anu's intensive labour for the duration could be taken as additional costs. In return, we received Joydeep Ghosh's 'thank you'. What a joke! Even a junior artist with just two dialogues in a day was sent back home smiling with five hundred rupees nicely tucked inside his pocket. Another girl, who had merely copied down dialogues from my book for the characters to say, was handed out five thousand rupees. But there was nobody to give me even five paise. One day out of sheer desperation, I asked Joydeep Ghosh, 'Dada, won't you pay me something?' His assistant replied, 'Usually it is the lead in our films who pay us money. You are the hero of this film. You should be the one paying us money. Why don't you write us a small cheque?'

I was rendered completely speechless.

It was not anybody's fault but that of my own fate. I had been born with such an ill fate that anybody and everybody ripped me off according to their wishes. Out of this episode, I benefited in a small way. Using the shoot as an excuse, I was able to revisit Chhattisgarh again, which would perhaps not have happened otherwise. Unfortunately, I had nobody left to visit; neither Ram nor his Ayodhya existed anymore.

We stayed at a small government rest house near the Durg station. Joydeep Ghosh had his reach in higher places. He had arranged for this through his contacts. From there, we travelled towards Dalli-Rajhara in a hired jeep on the first day. The Shaheed Hospital had by then grown into a huge establishment. New departments had opened, expensive instruments had been purchased. The number of healthcare workers had increased, similar to the rise in the number of patients. Patients would swarm from far and wide to avail of affordable health care facilities. All that was fine, but the former excitement seemed to be missing. The union office bustled with people once. Its corridors now stood glaringly empty like an abandoned town. The field in front, which the workers had named as Lal Maidan, was lying desolate like the quiet crematorium ground left empty after the bodies had been cremated.

The Union secretary Sahdev Sahu was still there, like a lonely guard in this vast crematorium. There was no one around, only memories and an eerie emptiness. He was present like a living corpse, hiding within him forty years of voiceless history from 1977 to 2013, along with the files, the documents and the furniture of the Union office.

He had once seen the workers rising in a movement like the foaming waves at sea. He had seen the thundery fisted hands carrying hammers, shovels and spades, as if advancing towards the skies in extreme arrogance to tear away the sun, in hopes of unsettling the orbit of the oppressor and the oppressed. The hills and forests of Chhattisgarh used to tremble in their roar for Inquilab. The protected fort of the feudal lords would shake in fear, almost as if their end was near.

Everything had gone mum. No longer could one see rallies of men, women and workers, marching on the roads in front of the Union office onwards to Khadan, on whose shovels and spades the rays of the morning sun would be refracted. Their strong muscled legs would make the soil on the roads fly, the ground would shiver under their strength. Everything had been silenced by the bullets fired from the local guns of the murderous lords. Like Shankar Guha Neogi's chest, which had been shattered with bullet holes, the organization was in tatters. The Chhattisgarh Mukti Morcha was now a dying flame about to go out completely. There was still some smoke left, but nothing compared to the bright razzle-dazzle of the past.

When Neogiji passed away, he was survived by his two young daughters and a son. I heard that his eldest daughter, Kranti, had completed her LLB and was now practicing at the Raipur Court. His youngest daughter, Mukti, was the head of the Dalli Municipality Parishad. It was under her initiative that a tall wall with an iron gate had been built around the place where lay the altar of Neogiji and eleven martyrs from 1977. Different trees had been planted. A person had been hired to look after the place.

Mukti, who had been of a tender age then, recognized me instantly. Finding me, she vented out all her suppressed grievances, 'I had asked for a ticket to run for the elections on behalf of the Mukti Morcha, but was denied. Congress came to know that I wanted to run in the elections and said that they would give me a ticket. I fought from their seat and won. They appointed me as the head. Let's see what happens next.'

Ashadidi also recognized me. So did Faguram Yadav, Janak Lal Thakur and Chabilal Sau. It was obvious that Dr. Saibal Jana would recognize me. Everybody reminisced about the old days. They remembered the role I had played in the movement. My role was akin to the role played by the squirrels in helping Rama build a bridge across the ocean between two countries. I was happy to find out that they still remembered it.

After this we went to Kanker. The town had now expanded in both length and breadth. If Dalli was my heart, Kanker had been my two lungs. Every nook and corner of this town was painted with my memories. I used to love Dalli, but Kanker loved me back. The sight of the natural unadulterated beauty of the little town of Kanker brimming with life brought to my lips the phrase, 'If there was paradise anywhere, it was here. It was here.'

At one point of time, there were a lot of people from Kanker who were known to me. But I did not have the time to look for them. The sun was slowly sinking and the light was growing dim. There would be no point using the cameras in this light. The only two people who were able to give bytes for the documentary were Nazeeb Qureishi and Saroj, the owner of the Punjab Hotel where I used to spend my nights whenever I came to Kanker and who was friends with both Nazeeb and me. Together they nostalgically recollected some memories of their 'Bengali Dada Manoranjan Byapari'.

The next day, I caught hold of the Bengali lawyer Vishnu Prasad Chakrabarty. He also spoke for a bit, although not a lot, it was enough for me. I had my own intuition about people and could tell from their body language how happy they were on meeting me after so long. They had carefully preserved the memories of the relationship they shared with me so many years ago in their hearts. This filled me up with a sense of warmth. I realized, even though I was not physically present here, I was present in their leisurely discussions and would stay so for many more years. This was the biggest gift from my Chhattisgarh travels.

NOTE

[1] Amlaki (Indian gooseberry), a sour fruit; haritaki (chebulic myrobalan) and bahera (bastard myrobalan) all possess valuable medicinal qualities.

CHAPTER 27

The Patna Literature Festival

My transition from a 'person' to a 'subject' had a direct influence on my increasing worth. The intelligentsia all over the country started lovingly inviting me over—like a crow singing in the voice of the koyel—to see me. I had already visited Delhi, Maharashtra and Hyderabad. I was told that Bangladesh and Australia were also eager to invite me. But, how was I to go without a passport?

A new craving was slowly branching out in my heart. I wanted to board an aeroplane at least once in my life and fly up to the sky. In my destitute condition, such a luxury was impossible by my own means. But the people who invited me from different places were sitting on a mountain of wealth. Sponsoring a single plane ticket was insignificant for them. So I made a vow to myself that the next time I was called for an event outside Bengal, I would go only if I was offered a plane fare.

One of my acquaintances, whom I had met on the road, approached me one day. He said, 'Your wish will be fulfilled this time. There's an invitation from Bangalore. You will have to attend it.'

I almost danced in joy, 'Will we take the flight?'

'No, the train.'

'Then I won't go.'

'But first listen to the entire thing.'

'All right.'
'From Bangalore, we will go for another event. That will be in Delhi. There is an event at JNU.'
'Oh, I am sure we will take the plane from Bangalore to Delhi then?'
'No, for that too we will have to take the train.'
'Then how will my wish get fulfilled?'
'The return journey from Delhi to Kolkata will be in a plane. I have already finalized everything. Just pack up your things.'
I put my faith in him and a spring of hope started brewing in my heart. I applied for a week-long leave at my workplace. I shared the good news with everybody at home, in my area, at my workplace.

I borrowed some money from a friend and bought a new bag. It was a seven-day long trip, just any bag wouldn't do. It should be large enough for a week's supply of clothes. I spent around ₹12,000 on the bag. I also bought some kurtas, pajama, vest, underwear, towel and a shaving kit and some medicines in case I happened to fall ill. Anu was very meticulous. She put together oil, soap, and shampoo that would last me a week and neatly packed it along with the rest of my luggage.

I started packing two days before the intended date of departure, and it seemed as if we were preparing for war. We did not have a cobbler in the area we lived in. Anu spent two hours and twenty rupees on a shuttle taxi, to get my shoes mended and polished from Mukundapur. Her strict orders were that I wear the shoes with trousers and the slippers with my kurta.

When Anu came from Chhattisgarh to Kolkata, she did not leave even a single thing behind, be it the grinder or the broom. Had she known that I would have to cook my meals in Bangalore and Delhi, she would have perhaps packed the grinder, the chopper and other such things too. Despite that the two bags she had packed, one small and one big, were no less than fourteen kilos. Having packed everything, I now waited for dada's call on the said date. I was supposed to leave for Howrah as soon as his call came and then wait under the big watchtower upon reaching. Thereafter, the three of us—dada, the person accompanying him and me—would board the train for Bangalore.

That desired call, however, never came. Morning turned into afternoon, afternoon turned into evening, and evening descended into night; the call never came. There was no news that day or the next or the day after that. There was no way of knowing what had happened to the man. I did not know much about him. He had never shared facts like his address, what his kids did or his livelihood. It was not in my nature to show curiosity about somebody else's personal life. Our interactions were limited to only that for which we had come to know each other. If he ever chose to share something personal, I would listen but I would never probe on my own. As a result, I hardly knew anything about him. After we met at an event, he became a regular at my place and would sit for hours, drinking tea, smoking cigarettes and chatting. Our discussions would span topics of society, literature and politics.

After this incident, he disappeared from my life with the suddenness with which he had appeared. Initially, I was worried that he must have fallen into some deep trouble. I kept calling him on his mobile, which kept ringing but nobody received it. One day, when I decided to call from my wife's phone, he received it. From his voice it didn't appear as if he was unwell, but he cut the call as soon as I tried to speak. A person entered my life like a whiff of wind, stayed for a few days and then disappeared without a trace, just like air. To be honest, he did actually leave behind a blemish which would always remain. Perhaps he had been put under pressure by some higher official to cancel my event, a pressure he had been unable to reject. This could have happened with anybody. If he had just made a short call and told me, 'Sorry Dada, I won't be able to take you. A small problem has arisen ...' Just one call would have solved it all!

I knew full well that West Bengal was not the only place which had seen a rise in my oppositional camp. The same was true for the rest of India. This was not necessarily a bad sign. This was Newton's third law, as the number of your friends would increase, so would the number of your enemies. It would be unfair to stop making friends for fear of making enemies. I welcomed both equally, simultaneously, baring my chest for my enemies to land their blows upon.

* * *

There was a gentleman from Delhi, by the name of Bajrang Bihari Tiwari. He was a Delhi University professor who wrote on Dalit life and literature. It was because of one of his writings published with *Kathadesh* that the Hindi readers all over India came to know about me. He gave me a call one day, 'Byapariji, Namaste! How are you?'

Author interviewed by Bajrang Bihari Tiwari, Department of Hindi, Delhi University.

He added, 'A couple of organizations along with the Bihar government and *Dainik Jagran Patrika* are planning to arrange a programme 'Bihar Divash' in Bihar. Under its banner, a Patna Literature Festival will also be organized. This programme spanning three days, will be attended by delegates from almost all the states in India including Delhi, Bihar and Kolkata. There will be people from Pakistan, too!'

I said, 'Seems like a grand event.'

'Yes, a grand event.' He continued, 'I have been given the responsibility of choosing just one Dalit writer from all of India. This has put me in a great dilemma.'

I smiled and said, 'Why? Are you not finding anybody appropriate for the event?'

He said, 'There are people. In fact, Maharashtra, Gujarat and even Delhi are filled with such Dalit writers. But .... According to me, none of them are truly representative of Dalit society. They are all professors, or government servants who know nothing about hunger or pain. What I mean is that they may be Dalits by societal standards, but financially they are quite well off. If I could choose ten, I would definitely have chosen from them too. But I was given the option of picking only one, so I chose you. Please don't say no. I have already proposed your name. They will call you, and this is a matter of my reputation.'

No, I did not have anything else to say. Bajrang Bihari's logic behind choosing me was irrefutable. There were hardly any Dalit writers like that.

I told Bajrang Bihari, 'I will go. I won't say no. But only on the condition that they sponsor my plane ticket. I could return back in a train, but I have never been on a flight. By your grace, I would love to fulfil that desire.'

They agreed and as a result, I was able to see the houses, mountains, rivers and people down there from a bird's eye view. My request for a window seat on the right side was also fulfilled. The only regret was that I was not able to see the Himalayas because of the cloudy skies, even though I would have really loved to. That I would fly one day was a thing of wonder not just for my family but also for the village of Khudirabad. Ajit Dalui's mother, my neighbour, started trembling in fear. She came and told my wife, 'Bouma, forbid your man from flying. What if he falls down while flying at that height?'

To be honest, it is not that I was not plagued with the fear of death once the plane reached the clouds. But the fear was interspersed with hope that if death came, I would not oppose it for it would be a grand one! If the person who was fated to die by coming under a bus or a lorry, or by getting hit by knives, bombs or bullets, or just by starving, died in a plane accident it would be as holy as dying under Jagannath's chariot wheels. I had not been able to do much for my wife and kids. They would perhaps get around ten to fifteen lakhs from the life insurance company. They would live comfortably. But if it were that easy to get your wishes fulfilled! This damned life was such that there was neither any chance of me living life king-size nor dying in a grand way.

With no provisions for a public vehicle to take me from my house to the bus stop, I was compelled to hail a taxi. My two accompanying bags were very heavy. My wife and Sabitri Dalui, a neighbour, came to witness my final traumatic moments. When my taxi came to a halt, I reached the gate with my bags. I had been told to report two hours in advance for the security check. One was permitted to board the flight only after going through all this hassle. Accordingly, I reached two hours early. It was time to say goodbye to my wife. She waved me a teary farewell. For jatra performances, in a similar situation the actor playing Abhimanyu would sing before entering the chakravyuh, 'Bid me farewell, O beloved, so that I may emerge victorious in the battle.' I too whispered the same in my heart. I would be the only Dalit person sharing the stage with some of the biggest scholars from all over the country. I was determined to make a mark before I left, so that I would be invited to such an event every time it was organized.

There was a security guard at the gate. I showed him my ticket and my voter id card. I told him, I was barely literate and didn't speak English at all, that I was travelling by air for the first time, and asked him for guidance. Honesty always wins! He immediately guided me saying, 'Go straight and then take a right. You will see a counter. Ask anybody, they will show you Jet Airlines. Hand over your tickets at the counter. They will guide you through the next steps.'

I was then asked to wait in the queue. My big bag was deposited. A machine was used to search my body. Finally, I was shown another gate and asked to follow it inside. There was another security guard at this gate. He, in turn, examined something, after which I was able to proceed towards the waiting area. Almost two hours passed in this entire course of action. Then we were put on a bus which dropped us till the aeroplane. It was a small flight with a small stairway. Nevertheless, I felt a sense of elation climbing those steps to enter the plane. Was this the stairway to the heavens that Ravan had coveted to build? The scientists managed to achieve what Ravan failed at! And now I would finally reach the heavens!

My heart felt weird. I kept remembering my father's face. In his life, he had never been able to travel legitimately even in the third-tier chair car with a ticket. So many times, in the hot June afternoons, I have had to walk all the way from Rajdanga Khal Par to the Bharat TV Company near Jyoti Basu's house in Hindustan Park in order to reach my two-to-ten shift, just because I did not have twenty-five paisa in my pocket. That same me was about to board an aeroplane today, to fly atop the clouds, from where I could easily touch the moon or the stars just by extending my hands. I was grateful. My heartfelt thanks went towards Bajrang babu!

My seat was near the window on the right; the seat on my left was empty. Why was nobody sitting on that seat? Was it because I smelt of sweat? Or I did not look like a polished babu? I didn't care, as long as I had my seat to sit on. My whole body was ecstatic. I had spent my entire life walking over mud and dust. Destiny had given me wings today! I was floating in that happiness. How did it matter that the seat beside me was empty?

I would be lying if I said I wasn't even a little bit uncomfortable. I was like a fox cub amidst a herd of tigers. From the attire, body language, way of speaking of the people around me, I could tell that none was of my station. Their wealthy background was evident from their attitude. So instead of looking at them, my eyes went outside the window. Down below, I could see the city of Kolkata. The huge buildings looked tiny like cigarette boxes. I could see the

Indoor Stadium, the Shahid Minar. It had been my dream to climb atop the Minar and gaze down at Kolkata. People who had already done so had told me many times that I wouldn't be able to do it, that it was too high and my legs would give up before reaching the top. The same Shahid Minar now looked like the size of my thumb. Its size which was its pride seemed insignificant as compared to mine. The head that it held up so high was now under my feet.

As soon as the city ended, the scenery changed to that of rural India. Everything was green, some unknown river flowing between them. The plain in between the rivers and the mountains looked squarish in shape, like boxes of hopscotch drawn by kids at play. I assumed each box to be the boundary line of a district.

Many years ago, I had read in Jajabar's book *Drishtipat* that the airplane had given us speed but taken away our emotions. I understood the inner meaning of those words that day. To board the plane, it had taken me one hour and twenty minutes. But I reached Patna from Kolkata in the blink of an eye. Where was the excitement of travelling, the one that was there in train and bus rides? This was the fun of staying close to the land. The train would stop at different stations and the atmosphere would immediately be filled with the sweet cumulative chorus of hawkers ferrying tea and other goods like pleasant background music. These sounds alone could enliven any dead town in the middle of the night. The heart would get rejuvenated with a new vigour. Realization would strike anew that our country was so huge, so diverse were its languages, clothing and culture. Sitting in the train or the bus, even for a moment, one could touch these things albeit symbolically. The same joy was not available in a short airplane ride.

Finally, I reached Patna airport. The total time taken had been one hour and twenty minutes, almost equal to the time I usually took to reach Jadavpur station from my home. There was a file of mobile passengers in front of me. I followed them outside. A man had laid out a table, and was sitting with a bouquet of flowers and a bottle of water. There was a placard in his hand saying 'Manoranjan Byapari Welcome!' As soon as I went near him, he handed me the bouquet and the bottle. The other person ushered me to the car which was waiting. He opened the gate for me and asked me to take my seat. He went and occupied the seat beside the driver. I was a bigwig for him and he did not dare sit beside me!

The cold air that hit my face upon opening the car door told me that it was not an ordinary car. Now my whole body cooled down. The AC was on, and the 42 degrees temperature outside in Patna could not even touch me inside the car. Those who rode such air-conditioned cars and lived in air-conditioned houses, what care did they have whether the global temperature was rising or falling? They could easily destroy miles of forests for their own needs!

The car reached the guest house in twenty minutes. Here too arrangements had been made to receive me with a lot of pomp and show; some officials working with the Bihar government had turned up for the occasion. In the way they were dressed and moved, it was evident that they came from comfortable and educated backgrounds. I did not count how many floors the building had, but I was kept on the tenth floor in a well-furnished room. I reached on 22 March 2013, the same day Bajrang Bihari reached from Delhi. He was put up in the room next to mine.

Apart from him, I knew nobody else. Soon we left for the Patna Planetarium hall room, where 'Navaras', the Art and Culture Department of the Bihar government, in collaboration with *Dainik Jagaran Patrika* had arranged the Literary Fest: Patna Literature Festival. The huge hall of the Patna Planetarium was filled with celebrities from all over the country. Chief Minister Nitish Kumar was also present. My identity among these scholars was, in the words of *Dainik Jagaran*, 'Manoranjan Byapari, the able representative engaged to create an India enthused with the working-class spirit.'

I don't remember exactly where I had encountered these lines, but there was a couplet that went like this, 'If you don't know how to shine, don't give people the opportunity to laugh at you.' During the two days, 22–23 March, I remained dull, hidden in the crowd of speakers and audience like an ordinary person, unknown to all the people in Bihar. After my session on the 24 March, 9.30–10.30am, the way *Dainik Jagaran, Hindustan Times, Prabhat Khabar,*

Apna Bihar Patrika and many news channels started creating a hullabaloo over me, there was no way I could have remained unknown. Satisfied with the audience reaction at the end of the event, Bajrang Bihari, who had proposed my name, directed Sanjeev Kumar's oft-quoted dialogue from *Sholay* at me, 'I was not unjustified in bringing you from Bengal to Bihar.'

On 24 March 2013, as the needles on the clock ticked closer to the hour, I took a bath and got ready to head out to the battlefield. The stipulated time was 9:30 am. For two days, I had closely observed the movements and weapons of my opposition camp. Charu Majundar had once said, 'A proper investigation is the heart of a successful action.' So, in the previous two days I had gathered enough information about the kind of weapon that could be directed at me and the weapons I would need to defend myself.

The moderator for my segment was Bajrang Bihari Tiwari. I was seated in the audience. As soon as he took my name, I climbed up the stage with firm steps. It felt like I was entering a space that was referred to as the 'arena' in English—where the bull could be let in for the people to derive pleasure from poking it, riling it up or causing it to bleed. I silently observed Lord Krishna's *akshauhini* regiment in front of me. 'I was a body-less weapon-less' lone individual, like Eklavya. If I could defeat this army, I would be able to exit this vicious cycle. If I failed, they would rip me off and dance over my dead body. They would say: 'The fittest rules. These people are unfit; hence they have been rightfully placed at the bottom. They were given a chance to prove themselves, but look how badly defeated they were. Thus, no one can dispute the fact that they can't and they will never be able to compete with us. What is the need for you people to write literature and all that? Go and farm, pull a rickshaw, or be a porter bearing luggage. That is all you are good for!'

The first speaker was the famous writer Asghar Wajahat. This was the third day he had gone up on stage. The organizing committee had put him in something or the other every day. Perhaps he had already said what he wanted to in the previous two days, so he did not take much time that day. He finished his speech within five minutes saying that 'Dalits must not just write autobiographies. They should also write stories, novels, poems, etc.'

Now it was my turn. According to the rule, the host would ask me a question or indicate which direction he wanted to take the discussion towards. But I was that man who sang to his own tune. All my life I had paved my own way. That day was no different. I let his questions enter through one ear and go out through the other. Standing in front of the microphone, I thanked the Bihar government, *Dainik Jagaran* and the audience and then began introductions in my own style.

'Respected guests, I will answer Bajrangji's questions soon. First, I wanted to talk to all of you. Then I will read out something. Finally, I will answer Bajrangji's and your questions.'

My Hindi was not too bad.

> I will begin with a short story. It goes this way: once there was a huge debate about something in the Parliament, and a comment passed by a member was found to be unfavourable by the head who felt insulted. He said to the member, 'I hope you know who I am?' The MP answered, 'I know who you are.' 'Then I hope you know what is the difference between both of us?' The MP nodded. 'Then tell me, what is the difference?' The MP smiled and said, 'There is just one difference—just one—that you are seated there and I here!'
>
> Respected guests, seated in the audience, I have the same difference with all of you. You all are seated there and I am here. Each one of you has the qualification to replace me on stage at any given time. I can guarantee that that person would know more and would be able to speak more about art and culture as compared to me. There is, however, one difference between both of us. For you to make the trip from your seats to the stage will take only fifteen minutes, for me it took thirty-three years. I used to sleep on an empty stomach at the Jadavpur railway station by spreading out my gamchha and with a brick for a pillow. In that condition, I began my literary journey in 1981

via *Bartika* magazine in order to reach this respectable stage. Today, I have finally arrived!'

The audience burst out in a round of deafening applause. I was unable to understand the reason behind this applause. Was it an indication that the scholarly and skilful section of society seated in the audience had accepted me? That my words had hit its mark? Long back I had heard somewhere that one's weapon is one's own vulnerabilities.

The source of my strength was my crushed life. I was already at the lowest step of the staircase and did not have any more steps to descend. For lack of anything to lose, I was fearless. I told them,

> I come from a poor Dalit refugee family deprived of any governmental assistance who made their way from the other side of Bengal. My childhood was spent in grazing cattle. As I grew a little older, I waited upon tables at tea shops. Fast forward a couple more years, I worked as a porter, a rickshaw-puller, a crematorium ground assistant, a sweeper, a lascar in a truck, a night guard and in so many other roles. To curb the excessive pain arising from the cramps in my stomach because of hunger, I have also stolen and snatched goods many times. Life has not given me a chance to go to school. Instead, it has pushed me into the dark cell in a jail. Drawing out patterns in the dust on the cell floor, I was taught the Bengali alphabet. Thereafter, I became a writer, quite incidentally at that! Till now I have published around ten to twelve novels, 100 stories, 20 to 25 essays and a total of 5 to 7 poems. But I have found more fame after the publication of my autobiography, *Itibritte Chandal Jivan*. I don't know how much literary merit one can find in it, but one thing is for sure: it has a lot of truth. Harsh, heartless, cruel and ugly truth.'

Clap! Clap! Another round of applause. I had been able to win over my audience. I was dancing like little Krishna on the head of the Kaliya Nag and I was making these people dance. I had watched a film where a Kung Fu king (in the film Karate Kid, 2010) makes a poisonous viper mime its actions just through the power of his eyes. I had turned into this Kung Fu king. I was forcing my audience to listen to my speech. They would listen as long as I would speak. They were listening to me at my will, but believing it to be their will. They were not being able to detect my intention. I was pausing in between my speech to ask the audience if they were getting bored. To ask if they were getting delayed? 'Tell me, I will stop.' The audience would roar back in unison, 'Nahin nahin! Go on.'

> I told them that out of my twelve novels and hundred stories, not a single was fiction. A part of my life was scattered in each of these narratives. The boy with a torn sack on his shoulders hunting for food, the boy looking through dustbins for the entrance to Ali Baba's hidden cave, the boy being tied to his back to the lamp post and being beaten up as a thief for stealing a packet of bread, the man eating a meal at a restaurant and trying to escape without paying and being chased for it by a mad crowd with the cry of 'robber! robber!' the man being shunted off to jail on false allegations of being a wagon breaker by the police to fulfil their quota of arrests for the day—they were all me. These were my many split selves. I had written them all as characters in my stories.

The organizers were sending me frequent alerts, Bajrangji was constantly looking at the clock, time was literally floating away. It had been scheduled for an hour, I had already exceeded by twenty minutes. The programme was just not ending. The moment I paused, a bunch of questions would be hurled at me. 'How did you become a writer? 'What do you understand by Dalit Literature?''Why is there no Dalit movement in Bengal?''What are your future plans?''Where do you work ?''How does your family run?''Did you ever fall in love?' There were so many questions I felt I would be washed away by its force.

The answers to these questions could all be found in my book. I tried answering in short. Finally, Bajrang Bihari said to the audience, 'It is evident from your excitement that your heart has not been satiated with the question and answers. But my hands are tied and I have to end the session here. The schedule is tight, there are other events too. We will have to clear away the stage for them. If you want to continue the discussion, carry it on with Manoranjan Byapari outside where you will find a proper seating arrangement.'

I alighted from the stage and reached outside. A crowd followed me, people requesting for autographs, reporters asking me questions, cameramen asking me to pose. I was no longer unknown. I had become a voice of the whole of India's Dalit and poor people who had no agency for expression. I had won over Bihar.

Writing about that day's event, Nawal Kishor, the reporter of *Apna Bihar Patrika*, wrote, 'Manoranjan Byapari turned the event 'Anya ka Lekhan' into a huge success.' He started off the article in this way, 'Friends, personally the Patna Literature Festival did not have any significant value for me.' Why? Why was such a huge festival insignificant for him? This is because he was a Dalit, the kind whose hands would be burnt with a rod by the Savarnas of Bihar for trying to drink water from their wells. Although the Patna Literature Festival was a government one, the credit went to the Dubeys, the Chaubeys, the Mishras and the Tiwaris, who had selectively curated the list of invited writers, poets, playwrights, film directors from the Savarna group. The two or four Muslims and a handful of Dalits who participated, had been added to project an impartial front. Being few in numbers, their voices would get shrouded by the loud voice of the higher castes. Hence, this event was like a farce for Nawal Kishor, nothing more than a gimmick. Having reluctantly taken part in the event, his experience was evident, 'A man clad in a dull kurta-pajama has literally shaken the Brahmanvad and capitalistic system amidst a Savarna crowd.'

It was true. I had turned extremely fearless that day and cast cannonballs at the palaces of the opponent camp. Somebody had asked me, 'Why do you write?' In an unwavering voice, I had replied, 'I write because I can't murder anybody. If my body had enough strength to murder, I would not have written. I would have murdered instead.'

I had intentionally used the word 'murder' not 'eliminate'. But *Dainik Jagaran* reported that as 'My heart feels like killing them.' Kill, murder, execute, slaughter, eliminate—all have different meanings. What people made of my word at that instant I am not sure, but the whole hall room went quiet. It was so silent that a pin drop could be heard.

I said, 'I feel like murdering people who cut out babies from their mothers' wombs in the name of religion. I feel like murdering those that use caste as an excuse for burning the hands of a man with a rod for fetching water from a nearby well to quench his thirst after walking miles under the relentless afternoon sun. I feel like murdering the intruder who broke in through a hole in a broken fence to rape a three- to five-year-old infant girl whose mother had left her home to go to work. I want to murder those who evict a poor farmer from his little piece of land and seize it in the name of industrialization. I want to kill the people who burn houses and rape the wives and daughters of innocent Adivasis for the crime of claiming ownership over their water, land and forests and telling off the so-called civilized people to keep their usurping claws to themselves. My hands itch to murder these murderers.

'But I can't. My body does not have adequate strength anymore. So, I write. I want to create a group of heartless killers by wielding just my pen! I want people reading my books to develop this murderous rage—and accomplish that which I failed at!'

For this reason, my story was published with my picture on the first page of *Hindustan Times*. It was also published in the *Prabhat Khabar Patrika*, reported by Prabhatranjan.

CHAPTER 28

Literary Accolades

To say that I am from the Dalit community would not be enough. There are a lot of internal factions within the Dalits; maybe this number is around six thousand. The British Raj supported the caste system even though the four divisions of caste were not its creation: it was the contribution of the 'wise' Brahmins of our country.

I belong to the Namashudras, occupying a small portion within the six thousand other Dalits. The Namashudras are further divided into two sections: one sells fish and the other eats it. The two sections cannot inter-marry, just like a Kaora cannot marry a Bagdi, or a Bagdi cannot marry a Poundra Kshatriya. There are the Guru Gossains, who have made additional divisions. My cousin Keshav Byapari rose up the social ladder by becoming a disciple of Anukul Thakur. His guru tied a sacred thread around him. Although this did not turn my cousin into a Brahmin, he no longer remained a Namashudra. That's the reason he stopped eating at our place.

It was hilarious to see the lower-caste communities vying for the sacred thread. The place where I lived was a neighbourhood of poor people which had started developing over the last twelve or fourteen years. Every year labourers from the Sundarbans came to work here. One winter dawn, I woke up to the sound of people huffing and puffing. Stepping outside I saw five to six labourers carrying baskets of soil that had been dumped by a lorry. There was a cold wind but the upper bodies of these men were completely bare. All had a shiny sacred thread around them. Its colour was not as soiled as would be expected of people working in the mud. The thread looked like a recent import which had still not found the time to settle down on its wearer's body. How could so many Brahmins be carrying mud? If that be the case, then their caste was not averse to manual labour. They should rather be celebrated as true labourers of the soil.

A tea shop nearby had just opened up and the shopkeeper had put some water to boil. I went and stood there in order to observe these people better. Their skins were dark and they all looked rather stricken. But they guarded their sacred threads like precious jewels. I realized they were bare-bodied in this cold morning just to flaunt their threads; trying to scream out that they were higher in status than us. I went up to them and struck up a conversation. I learnt that the thread had been a guru's gift to them. One could land their hands on this *brahmashuto*— the god's thread—just by becoming his disciple. I did not know whether to laugh or cry. This was the first time I got to know that a *brahmashuto* meant the sacred thread.

Political parties like the CPM, the Congress, the Trinamool, BJP also had divisions. Some people were even associated with the Bahujan Samaj Party (BSP), a party which did not have a single panchayat seat here. Additionally, there was an anti-Mayawati sect of the BSP who would sing praises of Ambedkar and Kanshi Ram, and express displeasure at the five-crore necklace hanging from Mayawati's neck in order to flatter the Brahmins.

If the Namashudra community could be cleanly divided into two categories, then one would be the Matua sect and the others who were non-Matuas. On further dissecting the Matuas diagonally, one half would be the Thakurnagar group and the others would be its opponents. The former believed that the Thakurs of Thakurnagar were working for their upliftment, while the latter believed that whatever the Thakurs of Thakurnagar had done was for their own benefit.

I was a Namo but not a Matua which meant that I had not been initiated by a guru. With my income, it was difficult to raise my own kids, let alone support a guru, which was an expensive affair, akin to rearing elephants. Money had to be donated for his pilgrimage or for any festivals organized by him. In fact, I would prefer calling myself a human rather than a Namo. It might be better to explain what I mean through a story. Four kids from a school were playing on the field: a Brahmin, a Baidya, a Kayat and a Shudra. They were playing a game of pretend-horses. People were delighted that they had transgressed caste boundaries. However, it was only the Shudra boy who knew otherwise, as for every game he was the one expected to be the horse and carry the other three on his back.

This is how the world generally is. People would go around preaching sermons of equality and protest against the caste system but would never consider the Shudras as their equals. They would mix with them only to turn them into asses or horses. I was one of its biggest examples. This casteist society made me wash utensils, cut vegetables and cook every day, while another Grade IV employee from a higher caste was free to lead a much more comfortable life at the same workplace.

It is for this reason that I would introduce myself as a Namo. I didn't have any hesitation in saying that I hated a group of people from my own caste much more than the Brahmins. My neighbour could cheat me, harm me or be disloyal towards me. But what if the same was done by my brother? In that case, I would rather teach my own brother a lesson before lashing out at my neighbour. He would not be shown any leniency just for being my brother.

Guruchand Thakur had wanted to educate his own people. Ambedkar had wanted the people from the lower castes to be capable enough to get a job for themselves. Both these visionaries had hoped that this newly educated self-reliant group would become a trailblazer for the next generation and change society's dynamics. Unfortunately, many of these people completely forget about their own origins. Following in the footsteps of the Brahmanvads they were now busy chasing wealth and status.

The group which had cared to remember would mention Guruchand Thakur's contribution and celebrate Ambedkar's birth and death anniversary regularly. They would write stories and poems. They would criticize *Manusmriti* and Brahminism in the harshest language at gatherings and seminars. Unfortunately, what they did not do, but which was more essential, was to reach out to their destitute brothers living around them. Nandigram, Netai, Nonadanga ... these came much later. Before everything came Babasaheb's words about paying back to society, which these people had conveniently forgotten.

My fight was for these unfortunate poor Dalits. I was fighting against capitalism and Brahminism, and for equality and respect. After being featured in *Khas Khobor* in 2000, I expected all the doctors, engineers, politicians, businessmen and influential people from our community—there were so many of them who regularly appeared on newspapers and television—to extend their hands in support. I hoped they would pull me up. But nobody came forward. Post *Khas Khobor*, other newspapers and magazines relentlessly published about me. I appeared on television multiple times. Plenty of people from the higher castes came to stand beside me, but none from the Namashudras; at least the other writers from my community could have come forward.

'Nobody will come.' This had been justly prophesied by rickshaw-puller and playwright Raju Das. 'They are afraid of you. Some are teachers, professors, big officers. Nobody published them, but your writings are continuously being published. They are worried. What if you surpass them? The higher castes don't have that fear. They are sitting a hundred steps ahead of you, in any case. They know that try as you might you will never be able to reach where they are in your life. Hence, they are not afraid to pull you through. Even if you move ahead five steps, their position will stay secure. All our intelligentsia on the other hand is still lying at the bottommost step. They do not possess the patience, the dedication and the practice that is required to climb higher. They have their jobs protecting them. They have enough resources to bribe. Gaining literary fame is not quite as easily earned. They do not understand that. If they could, they would question why they cannot write despite having good jobs, living in good houses, eating good food and being educated.

'The Vaishya system is in place right now. If a businessman can make profits by selling alcohol, he will do that. If he can make profits by selling milk, he will take that up instead. Similarly, if you can write in a way that your readers will pay money to read you, you will never be in want of a publisher. Instead of trying that, these people are trembling in fear and insecurity that somebody else will surpass them. The one who has the chance of going ahead will do so in any case, with or without help.'

Twelve years passed in this fashion. I was finally able to hear the kind voice of a dear kinsman after twelve long years. I got a call from the Hariguruchand Ambedkar Chetana Manch in North 24-Paraganas. Calls started coming from Bagula, Birati, Hridaypur and many such places. I was invited to various programmes as a delegate. My hands were filled with garlands, certificates and mementos by my loved ones. All this started only after *Ittibritte Chandal Jivan*'s success. Because of just one book I was able to find a place in the hearts of readers from Bengal and my very own Namashudra community.

The most notable event was the invitation to the Bardhhaman Book Fair. The host announced in a voice choked with emotions, 'It is our fortune that we have the guru and her student together on the same stage.' Mahasweta Devi was the chief guest. She was not aware that I had also been invited as a guest. We were made to sit beside each other. I did have a feeling of unease to be honest; it was as if a termite mound had been placed beside the Himalayas. Nonetheless, it was definitely a memorable day in my life. I had completed another full circle.

At the Bardhhaman Bookfair, 2013, author sharing the dais with his mentor Mahasweta Devi.

A few days after this, I got an invitation from Budge Budge, Majerhat. Amalendu Samaddar invited me over the phone. Nobody had ever invited me with so much affection. Instead, I had always been driven away by people. Hence, I never said no to anybody's invitation. I just rushed over wherever they asked me to. A friend, irritated with my behaviour, had once told me disgustedly, 'They call you and you go. Why? Are you a dog? Only dogs run this way when you call them.' I explained that I was a dog, guarding my poor Dalit destitute labourer brethren. If anybody tried to harm them, I would charge at them, and if necessary not even hesitate to bite their throats.

* * *

One day I received a call from a doctor in Durganagar who said that the MLA from Raipur, 'Mayawati's sister', will be going to Kolkata. I must come and be introduced to her and my books would be sold. The 'sister' would be arriving at the airport and I could be picked up from the airport.

I had to bunk work. Carrying ten to twelve books in my bag, I reached the airport at the stated time, but it was 2 pm when 'Mayawati's sister' arrived. Around twenty people had come on behalf of the organizers. For the return journey there were now only two cars. As soon as 'Mayawati's sister' boarded one car, around eight of the others rushed in with her. The rest of us were left to take the other car. I did not have any place to sit. Nobody was concerned about how I was supposed to travel. The person who had invited me over had been the first person to occupy the seat next to 'Mayawati's sister'. He called from his car and asked somebody to 'pick up the writer.'

Was there any place left in the car for this person to pick me up? This person nonetheless said, 'Come and sit on my lap.' That is what I had to do. It was difficult; my head kept bumping on the roof. I had to twist my body into a half-sleeping position. We reached Birati in this fashion in an hour. The car carrying 'Mayawati's sister' went and stopped in front of a three-storey building. She would eat and rest here. Our car stopped too. I alighted from the car and climbed up to the top floor, the bag full of books on my shoulder. Nobody knew me here; the only other person who knew me was with 'Mayawati's sister'. I had snacked a bit in the morning, but by now my stomach was growling with hunger. There was nobody to offer even a glass of water to me, leave alone food.

'Mayawati's sister' came around four o'clock and immediately launched into a speech. My host got so immersed in the speech that he completely forgot about me. She stopped after almost an hour and a half. The meeting ended. I saw that there was no need to remain any longer so I left. Just because of one call I had lost a day's wage and meal, and I was not even offered a drop of water to drink. It was not easy to believe that these people had entered this field with the aim of bringing about a change in the Dalit society. But because of a few such scoundrels, if I shut down my doors to everybody, how would the good ones enter? So, I was not able to shut the doors to my heart.

* * *

Thus when Amalendu Samaddar's phone came, I was not able to say no. Later I got to know that he was the BDO of Rajarhat. He picked me up in his car from the Bypass to take me to the event. On reaching the destination, I saw that a makeshift stage had been created with jute cloth on the rooftop of a house. The event had been titled as 'Felicitating Litterateur Manoranjan Byapari'. The whole event had the appearance of dullness with no shine or the dazzle of light. There was no microphone or the shutter claps of cameras. Almost half of the fifty seats arranged had been occupied by some young boys and girls with their mothers. The men were around twelve in number, all of them quite aged and retired.

There were two speakers before me. The topic was my life and literature. After the event, Amalendu Babu handed me an envelope and said, 'Our small contribution for your literary pursuits, so that the second part of *Itibritte Chandal Jivan* gets published soon.' Inside was twenty thousand rupees! My eyes were full of tears as soon as I held the envelope. I had never received money for writing, so this was a different kind of experience. It was not merely money but a pressure to produce more quality work. They were my readers who were left unsatisfied after the first part and wanted to know what came next, hence the request for the second part. 'Write, keep on writing. Don't worry about publishing it. That is our responsibility. This is your advance. Tell us when we can get our hands on your new book.' I never knew that so much love could be filled into one tiny envelope.

I was introduced to a kind man named Himanshu Biswas at this event. He was a businessman and quite well-off financially. He gifted me a couple of books out of which one was Taraknath Sarkar's *Hari Lilamrita*. He said, 'The way Harichand Thakur's life has been described here is too idealistic, one that has been adorned with unreal imagination. If you can, write a novel on this, so that people can meet Harichand, the real person, somebody who has worked among the Dalits in order to direct them in the right direction.'

I was also introduced to Suresh Biswas, a well-wisher of the society who had the same wish. Their requests compelled me to write the novel *Matua Ekti Mukti Sena* (The Matuas, a Liberation

Army) which was published from *Haate Bazare Patrika*'s Puja edition, 1420 (2014), and in the book format at the Book Fair of 2018 by Kolkata Prakshan. I firmly believe that I did a fair job with the novel. Some of the readers also called me to share their appreciation. I sincerely hoped to write someday a novel about Harichand's son, Guruchand Thakur.

* * *

The *Samasamayik Patrika* was first published in 2012. Under Sayandeb Bandyopadhyay's editorship, the magazine found a special place almost immediately among its readers for the topics covered and for its unique presentation. This magazine holds a special place in my heart for another reason—for acknowledging that my writing had market value. For a five-page article I was paid a sum of one thousand rupees, where previously I was paid one hundred and fifty rupees by *Pratikkhan* and four hundred and fifty rupees by *Manorama*. My value had definitely increased.

On behalf of the magazine, I was also felicitated with a shawl, a bouquet and a packet of sweetmeats at the 2012 Book Fair. In a way the Kolkata Book Fair and my life as a writer were almost contemporaneous. Apart from the years I was outside Kolkata, I had been to the Book Fair nearly every year. It was mostly to meet my acquaintances and writer friends annually as I did not have the financial capacity to buy anything even if I so desired. However, this time I was finally able to buy some books. I bought the entire set of Mahasweta Devi's writings for six thousand rupees and other books worth two thousand. I felt the adverse effect of such crazy buying on my domestic expenditure at the end of the month as my debt at the grocery shop rose—a hardship I had not anticipated during the time of buying when I was simply floating in the air. It was the first time I had found some literary recognition at the Kolkata Book Fair. It meant something to me as I had often wondered when I would find recognition like everybody else. Even if it weren't that huge, it still meant something and this happened because of *Samasamayik Patrika*.

The number 2013 is considered to be as 'unlucky thirteen', but it brought into my life a lot of luck. Around the middle of the year, the 26 June, turned out to be a golden letter day for me that could be flagged off as a brag-worthy milepost on the road of my life.

* * *

I received a letter from the highest seat of literature and culture in the state, the Paschimbanga Bangla Akademi (West Bengal Bangla Akademi), inviting me to read out from my works at their event. The name of the programme was 'Atma/Akkhyan/Samayer Sandhane' ('The Self/Narrative/In Search of Time'). The event would be attended by the Chairperson Saoli Mitra. Finding a place on this stage meant that I had been acknowledged by the Government of West Bengal, the same government who had been elected by around ninety million people from the state. It might seem like a small step to others, but it opened up a world for me.

On that day I knew that I would be flanked by two award-winning authors on either side: Sunanda Sikdar, who had received the Bankim Purashkar and the Ananda Purashkar for her book *Dayamoyir Katha*, and Sadananda Pal, who had received the Akademi Award for *Ek Matimakha Kumorer Atmakatha*. In comparison to them I was of a much lower status, having won no awards so far. Literary awards too had their own paraphernalia. I had heard that for the Bankim Purashkar, one had to present eleven copies of the book. It was not possible for small publishing houses who printed only three hundred copies of the first edition to do that. Only by trying one's luck at ten different places, could one net a fish. But where would one find the material capacity to send the books to ten houses?

That day I sat down in the corner of the stage with some hesitation. In front of me, the room was filled to the brim. They were, however, all my people, my readers. So, my heart did not flutter even once and my throat did not dry up. There were certainly some unfamiliar faces too, but they were like drops in an ocean. Anantada had once expressed a desire of organizing an event at the

Akademi: Manoranjan Byapari face to face with his readers. It did not materialize because of various reasons but something he said stayed back with me. He had mentioned how the Akademi events did not get much of an audience and about three-fourths of the room usually stayed empty. Upon receiving the invitation, I told him, 'You wanted to organize an event with me at that very space. Why not do it now? The stage will be theirs, but the programme will be yours. The proposal struck a chord in his heart. He started a campaign on Facebook and sent hordes of messages from his cell phone. He also informed all the people he knew from various organizations that 'Our Manoranjan Byapari will be on the Bangla Akademi stage on 26th of June.' The speakers, who were usually invited upon this stage, naturally attracted only the extremely educated group with their scholarly speeches. But this event saw the presence of people from the Nonadanga Basti clad in soiled clothes and rubber slippers, some of whom were rickshaw-pullers, or daily wage workers, or masons. In short, these were people whose life struggles, happiness, tears, love, resistance were the subject of my writing. It seemed as if all of them had stepped out of the pages of my books and reached here.

I usually avoided any close association with intellectuals. I was made aware of my coarseness even more when I was with them. Realizing the limited extent of my knowledge in their company pained me. Initially I used to make occasional trips to the College Street Coffee House. During those visits, I would get hounded by vessels of knowledge from all sides, who would pierce me with a volley of questions, 'Have you read Hobson?' 'Have you heard about Derrida?' 'Do you know of Noam Chomsky?' 'No, you haven't read Foucault?' To hide my own ineptitude, I finally gave up on the black coffee and erudite company at the Coffee House.

My friend Bappa had literally dragged me to the Jadavpur Coffee House one day. *Itibritte Chandal Jivan* had already reached this place before my arrival. As a result, I was received with a warm welcome and by a group of friends. Here I bumped into Gautam Bhadra one day. The moment he realized who I was, he pulled me into a warm hug. There is no need to stress on his tall stature. I was told that his book *Nyara Beltolay Kobar Jay* was priced at eighteen thousand rupees. What exactly was in the book that people paid that much money to read it? Giddy with emotions on meeting him, I said, 'Dada, have you read my book?' His eyes shining with a sparkle that made you like him more, he said, 'I have not. I have memorised it. Four times.'

I also got to know that the scientist Sujay Basu, writers like Sankar Roy and Tapan Bandhyopadhyay were also my readers. In fact, Sankarda and Tapanda had also written critical commentaries on my writing for various English magazines like *Frontier* and others, much before meeting me. That the upper middle-class people, against whom I direct a lot of venom through my writings, would make me one of their own was beyond my imagination. On that day, some of these friends from the Coffee House too had gladly taken up the responsibility of filling up the empty chairs in the Akademi hall.

Word was that a huge rally on behalf of the Namashudra community from the North 24-Parganas was also supposed to attend the event, but at the last moment a train blockade in protest of the Kamduni incident (where a college student had been captured by a gang of six men and gang-raped and murdered) prevented their presence. Through the efforts of Himanshu Biswas, some people from Budge Budge, Majerhat were able to join us. The hall was filled from one end to the other. The Secretary of the Akademi, Sekhar Bandyopadhyay, also attested that such a crowd had never been seen before.

I was the last speaker at the event. Sunanda Sikdar spoke first. She read out from her life story as had been inscribed in *Dayamoyir Katha*. Next spoke Sadananda Pal from his *Mati Makha Kumorer Atmakatha*. My turn came after both of them.

I was on the battlefield now. There was no audience in front of me, but the army of the oppositional faction. The first thumb rule of any battle was to injure the army chief, after which victory was inevitable. What would be the benefit of targeting the soldiers from the lower ranks? So, I directly aimed for the head, who was Saoli Mitra, the then Chairperson of the Bangla Akademi. I chose my words carefully, like choosing the right weapon to strike.

'Many, almost thirty years ago, a rickshaw-puller from Jadavpur with his hard-earned day's income of fifteen rupees bought a ticket at the Akademi stage to watch a play. The name of the play was *Nathbati Anathabot.*'

The words found its mark and hit by the canon ball of my rhetoric Saoli Mitra stirred in her chair. She seemed anxious to know how an ordinary man had been moved by her art. I continued, 'For an hour and a half, I was unable to move from my chair. The person who had tied me up to my chair, that very respected Saoli Mitra, is present here. I have nothing to give her apart from my utmost respect.'

The auditorium filled up with the sound of deafening applause. Everybody had welcomed me with their applause when I had first taken to the stage. Now they clapped again, doubly louder than the first time. Saoli Mitra also joined in. I said, 'I will take my revenge today. She had tied me up for one and half hours that day, I will return the favour today.'

The sound of applause was heard again. My friends, my readers, people from the same caste and class, were all boiling with excitement. The room which had been so dull till some time ago seemed to have woken up. I had already hypnotised everybody in the audience by then. Now their only job was to occasionally clap and keep up the tenor. It felt like I was joined on the stage by the poor eternally deprived Dalits who were denied all respect. In the way that each kick by the king of football Pele and each punch by Mohammad Ali meted out the anger and hatred of black people all over the world, my presence on this stage was a symbol of the victory of the labouring classes.

I finally drew out the final arrow from my quiver. 'Friends, you all live in good houses, wear good clothes, eat well, and have been to good schools. It is evident that you will write well, or else all your privileges would have been in vain. How could I write like you? The age at which you went to school, I was grazing cattle. When you went to college, I learnt the alphabet by drawing lines on the floor of the jail. You are ahead of me by one thousand miles and one thousand books. Despite that if the wheel of my literary chariot has moved ahead even by a step, don't I deserve a clap for that? For me it is akin to Sri Krishna's applause; the biggest reward of them all.'

The applause had been irrepressible that day. The small hall had been warmed up with emotions and heartfelt wishes. I had not been able to observe them individually, except for one person who was Saoli Mitra from whom affection seemed to be oozing out for me. I did it! I was able to earn the blessings of the great actress at the very seat of literature and culture. My victory was complete. The battle which I had initiated armed with my pen had proven to be a success. After alighting from the stage, the wishes from various known and unknown people filled up my life's empty sack. The burden of my humiliating life that I had been carrying on for so long was washed away in a wave of human outburst.

* * *

A young boy named Rajdeep came to me with the request, 'Dada, we have called for a gathering to protest against the state sanctioned violence on the people from the literary world. We want you the join us as a speaker.' The longing on his face did not allow me to refuse his request outright, but I said I would not be a speaker. On the specific day I sat down on a chair in a corner in the back. Right at the end my name was announced, 'Dalit writer Manoranjan Byapari is amidst us. We are inviting him to please come up on stage and say a few words.' Rajdeep had not kept his promise. Finding no other option, I walked up to the microphone on the stage and said, 'It would have been better had I not been called here. What do I say? I am not that educated. I only have my life. Let me share some learning from my own life.'

'Once Safdar Hashmi had gone to meet Shankar Guha Neogi. He asked him, 'What is the matter Neogiji? Whenever you gather for some rally or a meeting, the police come charging at you with rods and bullets. We tour the entire country staging plays that raise voice against injustice, but the government never behaves the same way with us.'

Neogiji replied, 'The day your voice will be able to scratch the surface of this oppressive regime, the government will not let you go. Till then you are safe.'
You all know who killed Safdar Hashmi and why. You also know the reason why Neogiji was shot to death.
I had once gone to Maharashtra for a conference. Binayak Sen's wife, Ilina Sen, was also present there. At that time Binayak Sen was in jail and I distinctly remember seeing a poster on the wall which said 'One has to face the danger of expressing oneself.' I feel that if you write something that does make a dent on the surface of this repressive regime, you will be compelled to bear the price of expressing yourself. You will have to go to jail; you will have to brave a bullet. If you are able to risk this then keep on writing. If not, don't. Namaskar.'
I was introduced to poet Sabyasachi Deb at the event. He said, 'Poet Sankha Ghosh is your reader.'
This was a statement that would obviously sound outrageous. Shocked out of my wits, I said, 'Which work of mine has he read? *Itibritte Chandal Jivan?*'
'Yes. That's how he recommended the book to me.'
I procured Sankha Ghosh's number from him and called him the very next day. One of my short story collections was about to be published in a few days and I was looking for somebody to release the book. Now my hopes touched the sky. What if Sankha Ghosh does it? There would be nothing better than that.
I had hesitantly called the poet on his landline number. Never did I imagine in my wildest dreams that the poet would receive the call himself! Naturally, I was totally flummoxed when I asked to speak with poet Sankha Ghosh and the voice on the other side said, 'Speaking.'
I spewed out everything in one breath, 'I got your number from the poet Sabyasachi Deb. My name is Manoranjan Byapari. The reason for calling you is that my anthology of stories is about to be released and if you would do me the honour of launching the book, I will be greatly indebted.'

I explained the launch would be at the Paschimbanga Bangla Akademi at a time that would suit him. My voice was shaking. The most prestigious poet of our times had agreed to launch my book! I agreed to wait till he was available. He asked, 'You will delay it for so long? Won't the book sell otherwise?'

I replied, 'If my book is honoured by your touch, my life will be worthwhile. I cannot let go of that opportunity. An entire lifetime is left for the book to be sold.'

Sankha Ghosh—the poet venerated by every other poet—spoke haltingly, 'I must tell you that I am one of your readers.'

What melody to the ears! What gratification! It felt like somebody had just now announced on the telephone that 'Manoranjan, you have won the best award for literature. The poet Sankha Ghosh is one of your readers. Did you ever think that you would have achieved such a huge honour in life some day?'

No, never. I did not have the audacity to dream of such a dream. I did not want anything else. What more could anybody give me? The poet Sankha Ghosh had touched my art, immortalizing it, and along with it my life.

* * *

The dream came true on 27 August, 2013—a never-happened-before kind of a day in my life. It was such a sublime day that would remain stamped forever in the deepest corners of the heart. An event was organized at the Jibanananda Sabhaghar in my honour. Adorning the Chairman's place at this event was the senior-most and most respected poet of our age, Sankha Ghosh. There were performances by Pratul Mukhopadhyay, the singer, who had bewitched people with his singing in the seventies. Rupashree Kahali read from my works and the entire event was hosted by Mihir Chakraborty. The event was being organized by two of my publishers, Boiwala and Kolkata Prakashan. The former had put together a collection of my short stories entitled *Manoranjan Byapari-r Golpo Somogro 1* (Manoranjan Byapari's Short Story

Collection 1) and the latter my novel *Amanushik* (Inhumane), both of which would be launched on the same day.

The Jibanananda Sabhaghar was quite small, because of which all the guests did not find a place to sit. The number of people standing was much more than those sitting. All were all my readers, my well-wishers. It was overwhelming for me to realize that they had come for me. Leaving all their work behind, spending money from their own pockets and being crushed in buses and trains, people had come from Bongaon, Barasat, Budge Budge, Jadavpur, Nonadanga and various other such places just because of their love for me. Professor Jaydeep Sarangi, reporter Chandrasekhar Bhattacharya, theatre artist Tirthankar Chanda, all these people had also come to talk about my life and writing. All had gathered in honour of a person like me, about whom Time did not care much.

Time! Time controlled everything of value. At times it would deem somebody to be worthy enough and dance with him on its shoulders. At other times it would slam a person down on the ground. There was nothing as powerful as time in the world.

* * *

The event started sharp at six-thirty. The Chairperson was welcomed, the book was launched, the songs were sung and selections from my works were read. Something happened, which was not only surprising for me but also for the audience. Nowadays, Sankha Ghosh did not deliver speeches at gatherings or conferences. He did not even get up on the stage at many events, but remained seated in the auditorium. Before accepting my invite today, he had put forth the same condition that he would not be asked to say anything. I had agreed, saying 'Your presence is all that matters.' The host for the evening Mihir Chakraborty was not aware of this condition and hence ended up requesting him to say a few words. To everyone's surprise, the great poet stood up with the microphone. After a long period of silence, he broke his fast with just two words at my event—but worth more than two crores, at least for me. Looking at the audience he said in his calm voice, 'Is there anybody among you who has not read *Itibritte Chandal Jivan*? To them, I have just one thing to say, every Bengali should read this book.' For a writer like me, it was the highest form of acknowledgement.

At the launch of his books, Sankha Ghosh and author and members of the panel.

Later, theatre artist Tirthankar Chanda added to the honours, saying, 'Manoranjan Byapari has surprised us by producing work that is at the same level as that of Gorki and Jack London.' Jaydeep Sarangi pointed out that I continue to work for fourteen hours in front of a sweltering fire. The government should prescribe my books in schools and colleges. Finally, reporter Chandrasekhar Bhattacharya did something that takes us to the *Mahabharata* when Yudhisthira was performing the Rajasuya Yagna. Though the eldest and the most famous members of the Kuru clan had been invited, Yudhisthira chose to touch the feet of Sri Krishna. Similarly, Chandrasekhar said, 'I, from a Brahmin family, would like to touch the feet of a Chandal. Just like Yudhisthira had considered Sri Krishna to be the most deserving of his respects, for me it is Manoranjan Byapari— my Manoranjanda.' Saying this, he really bent down to touch my feet.

Strangely, nobody said much about the two books which were launched at the event. People mostly spoke about *Itibritte Chandal Jivan* and its writer. Experiencing this made me feel that I had somewhat been able to touch the mark that I had aimed for.

* * *

Another memorable day in my life was 20 July 2013. On this day I met the internationally acclaimed doctor Binayak Sen at the Bharat Sabha Hall. In tandem with Shankar Guha Neogi he helped to build a modern health care facility—now known as the Shaheed Hospital—with the help of the workers in Dalli-Rajhara. This hospital eventually became the biggest strength for the poor Dalit and Adivasi population in the Durg and Bastar districts.

Binayak Sen had been jailed by the BJP government on sedition charges for the crime of helping the poor Dalits and Adivasis of Chhattisgarh. They would have wanted to keep him behind bars for life. Unfortunately, the power of public opinion defeated them. Ordinary people and twenty-two Nobel prize winners demanded his release. Senior barrister Ram Jethmalani rushed to the Supreme Court to get Binayak Sen released. By citing the reason that one could not be jailed for merely being associated with some Maoist leaders, the judge ruled against his imprisonment, thereby overpowering the vengeful state mentality.

I had met him only once in Dalli, seven days after Neogiji's death. I had perhaps spoken to him for not more than ten minutes. I don't even remember what I had said. But the memory of the brief meeting never dimmed in my memories. Sixteen years passed in the blink of an eye and we lost contact. I was able to recreate the memory once again, by finding the legendary figure in front of me after so many years. He had arrived from Mumbai and assumed a place within the audience.

It was five or seven years since I had last met Ilina Sen. I went up to Binayak Sen and said, 'I had met you in Dalli sixteen years before, a few days after Neogiji's death. I used in to live in Chhattisgarh then and was a member of the Chhattisgarh Mukti

Morcha.' He asked me my name and came outside with me and said, 'I have written about you, in fact, both Ilina and I have.' This was in *The Week* magazine, published five days ago on July 15, 2013. It seemed unbelievable and miraculous to me. All these events in one life, was it possible for real?

Dr Binayak Sen, poet Sankha Ghosh, Naxal leader Khokon Majumdar, Gautam Bhadra, poet Joy Goswami, theatre artist Saoli Mitra and the unrivalled writer Mahasweta Devi, all of them were my readers. Was it really possible? If that be the case, life I forgive thee. I will not have any more grievances against you; neither will I have any anger or wrath. I certify that you have passed this test and emerged successful.

CHAPTER 29

In Pursuit of *Parivartan*

J thought, or rather hoped that the new government which replaced the older one with the promise of bringing parivartan, change, would not be as heartless and inhuman as their predecessors. I am from the labouring class. I also write. I hoped that they would create a better system for me, so that I would have two square meals a day and enough time to write. This present government of ma, mati, manush, at whose helm was the honourable Mamata Banerjee, had taken a lot of initiatives to build up committees to create a space for innumerable artists, writers and intellectuals. They were all now recipients of allowances and opportunities, although they would have functioned equally well even without them. If she could sprinkle oil on already oiled heads, perhaps she would do the same for people who were bald, as that would be much more helpful.

She, herself, hailed from a very ordinary family. She had reached her present position after years of struggle. In my heart, I hoped that she would definitely turn her benevolent eyes towards a fellow fighter like me and extend a helping hand. If she did that, my struggles would become easier to deal with. Then, I would be able to write my last work, for which I had been born, for which I had become an author, for which I had survived so many storms. But who would deliver my word to Mamata Banerjee? There was nobody appropriate to be found. So, I decided to take matters in my own hand and reached Harish Mukherjee Road one day with my heart full of hope. It was Mamata Didi's humble abode. I felt like I had accomplished an arduous journey and reached the temple where the goddess resided. It was believed that just by reaching this place, one's life found fruition, their half-filled jars were filled up again and fortune came knocking at their doors.

Armed police forces were stationed right at the Kalighat Bridge. They stopped me to enquire, 'Where do you want to go?'

'To meet the Chief Minister.' It was 7 am, too early in the day. They said, 'Wait here. You can only go at 9 am. People are not allowed before that.'

I saw many people waiting and took my place with them in a corner. Right at 9 am we were allowed to go up to her gate. There was a seating room, filled with chairs. Almost a hundred people had come before me and were already queued up. I took my place behind them.

My turn came after an hour or two. I met a gentleman in the opposite room. He had a pleasant appearance and was bald in the head. I found out that he was the Chief Minister's secretary. He said, 'You will not be able to meet the Chief Minister today. You can tell me whatever you need to say.'

I told him whatever I had to say. I showed him whatever I had to show. I had carried along with me the newspaper cuttings from *Anandabazar Patrika, Times of India, Statesman, Prabhat Khobor,* and some books. I had also with me a copy of *Itibritte Chandal Jivan.* He saw everything. The shock was apparent. 'You are a writer? You don't look like one.'

I told him, 'I work as a cook. My whole day goes there. I don't get enough time to write. If she can give me a chance, I will be eternally grateful.'

He gave me a paper and a pen and said, 'Write these things and, along with it, your address, phone number and the name of the school where you work.' I did as instructed. He took it with a lot of warmth. I was also offered a cup of tea. Whether he delivered the papers to the Chief Minister's desk later or not, I am not sure. Many years have since passed; there has still been no parivartan in my life.

I made similar visits to the area's MLA and Minister of Power Manish Gupta, theatre personality Arpita Ghosh and the Chairman of the Borough Committee Tarakeshwar Chakraborty. I gave them my books and papers. Again, nothing worked. Instead, a large number of copies of *Itibritte Chandal Jivan*, which I had published with my hard-earned money, went to waste. I went ahead and contributed two articles for the *Angikar* magazine, which belonged to the MLA Sovandev Chattopadhyay. I also sent him the *Anadabazar Patrika* paper cuttings. Nothing again.

I was also quite well acquainted with the Labour Minister, Purnendu Bose. We had both fallen prey to a bad case of food poisoning near a river in village number 56 of Paralkot in the Bastar district of Chhattisgarh. I met him many years later in the Book Fair of 2011 and took the opportunity to gift him my books. He introduced me to Dola Sen and the student leader Sankudeb Panda with the remark, 'Having come from the faraway Dandakaranya, a place where people have not even heard of Rabindranath Tagore, this man has won over Bengal today. Meet writer Manoranjan Byapari.'

I also gifted my books to Joy Goswami, Kabir Suman and Bratya Basu. Bratya Basu was known to me from much before he became a minister. He was aware that I was a rickshaw-puller who had turned into a writer. He had even shot a programme with me for Kolkata TV along with Tathagata Dutta. My hope was that one of them would do something for me after reading the book. I did not expect much, perhaps just a small call to the Chief Minister. I don't know what happened to the books. As for my life, it remained unchanged.

The powerful never wanted a person from the lower castes to be able to uplift their status. Their hearts never acceded to doing something that would emerge as a competition to their high status. Not that they always did this consciously, their subconscious made them mechanically do many such things which they were not even aware of. Let's say that ten lesser-known authors have sent their stories to a major magazine in Kolkata. For obvious reasons, nine out of these ten people would have surnames like Chatterjee, Mukherjee, Banerjee, Chakraborty, Sengupta, Dasgupta, Ghosh,

Bose or Mitra. Only one of them would be a Byapari or a Bag or a Sardar. While selecting a story for a book reading, the editor would select two or three from the majority group. He would not even think of touching the writing by the Byapari, the Bag or the Sardar. Leave alone publishing, they would not even read it. The same rule applied while handing out jobs or opportunities. I had been at the receiving end because of this rule. Had I not been born into a Dalit family and had my surname been Banerjee instead of Byapari, I would have easily found people to back me, because without them in this country I was just a criminal by birth.

When the same me shows the audacity to compete against the Banerjees, the latter are obviously enraged. The story of the lower-caste boy, Budhiya, might be relevant here. This twelve-year-old boy ran the biggest marathon of this world—one which could leave even the strongest of the athletes breathless. Budhiya won the race, crushing casteism under his feet. A lot of people and organizations came forward in protest, conveniently hidden behind the mask of human compassion. They let out a howl in unison, 'This is unfair. This is anti-social. It is incorrect to make such a young boy run such a long race.'

Budhiya's mother did not have the capacity to feed her son twice a day. Budhiya would have died of starvation had not his mother sold him off to Birinchi Das for a measly sum. Where nobody else came forward with even a handful of rice, Birinchi Das slowly nurtured Budhiya's two feet to land a tight slap on the face of the casteist overlords. For this crime, Birinchi Das was shot to death and Budhiya's legs were rendered immobile by chaining them with countless legal sentences. He was no longer allowed to run, until he reached the age of eighteen. When left for so long, even iron caught rust. Who would have kept Budhiya groomed and fit in the absence of Birinchi Das? The wonder kid was lost to oblivion. The casteist overlords sighed in relief to see their status restored.

Not every higher caste person is so violent and crude, just like all poison is not fatal and every shit not as smelly. There are also those who would slam the caste system without budging an inch from their high positions. Their sacred threads remain intact, their surnames unchanged, yet in their defence, they mix with everybody and do not say no to food offered by anybody. These relatively soft-hearted people are not even aware which of their words or actions could prove humiliating for the lower-caste people. The Leftists have always been right at the top in denying caste. I was also respectful towards the Leftist ideology once, as I remain today. But after what I witnessed about the Leftists in Bengal, I would rather be an extreme reactionary than a Leftist. Let this Leftism be smashed.

CHAPTER 30

Boro Sahib's Desire to Felicitate Me

On 19 November 2011, a feature by Kaushik Sarkar entitled 'Having Painted His Life with His Pen, Manoranjan Byapari on the World Stage' was published on the fifth page of *Ei Samay Patrika*. Within two days, I received a call from Boro Sahib with whom I had last spoken during the Riju Bose fiasco over not mentioning Boro Sahib in the *Anandabazar Patrika* article, almost six years back. Ever since that, a long silence had crept in between us. Naturally enough, I was a bit astonished to hear from him after so long.

Nowadays Boro Sahib often came to the school. Previously, with his ministerial post, he never used to get much time. Since he lost his post, he had no other way to kill time. He came here to walk a bit, sit for a bit, or to play cards. This was how he spent time which seemed too heavy on him these days. The rest was spent recollecting the beautiful past. How wonderful the past three decades had been! During that time, he would be surrounded by sycophants all around. These would include promoters, contractors, adulators, bureaucrats and officers currying favours. Those days were long gone. Now he was all alone. When I reached his room in response to his call, I was immediately greeted with a gentle smile. My heart started trembling in dread. This was not an ordinary smile. It had the arrows of diplomacy hidden behind its veneer. The smile was not a stranger to me.

He said, 'I have read about you in the papers.'

What was new about this! Lakhs of people had read it. It was his next sentence that left me surprised. 'We will felicitate you this time,' he said.

I wasn't able to control myself. Without thinking about the consequences, I said, 'I do not want your felicitation.' My 'no' hit his senses like a bolt of lightning and his eyes flamed up in rage. Instead of grovelling at his feet in gratefulness for his noble intentions, this man who should have forever remained crushed under the feet like grass had declared an insignificant jihad—'I do not want!'

Controlling myself and carefully choosing my words, I launched a 'human' bomb on him, 'If you can, reduce the daily insult and torture I have been living with to bearable proportions and lessen my workload.' I did not wait to hear his response but pushed the door and came outside as soon as I had said what I wanted to. My heart felt as if it had been released off a huge load. There was a certain happiness in complying without any questions, but this was the first time I realized that the same was true for giving up. Rabindranath Tagore had renounced his knighthood. Just a few days back a bunch of intellectuals had renounced a lot of their medals, positions, awards and honours. Today, I realized the joy in that action. I felt like Alexander returning the kingdom to the defeated party with the nonchalant disclaimer, 'I have many, I don't need yours.'

Boro Sahib's 'Right Hand', the notorious colleague of mine, came to me and said, 'You did not do the right thing.'

'What thing?'

'Saying no to Boro Sahib's face. He felt utterly insulted.'

'Did he say so?'

'Does anybody need to say so? Didn't you see his face?'

'My sense of understanding has shrivelled and dried up after having to spend hours in front of burning stoves twice a day for almost fifteen years.'

I could fathom that even the Right Hand was feeling extremely humiliated. It was 8.30 pm and I had to serve food to the kids. My assistant who had been unwell for three to four months wouldn't be coming back. Apparently, she had been afflicted with leprosy, for which there was a provision for taking leave on full salary. It was now my sole responsibility to feed around one hundred and fifty mouths. If they did not get food on time or if I made even a tiny mistake, they would not spare me. I did not have the time to think whether the other person was feeling insulted or not.

The next day, just as I returned home after my afternoon shift, a call came on my mobile. An educated voice from the other end said, 'Can I speak with Manoranjan Byapari? Do you know me? I am Sailenda, Sailen Choudhury. I am sitting at your school. Can you come over to the school once? I had something to tell you. Will you please come, bhai?'

I knew Choudhury babu, though I had never spoken with him as there had been no need for that before. He was a senior leader of the organization for disabled people. This visually impaired person, holding a high post, would travel in a milky white car and be accompanied by two helpers at all time. Whenever he came, he would sit in Boro Sahib's room and meet the bigwigs for important discussions. Insignificant people like us belonging to the lower ranks did not dare have much opinion about him. I had therefore always tried to maintain my distance. Now that he was inviting me to bridge that gap, what was I to do?

I said, 'But I have to go somewhere else this instant.'

In an imploring tone he said, 'I will not take much of your time, give me just five minutes. Just meet me and leave.'

I was left with no other choice. He was seated in Boro Sahib's office as usual. Boro Sahib himself had been there till a minute back, but had left after their meeting. He said, 'I heard you are a cook at the school and you also write. We want to felicitate you.'

I said, 'I don't want any of those. If you can, reduce my workload, so that I get enough time for my writing. I will be highly grateful.'

He said, 'It is the World Disability Day on 3rd December. Let the event pass and then we will see what we can do for you. Even Boro Sahib has agreed to personally ensure that you get more time.'

I said, 'He said the same thing six years back in a programme called 'Tara-r Nojore' aired by Tara Channel. Six years have passed, he still hasn't done anything. He was a minister then and could have done a lot of things had he wanted. Since nothing happened then, how can I expect anything to happen now? I cannot believe his words anymore. If he really wants to do something, there are ten days left, ask him to do something now. Otherwise, I will not accept any honours from you all.'

Boro Sahib had given him the responsibility to get me on board. His reasons were quite clear. He wanted to sit on the stage with me beside him and give a byte to all the newspaper reporters and television cameras in a compassion-filled voice that: 'This boy came to me and told me that he writes. I could see he had a good hand for writing. Being from a poor family myself, I have a soft corner for these things in any case. So, I went out of my way to help him. I told him that he did not need to do anything but just keep up the writing and that I would make the necessary arrangements. I gave him the assurance that he could approach me with whatever need he has. Today he has reached a high place; his fame has spread all over the country. I am happy for him.' He had said something similar six years back in front of a TV camera. Human memory was quite weak, so he needed to remind people how he had helped turn a street person into a writer.

Sailen Babu left, greatly upset at my words. There was a time, when not just me but even the bravest of the brave would not find the courage to annoy a person like him. But now I had reached an extreme point of desperation and was eager to see how low they could stoop. These people would constantly look for some gaping holes in my schedule and thrust in some more extra work just like one would shake the tin of fritters to fit in more. At the present moment, there was no scope to increase my workload any further. The only thing they could do was terminate my job under some excuse. In any case I was slowly losing my capacity to keep up with the work. Even if they didn't suspend me, I was considering doing it myself. When Pintu Sen beat me up at a very young age, I had not realized the extent of the damage. Now that I was much older, it had returned back as a nagging knee joint pain, which was snowballing to unbearable proportions by the day. It was becoming more and more difficult to stand on these legs every day for eight to ten hours of work. If I really had to go, what was the point in keeping the babus satisfied?

Dr Prasenjit Baral from Apollo Clinic had tested my knee, prescribed medicines and injections, and warned me to not stand for more than twenty minutes or to ride the cycle. If I did not do as I was told, despite medicines and injections my knee would not heal. Hence my knee pain was not getting cured. How was it possible to travel the distance of twelve miles—three miles up and three miles down four times a day—from my home to the workplace without walking or cycling? There was no other transport available on that road. Also, how was I supposed to cook without standing? It was not possible to sit and cook in a kadhai where twenty kilos of rice was put to boil at once, with vegetables cooking on another utensil. This would then be followed by having to carry the heavy utensils from the kitchen to the dining space. Serving was also not possible while sitting. All things put together, there was no relief from standing eight to ten hours at a stretch. As a result, there was also no relief for my legs, making them weaker. I could at most stretch this for six more months with painkillers, or maybe a year. After that there would be no other option but to quit. I would have to say goodbye to my workplace, fulfilling the wishes of ill-wishers on all sides.

After Sailen Babu's departure, a lot of other people from his organization tried reasoning with me for days. But for me, it had taken almost three decades of immense patience and self-control to reach where I am today after striding through muck—a place I held with a lot of love and pride. I was not ready to give it up this easily. This was also because this place of pride was not mine alone. It belonged to the entire Namashudra community. Today, I was the jewel of my community and the recipient of their heartfelt love. Bengali Dalit society had understood that while Maharashtra had Ambedkar and Uttar Pradesh had Kashiram and Mayawati, Bengal did not specifically have anybody. The realization that the Bengali Dalit community was slightly behind the others in the Indian context had generated a sense of inferiority complex within the group. Leaving aside politics, even in the matter of Dalit literary output, languages like Marathi, Gujarati, Kannada, Hindi, Tamil or Telugu were far more advanced than Bangla. That there was something called Dalit Literature in Bengal was unknown to even the Bengali intellectuals, let alone people from other states. Traces of this concern could be found in the writings of many writers and intellectuals.

The fact that Bengali Dalit Literature indeed exists was established with proof by an *EPW* article not just in India but also the world over, under the penmanship of none other than Manoranjan Byapari. This was a truth nobody could deny today. One had to acknowledge this claim by gulping down the embarrassment that it was there all along, just that nobody had any knowledge about it. Although this was the larger truth, a smaller conflict had sparked off between Bengal and Maharashtra over the question of supremacy. The Bengali Dalit community was of the opinion, 'We agree that you are far more advanced in this area, but our Manoranjan Byapari's writing has been published with *EPW*. Have you been able to get your work published by such a prestigious publication like us?'

In reply, they had said, 'What about the Tamil writer Bama? She was published with *EPW* much before you people.'

Bengal's retort was, 'Bama might be a Dalit by birth, but not at all by her financial status. Our Manoranjan Byapari is a Dalit in all regards. He has never been to a school, he has driven a rickshaw, yet his writings have been published by reputed publishers.'

This debate had been doing rounds in the Dalit intellectual community all over India. A question had been floating underneath its surface about who would take up the leadership role of the Dalit community? Each community was eager to establish their supremacy, disregarding the others' position. The reason why the Namashudra community considered themselves to be superior was because compared to the other Dalit groups they had more people who were educated, affluent and with government jobs. Their people had once shaken the foundation of the British rule with their engagement in the Indigo Revolt. The first person to have measured the height of the Himalayas was a Dalit. The community had religious teachers and social reformers like Harichand and Guruchand Thakur. They had mass leaders like Jogendranath Mandal, barristers like Kumud Mallick, CBI officers like Upen Biswas, professors like Achintya Biswas, poets like Anil Sarkar, visionaries like Anil Ranjan Biswas and actors like Goutam Haldar. In short, out of all the coveted positions in society, one or the other seat was gloriously occupied by a Namashudra. The poet Binay Majumdar, the poet singer Bijoy Sarkar, the revolutionary Hemanta Byapari, doctors like Hrishikesh Majumdar and Sunil Thakur were all gems of the Namashudra community.

They were lagging behind all these years because of one reason, for having no writer who could contend with the higher castes at the same level. The few that were already present had not achieved much success, being reduced to the pages of one or two Dalit magazines like patients suffering from rickets. Pressed by the need, the Dalit community had so far managed with Adwaita Mallabarman, a member of the Malo community. That gap had finally been filled by Manoranjan Byapari, even if by a fraction. His writings, about the life of the lower castes, were now published in newspapers dominated by the higher castes even though he was a Namashudra himself.

A leader from the Dalit community, Sukriti Ranjan Biswas, had advised a hall full of people at an event at the Moulali Yuvak Kendra to read *Itibritte Chandal Jivan* even before Rabindranath Tagore. The film director from Jamshedpur Bidyarthi Chatterjee had said at a programme that to experience Dalit life thoroughly and know about the struggles one should watch the movie Joy Bhim Comrade and read *Itibritte Chandal Jivan*. Similarly, Dalit sympathizer Ananta Acharya had been carrying the book to various meetings as Dalim Maulvi had carried the Quran.

These days the CPM had become more proactive in bringing back the Dalits, Namashudras and the Matuas from the Trinamool camp to theirs. These communities had been allies of the CPM all these years despite the oppression, but had turned their backs on them in 2011. It was no longer unknown to the CPM comrades how much these communities adored Manoranjan Byapari. If he were brought back under their shelter, some amount of the damage could perhaps be controlled. This felicitation event was a part of that trickery. If I could be passed off as 'their' people on the stage, a lot of the work would be done. Even if nothing happened, the opportunity could be used to isolate me from the rest of the community.

Under such circumstances, as I lay in wait having taken the vow of not sacrificing my head on their altar, a letter arrived on my name. It was from the Rajya Pratibandhi Sammelani adorned with Boro Sahib's signature. Among many other things was mentioned, 'On 3 December 2012, as part of the World Disability Day, we want to honour you for your work in literature. The event will be attended by the former speaker of the Lok Sabha, honourable Somnath Chatterjee. We will be highly honoured if you accept our invitation.'

I was in a fix. Even a request by a king turned into an order and everybody knew the repercussions of rejecting the king's orders. If the matter could have been handled verbally, it would not have been a problem. But now a letter had been sent and as a result, my decision along with the reasons had to be informed in writing. Here I was thinking that I would last it out for six months or a year, it seemed like they wouldn't even let me last for a month or six weeks. Their strength was in numbers; I was alone. Was there any effective solution?

Finally, I told Boro Sahib's Right Hand, 'All right, I will go. But if I see that lies are being spewed about me with me seated on the stage, I will immediately stand up and protest. I will disclose all the truth. Then, we will see.'

He said, 'I hope we can at least mention that you are a cook at this school?'

'Yes. But not that I have become a writer while working as a cook. Or that I have had any assistance from all of you. If that is said, I will protest. I have been writing since 1981. On 20 November 1981, *Jugantar Patrika* gave me the recognition as an author. I joined the school only in 1997. Before that, one of my writings was published in *Pratikkhan* which was later translated into English for *Frontier* and in Hindi for the book *Sangharsh aur Nirman* published by Rajkamal Parakashan. So, to say that I have become a writer while cooking is an utter lie, one that is spread by everybody here. The actual truth is that this school is making a writer wash utensils and cook.'

All the poison that I had kept suppressed in my heart for so long at last found its outlet, turning the Right Hand's face like a sky overcast with dark clouds. I finally felt quite fearless. I did not submit anything in writing but verbally confirmed that I would be there. Consequently, I landed up at Rani Rashmoni Road—a road named after the illustrious woman who was born into a fisherman's family—where the event was being organized. I was hoping against all odds that they would not ask me to come up on the stage. I reached behind the stage and sat down without drawing too much attention to myself. My ears remained glued to the sound of the microphone. The programme was being hosted by the person who had migrated from Bangladesh in 1972 and was now an important leader here. Somnath Chaterjee was seated on the stage with many others, which included Boro Sahib.

After a long time, I was summoned. As soon as I got up on the stage, I was given a bouquet of flowers, an address of honour and an envelope which had a cheque. It was announced, 'ManoranjanByapari is a Dalit writer who assisted in the food department at the school.' I stood there as long as the address of honour was read. I dismounted as soon as they showed me the way out. They did not give me a chance to speak, not that there was anybody who would listen to me. But I did take advantage of the opportunity and handed out five newspaper cuttings to Somnath Chatterjee, although even that did not lead to anything.

At this point, it is highly tempting to share what was written on the address of honour, so here it is:

'To the distinguished member of the Dalit Literary community, Manoranjan Byapari

Sir,

In this shining fanciful world of glamorous globalisation, your life has been constantly flowing with a rich bunch of rare narratives. Your relationship with institutional education is that of an adversary. Despite that your knowledge on various subjects, right from nature to people, bears testimony to your creative impulses. In the true sense of the term, you possess a strong personality of intellectual beauty, in whose lap resides the heartfelt experiences of the indefatigable spirit of human strength.

Despite being constantly hammered by an overtly superstitious and rigid society which has grown up on the establishment of bitter transactions of class and caste oppression, you kept your pen immersed in creativity.

.... Professionally your identity remains as a hostel employee at this school set up by the present state government under our organisation's initiative; and in the field of literature, as our teacher.

... Please accept our honours and continue advancing in the path of wonderful creations with a healthy and long life, we present you with unadulterated love and respect from the bottom of our hearts.'

As the programme ended, life returned back to the way it was. I continued being extorted twice every day for two handfuls of rice. In the blazing heat of the summers, fire hurricanes still raged around me. I had to cook two meals every day for anywhere between two hundred and fifty to three hundred people. My work continued taking away almost ten to twelve hours of my day. This country, these times and this society kept denying me the minimum opportunity for food and education. My crime was that I was a Dalit of the clan of Shambuk and Eklavya. Within the casteist system, this was an unpardonable offence. But if they refused to change themselves, my pen would also keep firing cannonballs like before. This war would not end.

CHAPTER 31

The Bangla Akademi Award and Other Honours

*M*y life finally completed a full circle. Yes, it took a bit more time than expected, but it happened. Otherwise, people would have stopped having faith in the belief that perseverance leads to success eventually. Everybody would have pointed their fingers at me and justly noted, 'What about that man who toiled relentlessly but eventually found nothing!'

As a person I was still the same, but in terms of my societal presence my life was no longer one of insignificance. It had instead become like a proud adornment. It had provided many people with the strength to puff up their chests with confidence and hold up their heads high. I was in Meerut, at the residence of a local doctor who was also a friend. This friend, Goutam Biswas, was a Chandsi doctor. It is important to mention that the Chandsi treatment for piles, fistula or fissure was discovered by an individual from the Namashudra community. Goutam Biswas's guarantee to patients who had failed everywhere else was that he would heal them within a stipulated time. It is at his place, I got a call from Sekhar Bandyopadhyay, the secretary of the Bangla Akademi, 'You have been selected for this year's Bangla Akademi Suprabha Majumdar Memorial Award.'

Neil Armstrong had said about his journey to the moon, 'It was a small step for man but a giant leap for mankind.' While receiving the award at the Bangla Akademi stage on the evening of 11 January 2014, I felt the same way. The prize money was only twenty-five thousand, barely anything after thirty-four years of tireless penmanship. But in terms of societal prestige, the award was priceless. It was a huge honour for a person who had never once set a foot inside a school. The prize trophy was handed over to me by Bratya Basu, the Education Minister, and Saoli Mitra, the Chairperson of the Bangla Akademi. Among the six million Namashudras of Bengal, I was the first one to get this award for Bangla Literature. This was a huge win for the entire Namashudra community, after facing years of neglect and subjugation.

Receiving the Suprabha Majumdar Award 2014 from Saoli Mitra in the presence of Bratya Basu, education minister, poet Joy Goswami and writer Nabaneeta Dev Sen.

A community, whose entire population was around 30 million including both sides of Bengal, had not left much mark in the domain of literature, despite having contributed to various other areas of society. One reason could be the financial constraints because of which the educated Namos never found much interest in it. After having struggled so hard to gain an education, it must have made more sense for them to invest it on something that would pay back. However, this was also true, that a stirring had been generated within the deepest sections of the society to fill up the gap. The gap was emerging to be a tangible presence.

The most unfortunate people in India were the writers from Bengal. Over here, however important the author might be, it was impossible to run a family on a writer's income alone. Everybody needed an additional means of income. The number of newspapers and magazines that was produced from the region was countless. The publishing houses were compelled to pay the price of the paper and the services of the compositor, the proofreader, the binder and the book distributor. It was only when it came to paying the services of the authors that they would start grumbling about what a small establishment they were and how poor. For this reason, the literate people, especially the ones who were intelligent, usually avoided this field.

I am not a writer in the traditional sense. After learning to read and write, I merely started filling up the surface of a white paper with ink. That is how I became a writer. Since then, I have been referred to by various names like a Dalit writer, a protesting writer, a progressive writer, or even a representative of the life of the working class. The biggest reason behind this has been my autobiography *Itibritte Chandal Jivan*. Its literary worth could be left to the critics to decide, but in terms of reception, it garnered a lot of love from all quarters, leading my being selected for the Bangla Akademi award. Additionally, it also won the love from the ordinary, less educated people from the Namashudra community. They finally found their own writer who was honoured by higher-caste society.

* * *

I received an invitation to attend an event in Lucknow. A few months ago, the *Dainik Jagaran Patrika* had been a sponsor at the Bihar Diwas organized by Navaras, the Art and Culture Department under the Bihar government for which I had been an invited guest. They had seen and heard me at the programme and now wanted me to be a part of their event. This was the same Lucknow where forty-seven years ago I had come to work at the Loco-Rail Engine repair factory for a measly sum of fifty rupees. My job had been to clear out the ashes from the railway tracks into a basket. I had left heaping curses on the place. Today, I was being provided a dignified stage in the same city where I used to clear out dirt from the tracks as a petty labourer. The camera flashes were enough to turn anybody blind in the eye. The best of the country's meritorious people from various parts of the country had come to sit in utmost stillness and listen to me.

My role here was as a cultural ambassador of the Dalit-poor-labouring class people to raise their issues amidst a gathering of gentlemen. I was here to ask for a remedy. To warn them: 'Be careful! Give people their due credit. There is still time. Or else, the anger which they have so painfully suppressed for thousands of years will light up like a gunpowder one day and blast the opponent's safety net.'

Just a few days before the Lucknow event, I travelled to Mumbai. Ilina Sen, Binayak Sen's wife and a respected professor at the Tata Institute of Social Sciences, had invited me over as a distinguished speaker at one of the events being held at her esteemed institute. While everybody else presented their speech in English, I was the only one to speak in the Indian national language, Hindi. The audience comprised professors of different universities from places like Delhi, Kolkata, Mumbai, Bhubaneswar. Binayak Sen was also in the audience, whose presence was of extreme importance to me.

Immediately after the Mumbai event, I took an Air India flight to Dum Dum and from there boarded another flight for Silchar. This was to attend another event at Karimganj, organized by the Sandhani Yuva Sangha. To escort me, Baniprasanna Mishra of Karimganj flew down from Silchar to Kolkata. He was a former director of North Bengal University, now retired. My speech was the same everywhere; I spoke about my life and my works. What else could I talk about? For other matters, there were plenty of able speakers. But there was hardly anybody to describe in detail the tears, sweat and blood of the people occupying the lowest rung of the society. The simple reason was that to speak of such issues one had to first experience them. To experience them, one had to approach these people, meet them and get to know them. But not everybody's societal position allowed them to do so.

I spoke about these unsaid truths about the community to which I belonged. I shared the narrative of the unbearable and unspeakable conditions of my personal life and the extreme neglect and insult I had faced. I used words to paint the naked picture of heartless rulers and the existing oppression underlying society, aiming to pierce casteism and capitalism with the venom in my words. There were many people who spent a lot of money to take me to the different parts of the country to hear about these unfavourable truths directly from the horse's mouth in a language that was easy to understand. Where my father did not have a cloth on his body, a pair of slippers on his feet, food in his stomach or oil in his hair, not even the bare minimum means to buy a third-class railway ticket to travel fearlessly, his son's sponsors would ferry him in airplanes or air-conditioned first-class railway coaches.

Although I went to a lot of places, I never had the time to look around. My organizers would pick me up in a car from the airport or the railway station itself and thrust me into a well-furnished room of a ten-story hotel. From there, I would be taken directly to the stage and then back to the hotel. Finally, I would be taken back to the station or the airport. I was not provided even a minute extra as long as my sponsors' needs were met. Time was valuable. From what I had been told, the expenses of one day of lodging and food would be more than a month's salary for a person like me. Ilinadi, however, made provisions for me to have a small tour of Mumbai. She provided me with a car, a driver and her own daughter as my guide. By her grace, I was able to visit the Gateway of India, the Haji Ali Dargah, view Lata Mangeshkar's residence from the outside and see many other such touristy places. Mumbai was truly a city of dreams—the one that we knew as the golden city of wealth, fame and luxury, thanks to the world of cinema. There were countless stories of youngsters who came to this city lured by its charms but left in disappointment.

On the day of my departure, I boarded the flight at around 8 pm to reach Dum Dum in two hours. The plan was to spend the night at my friend Raju Das' house and then take the flight for Silchar the following day at around 1 pm. As luck would have it, my flight was rerouted to Nagpur. I was forced to spend a miserable night, in extreme cold temperature within the airport premises with no water or food. The flight left Nagpur the next morning and reached Dum Dum at 10 am. I was left with only an hour's time in between, given that the reporting time for my next flight was 11 am. Baniprasanna babu had already made his way from Silchar two days back and was waiting to take me with him. My wife, dear friend Ananta Acharya and Raju Das had also come to visit me, with a tiffin carrier filled with food, which I ate at the airport itself, after which I finally left for Silchar.

I was quite well versed with the entire process at the airport now and it did not worry me. This was my seventh air travel. I now knew how to put on my seat belt, how to look around with a deadpan expression on the face. Once, I had even scolded a traveller from Saudi Arabia who was using his mobile phone during the flight and made him turn it off. This time the journey was for seven days. I had been to many prestigious events as a guest, but the warmth that I experienced from the people in regions like Silchar, Karimganj and Suprakandi was beyond description. One of them had taken me in his car to see the Bangladesh border. I had seen the other side—my original land of birth—from this side. After having migrated from there as a child, I never found the chance to go back and perhaps would never have a chance to go back for lack of a passport and visa. The documents one needed to apply for these were not available to me.

My father was an illiterate person who had no idea about the seriousness with which certain documents needed to be prepared and preserved carefully to be able to prove oneself as a citizen of India. We had come to this country in the year 1952 or 1953. The government did distribute the papers at the camp in Bankura named Shiromoni where we were put up, but everything was destroyed as we moved from place to place after the dole stopped. We did not have any house or any trunk to safely store these papers. Tied up in a cloth bundle and tucked away in the straw shed, nobody knew when these papers had decomposed. Since then, we had become citizens of this country but without any name or identity. As for ration cards, our names in the electoral list or land deeds—we had none. A single scratch of diplomacy on a piece of paper had snatched away everything from us.

The river Surama had been identified as the border of both the lands. Standing at the edge of the river on the Indian side, I observed with an aching heart the houses and people on the other side. I could not stop my eyes from filling up with tears. There were a couple of kids playing. Some people were washing clothes in the river or taking a bath. The place where I was standing was so close, if I wanted, I could have swum to the other side in a minute—to my beloved homeland—the land believed to be even more superior to the heavens. But I would not be allowed. The border security forces waiting with their fingers aimed on the rifle trigger would immediately shower bullets directly to my chest and head. None of them were Bengalis and had never experienced Partition. Therefore, none of them would understand my pain. They did not know the overwhelming attraction one had for one's own land. For them, such emotions were unreal and meaningless.

Did they then allow nobody on the other side to come here? Thousands of people still travelled on the basis of illegal money transactions carried out in the darkness of the night. I did not want to go that way. Why would I even go? For the people on the other side, I was an infidel, a malaun, a kafir, a Hindu. They would not embrace me as their brother. Had they done that, the Partition wouldn't have happened in the first place.

Who was responsible for the Partition: Jinnah or Jawaharlal? I don't want to get into that argument here. Instead, I can say who benefited from the Partition. First and foremost, the higher castes of this country who managed to win the biggest share. During that time in Barisal, Faridpur, Khulna and Jessore of East Bengal, under the leadership of Harichand's son Guruchand Thakur, a mass awakening had been noticed among the Namashudras. They announced a rebellion against the dominance of the Savarnas and against religious oppression and started slowly advancing to the front ranks as an organized and powerful community through the new Matua religion. They were eager to make a mark everywhere including the arts, literature and politics in order to prove themselves. As the undisputed leader of this untouchable Namo community, Jogendranath Mandal came to the forefront.[1] He became an associate of the leader of the untouchables, Babasaheb Ambedkar, in Maharashtra.

Ambedkar's name was a subject of wide discussions among the masses as being the biggest opponent of Mohandas Karamchand Gandhi, the mass leader who was worshipped as a Mahatma and was the biggest protector of upper-caste interests. Babasaheb stood up against each step of the Gandhian principles with the weapon of his sharpened logic. Having found Ambedkar in the lead, the until now muted Dalit underprivileged class of people found their voice and started making demands for electorates that would be reserved for them alone. The stories that we are fed in the name of the independence struggle are actually balloons filled with the air of lies. What was the struggle about and how many people died for it? The list was not even as long as the number of lines on our fingers.

This is a huge country, with a population of around three hundred and thirty million and a rich soil, beneath which was the treasure trove of mineral resources and above which the storehouse of crops. Who would leave such a golden land just because a couple of people went around chanting slogans of 'British Leave India' and a group of emotionally charged youngsters charged with their tiny mosquito sized pistols? There were no bombs dropped from airplanes or villages burnt by the charge of the canon brigade. Huge numbers of people were not reduced to corpses. Was the British government this calm, well behaved and merciful? Didn't they use the same 'mercy' to become the lords of an empire over which apparently the sun would never set?

Actually, after experiencing a major setback in the Second World War, the 'well-meaning' English men spread over in their colonies all over the world, were left with no choice but to return back to their country in order to rebuild it. They were forced to vacate their thrones from Africa, where the natives had pleaded with the British government to stay back for a few more years till they became more competent in ruling their own countries. This was the same reason India got its independence, but what the British did to this country did not happen elsewhere. They left our country in pieces. Strangely enough, it was something that had been popularly demanded by the people of the country themselves, the British being mere facilitators.

While drafting the Constitution on how to run this newly independent country, the people from the higher castes did not want Ambedkar to have any place in the committee. One huge conspiracy started brewing against him and he was defeated in the elections. Jogendranath Mandal used this opportunity to invite Ambedkar, the Mahar from Maharashtra to East Bengal. Ambedkar was elected from Mandal's former seat. Jogendranath had realized that to protect Dalit rights, Babasaheb Ambedkar was a far more eligible candidate than him.

This incident landed a huge kick on the upper caste ego. The Namashudras from East Bengal became an eyesore to them. They feared that if the Mahars and the Namos were united, it would pose a huge threat to brahminical power. For this reason, during the Partition, they pushed the Namashudra dominated areas like Barishal, Faridpur, Khulna, Jessore to the side of East Pakistan. If the country had really been partitioned on the communal lines, these four districts should have stayed in India and the Muslim-dominated areas like Malda, Murshidabad and Nadia should have gone over to Pakistan. To satiate their feeling of vengeance, such an occurrence was prevented. For this reason, a powerful Dalit group was left scattered. Around 30 million of them made their way to this side. These people were then dispersed in Dandakaranya, Maharashtra, Nainital, Meerut and West Bengal, left to survive on the railway lines, the banks of canals and footpaths.

This scattered group was thus left powerless and the higher-caste interests safeguarded.

Another interest had been protected through the Partition, one that was more provincial. Had both the Bengals stayed together, their size would have been such that it would have yielded at least one hundred and twenty constituencies and only Bengali MPs would have been elected to go to the Parliament in Delhi. No other state would have had that many MPs. In reality, however, any party which came into rule in West Bengal had only one complaint which was against Delhi's step-motherly attitude towards them. If the former had been true, hundreds of MPs would have stood up together for Bengal and caused tremors in the hearts of the big leaders from Delhi. This fear was also no longer justified. With two parts of Bengal on the other side and one part here, the Bengalis would never be able to hold their heads high in this fragmented state. They could only if both the Bengals were united. Even Germany, which was partitioned at gunpoint, was united after so many years. Their language, food, attire and culture being all same, the unison had been smoother. Our language, food, attire and culture might have some similarities, but the barrier of religion came in between as a huge obstacle. For us, getting reunited won't be easy. Nothing else can create differences between people like religion.

I sometimes think how Israel, whose present population is only eight million, was also not a country previously. They had been driven from one part of the world to another as refugees. The German Nazi leader Hitler had put countless Jews in gas chambers and killed them. According to hearsay, their numbers were more than six million. For us Namo people, initially ten million came over to this side while 30 million remained on the other. If forty million people had stood up together, we would have easily been able to form a country of our own even by sacrificing ten million. On this side, our identity was reduced to destitutes, refugees, infiltrators, displaced people and Bangals. On the other side, we were identified as infidels, kafir, malaun and Hindus. Neither side had truly accepted us as their own. Then which side did we actually belong to? If neither side was ours, why didn't we just create a new side? If the eight million Israeli people could, why couldn't we, who were forty million in numbers? This is because by race we are Bengalis. We do say we are a race of the fearless, but history has a different story to tell. It is said that Lakkhan Sen, one of our kings, fled when a few Turkish soldiers came to his palace.

Three of our leaders, M.N. Roy, Rashbehari Bose and finally Subhas Bose, all fled from the country. As for other countries of the world, be it Lenin from Russia, Mao Zedong from China, Fidel Castro from Cuba or Ho Chi Minh from Vietnam, none of them fled their countries to a safer zone. They stayed undercover among the masses, organized them, fought back and finally won victory.

The Namashudra leader, Jogendranath Mandal, told the Namashudra people on the eve of independence, 'Do not leave the country. I am with you all.'[2] Pacified by his assurance, a large population of the Namashudras decided to stay back on the other side of Bengal. Then one fine day, he resigned as the Minister of Law and Labour in the Pakistani cabinet and left for India, leaving the Namashudras of East Pakistan like a herd of sheep in front of a starving lion, he fled to India himself. He chose to save his own life at the cost of lakhs of Namashudra lives. They were rendered helpless, with no way to stay back or to make their way to this side. Even those who managed to escape through secret passageways found no shelter or acceptance.

Mujibur Rahman, another leader, announced jihad against the Pakistani government. Thereafter he was arrested by Pakistan and imprisoned. The people he left behind died at the hands of the Khan and Razakar militia like poultry, while he stayed far away from the battlefield.. Finally, the Indian government fought the Khan army, rescued the country from them and handed it over to him, although, his fate did not allow him to enjoy this good fortune for long.

One could also mention Satish Mandal. He was the person who along with Ram Chatterjee had toured the Bengali areas of Dandakaranya and encouraged the settlers there to move to Marichjhapi. A hundred thousand people made the move just on their words. The day the Left Front government surrounded the island with forty launches, the first person to swim and escape with Madhu Malakar was Satish Mandal. His associate Madhu Malakar now lived in Paralkot and the latter in Raipur These lucky two made the trip to Marichjhapi and returned safely; while there remains no trace of the four thousand seven hundred and twenty-eight people who followed in their footsteps. Nobody knows what happened to them.

* * *

Even though Karimganj was under the state of Assam, it was dominated by those who spoke Bangla. Had I not been told this fact, I wouldn't have known that it was not part of Bengal. A lot of huge banners were put up around the city, with my face plastered on all of them. People were invited to come and listen to a man who evoked wonders. The event went on for more than a week with a number of programmes including singing, dancing and theatre, and one whole day set aside for me. There was no limit to the time available, be it two and half hours or more. On the first day of the event, a colourful procession was brought out with almost a thousand men and elephants to tour the entire city. Just the presence of the women in this procession was enough to catch one's attention, all dressed in vibrant colours. There was also a group of boys dressed in their military uniforms marching along to the beat from the accompanying band.

The Sandhani Yuva Sangha had been formed in the fifties to trace their missing favourite leader Subhas Chandra Bose. Many of the founding members of the organization were now no more. The ones, who were alive, were all very old. The new generation had shouldered the responsibilities of the organization with the promise of completing the task. Sandhani Yuva Sangha had not been able to trace Netaji. But the organization had now taken up a pioneering role in carrying out social service in the area of Karimganj and celebrated Netaji's birth anniversary with a lot of pomp and show every year.

The procession had both Assamese and Bengalis from Assam participating by upholding their own cultural stamp. Some of the girls, dressed in the traditional hilly attire, were dancing down the road. The Bengali women had joined in their traditional white sarees with red borders blowing the conch. Drums, kettledrums and other instruments were playing alongside. A group of small kids had come in their school uniform and distributed along the length of the procession with a banner mentioning their school's name in their hands. They were dancing and singing down the road like a frolicking hilly fountain.

The entire population of the town had joined in the procession. Those on foot were walking at a steady pace, the ones who could not were standing by the road watching the procession pass. A couple of girls were sprinkling flowers on the way. Conches were being blown. Smaller groups of folk artists were dancing along the sound of the music, demonstrating various dance forms from Assam and Bengal through their wonderful performances.

Jugasankha and *Samayik Prasanga*, the Assam equivalent of *Anandabazar Patrika*, later brought out an entire page feature on me with my photograph. In addition, the Sandhani Yuva Sangha digitised my speech and played it on loop at various parts of the city. Apart from Baniprasanna Mishra, here I also met people like Shyamal Ranjan Deb, the editor of Sandhani Yuva Sangha, Rathish Deb and a few others, whose warm hospitality I will never forget. I also received ten thousand rupees in cash, a shawl and a blanket, a saree for Anu, flowers, garlands and an ocean full of love.

NOTES

[1] Jogendranath Mandal (1904–68) was a Dalit leader in East Bengal. He was elected to the Bengal Legislative Assembly and in 1937 supported Muslim League government in Bengal, believing that Dalit interests would be better safeguarded by Bengali Muslims, with whom they shared socio-economic concerns, and not with the oppressive caste Hindus. He was instrumental in

getting B. R. Ambedkar elected to the Constituent Assembly in 1946 from Bengal when there was no chance of him being elected elsewhere. He also formed a branch of Ambedkar's Scheduled Castes Federation.

2   In the run up to Partition, he encouraged the Dalits to remain in East Bengal. He himself became Minister for law and Labour in the Pakistani cabinet. Increasing Islamicization in Pakistan made his position untenable, and he resigned his post and left for India in 1950. In East Pakistan, the Dalits, the bulk of whom were Namashudras, faced extreme hostility and violence from Muslim Bengalis, and they also left for India. The author's family was part of this movement of refugees.

CHAPTER 32

An Interview with 24 *Ghonta*

A TV reporter who worked at the 24 Ghonta news channel lived in Mukundapur. His superior ordered him to locate a writer who lived near his area and interview him.

'Where does he live?'

'Arre, he cooks at that school for the deaf and mute.'

'He cooks? But didn't you just say that he was a writer?'

'Yes, he does both. I have heard that he used to be a rickshaw-puller before this and has also been to jail.'

'An interview with *this* person!'

'Yes, the CEO has personally put in a request, so I would advise you to leave everything else and get this work done as a priority.'

The reporter called me on my mobile. He said, 'I am calling from 24 Ghonta channel. I urgently want an interview with you. When will you have some time?'

I said, 'Come over this evening.'

After a moment's thought he said, 'Not today. Could I come tomorrow?'

'It will be better. I am on leave tomorrow, so there will be no hurry. I will be home all day. You can come whenever you want.'

'You have a day off tomorrow?'

'Yes, tomorrow being Sunday is my weekly leave day.'

'Then how will I get pictures of you cooking? I also needed that.'

I said, 'Then you have to come before nine in the morning. After that it will not be possible as we generally finish cooking by then. We begin again in the evening at six. Call me before you come. I will be at my workplace.'

'We will come around eight-thirty in the morning. Please be there.'

Many of the Bengali channels had invited me once or twice, but most of them were not such big names. Among the big ones, ABP Ananda and 24 Ghonta had never invited me. I was a little surprised to find the latter come forward on its own. Did this mean that they had come out of their ultra-conservative state finally and opened their doors to the untouchables?

Who did not like publicity? Maybe there were people who did not want it, but I had no qualms against it. If not for the publicity, would there have been as many people buying and reading my books today? I was one of those lucky few who had received bountiful support from the media all over. It was true that they had also used me for business purposes, but without them I would have remained unknown. There was no denying the fact that I was truly grateful to my readers, my publishers and these news channels and reporters.

I remember going for the twenty-third annual programme of the Dalit Sahitya Sanstha, though usually, I did not like going for such events. Writing since 1981, I have had many highly educated people criticize my works, but it was nothing in comparison to the fierce attacks I received from the educated people of my own community. The year Meenakshi Mukherjee published with me in *EPW* (13 Oct 2007) and people all over India started adding the epithet of 'Dalit writer' before my name, the ones who came forward in opposition were writers from the Dalit community who were either teachers or high government officials, who had not yet managed to win even a single award despite publishing many books with their savings. These people had questioned, 'Manoranjan Byapari is a writer? What does he know about writing? What does he understand about the definition of Dalit? Does he know what Dalit Literature is? His rise to fame is simply a publicity gimmick funded by the Brahmins. Otherwise, he is just an air-filled balloon, with no real substance inside.'

The Dalits, especially the Namashudras, who loved me deeply, were the ones who ardently read my works and found these to be thought-provoking. As for the others, the ones who were writers themselves, they burnt in envy. I, therefore, tried to avoid the gatherings of Dalit writers as much as I could. But I couldn't avoid this particular occasion, because one of my acquaintances was supposed to come to this session. He was not a fellow writer, but my reader and it was important that I met him. He was a strange soul. He worked in the navy, spent six months on water and six months on land. Goodness knows from where he had heard about me, but he landed up at Mukundapur one day and collected a number of books from me. He said that he was taking his ship abroad and would meet me after his return.

I met a new person almost every other day. People made so many promises. Phone calls came from unknown numbers. It was not easy to remember everything. So, I didn't ask for this person's name, not really believing that he would come to meet me later. So many of them said such things but hardly anyone kept his word. After a great many days, I received a call from an unknown number, 'Dada, can you recognize my voice? Do you remember me? I am now crossing the Suez Canal. Before sleeping, I thought of reading your book. What have you done! Who writes these things and how! Now I have lost my sleep. I am not able to let go of the book. The moment I come back, I will come and meet you and take more books from you so that I can give these to all my acquaintances.'

There was no word from him for almost three to four months after that. After landing back in Kolkata, he called me once again, asking about my state, reminding that he had called me and enquiring if I recognized him. To be honest, I wasn't able to do so immediately. The other two calls he had made were from different numbers. It was saved as my 'Navy Brother'. This was a new number. Yet, I said, 'Yes. Tell me, how have you been?'

'I am fine. I will go to Jadavpur University in the evening today for some work. Will you be able to come? I can then meet you.'

Jadavpur was a favourite place. The Coffee House was filled with a lot of poets and writers known to me. I had not met them in a long time. I told him I could meet him there and he said he would call ahead. The phone call came around seven in the evening. 'Dada, I got caught in some urgent matter. I am coming now. I have some work at College Street. You can sit in my car and we can talk on the way. After my work, I can drop you back at Jadavpur.'

I had still not fully recognized him and grew a bit suspicious. My mind started weaving all sorts of crazy scenarios. What if I sat down in the car and it started moving? What if after moving ahead some distance, two more people boarded from either side of the car? The owner might say, 'No worries! They are known to me.' And then, what if the car took an unknown bend, a road that was more secluded, lonely and dark? Say, the two people sitting behind pressed the metal pipe of the gun on my stomach and said, 'Don't make a single sound. Come with us wherever we are taking you.' What if all this happened? What if this was my enemy camp's doing? What if they killed me and disposed off my body on the railway track? The fear was not just mine but Anu's too. So, I told him that it was late, I was not well and if we could meet some other day?

After a few days, I received a call again asking me to come to Jadavpur. I made an excuse about being at work. Ten days later, another call came saying he was coming to Mukundapur. So, could we meet? He would come around 6.30 pm.

On that day, I had to go to Mukundapur in any case. For the Lucknow event being organized by *Dainik Jagaran Patrika*, the organizers had sent me the airplane ticket via mail. I could use the email id of any cyber café to take a print out. I decided to meet him when I went to pick up my ticket from Mukundapur. His enthusiasm was such that it did not seem like he would rest till he had met me. I promised to be there and told him that I would wait for him under the auto stand shed.

It was a winter evening. There were fewer people on the road than usual. A thin mist was slowly spreading over the evening darkness. At the pre-ordained time, I reached the auto stand on my cycle. Immediately a phone came, 'Where are you?'

'There, where I said I would be, under the shed of the auto stand.'

'There are too many people there. We won't be able to talk properly. Come to the field behind 1A bus stand. You will see a red car waiting, it is my car.' This huge field was called the FCI ground. It would be completely empty at this time. The kids who played football here in the evening, the elderly who took a walk and the young men and women who chatted amongst themselves, would have all gone back. In the dim light of the descending darkness, almost drowned in the overhanging mist, I found the red car waiting on one side. I was worried whether I should go or not. The road ahead went towards Ruby via the Netai Road. There were no people or vehicles on that road. What if the car escaped that way after causing some mishap? Whatever be the case, I took my bicycle up to the car and immediately recognized him. This was my reader. My own blood.

He asked, 'Have you got the books?'

'You didn't say you needed books. If only you had said something over the phone.'

After thinking for a while, he said we would go to my house. I could lock my bicycle for the time being and pick it up when we returned. The road to my house was filled with potholes. Reaching my place in fifteen minutes, he picked up a couple of my books. 'What is the price?' After calculating, I said, 'Thirteen hundred and forty rupees.' He took out a bundle from his pocket and extended it towards me. 'Keep this,' he said. It was five thousand rupees.

'Why so much?'

'I am giving it to you. Leaving aside the thirteen hundred and forty rupees, you can use the rest. Buy some paper and pens.'

He did not have a cup of tea. Neither did he click a single picture with me beside him. He did not even share his name or address. Silently, without brandishing himself in any form, this compassionate human being took his leave. His name, as I later found out, was Nisith Sarkar. This thought came to me later, frequently, that it would have been a major mistake on my part had I not met him out of my misplaced fear. I would have borne the burden of that misconception all my life. My friend would be tainted by the unfounded suspicion of being a foe. It was this friend who was supposed to come to the Dalit Sahitya Sanstha's event before leaving for his next assignment at sea. There was no telling when he would return to India next. He wanted to meet me once before leaving hence I had no other option. My friend Anantya Acharya would also be at this event. From Ultadanga, we both boarded a bus headed towards our destination. I told him on the way that I would stay away from the stage and refrain from giving a speech.

I was always embarrassed with myself. When I was born, nobody had put any honey in my mouth. As a result, I did not speak the language of sweetness. Even when I wrote, the venom oozing out from all the suppressed pain in my life got accumulated at the nib of my pen. Many people did not like it and in most cases whatever I wrote or said ended up creating a huge controversy. I had no intention of stirring up any controversy that day. Alas! I was not able to avoid it. An official from the Kalyani faction of the Dalit Sahitya Sanstha announced my name on the microphone and kept on urging me to speak. I was compelled to go up to the dais and as expected, a writer started seething in anger on hearing my speech. I had said that compared to Hindi, Marathi, Gujarati, Kannada, Tamil and Telugu, Bangla Dalit literature was far behind. I had blamed it on the Partition. The most aware and well-organized Dalit group in Bengal was that of the Namashudras. Apart from the Mahars, the community that had extended their support to Babasaheb Bhimrao Ramji Ambedkar was the Namos. They were the ones who elected Babasaheb for the Constituent Assembly. Because of Partition, the same community was scattered all over India. At that time, their biggest crisis was regarding their very existence—where would they live and what would they eat? It had eventually taken them fifty-six years to merely overcome the crisis and become independent again. No other Dalit community from India had to face such a problem, making it much easier for them to tread forward.

The writer was enraged. He wanted to use the opportunity to show Manoranjan Byapari his place. He said, 'In my *Dalit Patrika*,

I have published a book list of hundred Dalit writers. The list has come to include at least one thousand books! Despite that the higher-caste people keep prattling that Bengal has no Dalit literature. Now, some of our own people are also playing the same tune. They have shifted allegiance to the Brahmanvads. The reason that our books don't get sold is due to the lack of publicity.' There were around a hundred people in the room. Pointing towards them he said, 'If I get this many readers, I would willingly give up the Rabindra Puraskar.'

He received a lot of applause. I felt like saying, 'Sir, Charandas Thief had said that he would not eat on a golden plate, he would not ride an elephant, he would not marry a princess, and he would not become a king. It was mainly because these achievements felt unattainable to him. You are talking about the Rabindra Puraskar? If that is a big enough vow, I will give up the Nobel Prize or the Booker or the Magsaysay Award. These are shallow accolades. These might win a person the applause of the fool, but the really wise ones would just smile and say "grapes are sour".'

I had not by any stretch said that Bangla Dalit Literature does not exist. My claim was that Dalit Literature from Bengal had not acquired any notable achievements yet. The collection of timeless works that existed within mainstream Bangla literature—one could list out at least hundred titles in one breath—did not have any worthy competitor amongst our works except for, say, *Titas Ekti Nadir Nam*.

There was no merit in stealing from one's own house. Hence, saying that it was a conspiracy of the Brahmanvads, would not do. It was important to accept our weaknesses. We haven't been able to, but that does not mean that we have lost all faith. We were trying, learning and writing. Striving in this fashion, we would one day reach the highest pinnacle of literary accolades. What was the shame in acknowledging this? For thousands of years the doors of educational institutions were closed for us. The door had just opened slightly, with some light spilling in. In that light, Dalit life was slowly getting illuminated and discussed. After striving for our whole lives, this place that we had finally managed to reach would serve as a stepping stone for the next generation to rise even higher. We have had to wander in the dark. The next generation would at least get a bamboo ladder or a concrete stairway within their reach. If they so wished, they would definitely reach the position we have yearned for. The way forward lay in smoothening out the way and inspiring each other to stay enthusiastic about that which had still not been achieved. Instead, if we kept blaming each other, the target would move farther away and we would never be able to fulfil our dreams of reaching the summit.

Securing a job for oneself provided some amount of stability. People took up jobs as teachers, professors or in other good positions. A friend of mine had once told me—in fact he had proven his point through calculations— that, 'Say the marks cut-off for a job was hundred. One from the higher castes with this score would easily get the job. If they had ninety, they would hound some uncle or relative to get them the job. Those with eighty would find themselves some political connection to acquire the position. But if they had seventy, they would be unable to do anything. For the same job, a lower-caste person would need only fifty. If they had forty and some personal or political connections along with the means to pay a bribe, they would still end up with the job. So, we can see that even with seventy, the higher- caste person might not get a job which a lower- caste person with only fifty might end up getting it.'

Various such debates were ongoing, with both parties armed with their own logic. But I was not against the reservation system. I lauded Eklavya's skill in shutting up a dog with his arrow rather than Arjuna's skill of shooting the fish in the eye. Apart from a good teacher, Arjuna had many other advantages. Eklavya had nothing. Despite that he had been an achiever and all because of his own tireless labour. For a child from a higher caste, the means to acquire education was readily available. The mother of the lower-caste child might be a maid in a domestic household; his father might be a rickshaw-puller. For his education, he would have to depend on second-hand books and a kerosene lamp. Getting a fifty under such circumstances was equivalent to five hundred.

I had an objection against the distribution of opportunities under the reservation system. A lower-caste person, who had acquired a job, would be capable enough to educate his children. Why then should the children too be given the same advantages? But it was mostly the government's fault for having created a system where the children too would get the same benefits. It meant depriving the kid from another poor destitute family for whom these opportunities would matter more. According to me, a bill should be passed to obtain an affidavit from the candidate that nobody from the previous three generations of his or her family had held a government post, before offering them the job on a reserved post. If one submitted a false document, he or she would be immediately dismissed from the job, jailed or fined. Thus, the children from the lowest echelons of the society, whose education had been acquired through great pains, would be benefitted.

Everybody right from Babasaheb Ambedkar, to Guruchand Thakur, to Periyar Ramasamy Naikar, to Mahatma Jyotiba Phule had all hoped and aimed to save the Dalits from upper-caste oppression. Towards that end, they had spent an entire lifetime fighting a severe and uncompromising battle. Having lapped up the benefits of their struggles, a couple of people had bloated up like leeches. These people were of no use to their Dalit poor brethren. They were more engaged in acquiring wealth and luxury of their own. Beyond themselves and their own family, they loved nobody else. To allow this group of people to continue to partake of such opportunities by dangling the Dalit card seemed unfair.

Babasaheb had created the opportunity for reservation within the employment system. He had hoped that the ones who would become financially stable would take the initiative of giving back to those who had none and thereby set up a cycle. He had said, 'Pay back to society'. But all of them had only squeezed out as much as they could. During the last stages of his life, this regret had been apparent in his voice when he had said that it was the educated people who had duped him the most. Naturally enough, if they did not do anything for society, why would society do anything for them?

Today the moment had come to support the deprived among the Dalits and not let the privileged Dalits continue to take the advantages—keep lapping from the honey pot reserved for the Dalits, without being of any help to the rest of the community. This was the reason that many Dalits had come together in protest. The idea was to tag this group of people as 'salaried' and socially boycott them if needed. The Dalit community had enough brawn to fight those outsiders who were harmful for them, but it was not possible for them to fight their own. It was hence important to identify this latter group and isolate them from society. These government employees holding high-ranking posts had become the biggest problem for us who were desirous of literary fame. It was not as easy for an aspirant to find literary acknowledgement as it was for a person seeking a job under the reservation system. The competition in the former case was quite tough. One could not succeed there by just getting 33 on 100. One needed to get the full marks. There was no one to show kindness in this field. Nobody to give away even an inch of space for free. One had to win their position through merit alone.

Many people among us gave the excuse that we are first generation learners. As far as I am concerned, this does not mean anything. The books one read from Class One to the stage of graduation were the same as that of our teachers. Then how could one be less than the other? The lack was in terms of personal interest, of the devotion and concentration in mastering that mastery. But more than anything else, it was the tendency of people to expect things easily without any extra effort. This tendency has become enmeshed in our blood. We would rather become the disciples of a guru and take shelter under his feet with the hope that he will make everything right for us, without our having to move a finger. But the truth was that he who could not solve his own problem, how could he solve my problem?

We bribed gods like Kali and Shiva with the promise of making a five paisa donation if they granted us a job or a lottery prize. We never once realized that god was not an idiot who would give us a job for a monthly salary of twenty-five thousand rupees or a lottery worth ₹500,000 in hopes of getting a five paisa contribution.

The biggest pilgrim site for us Namashudras is Thakurnagar in West Bengal. The descendants of Harichand Thakur fled from the other side of Bengal and bought some land here to build their houses. To increase the height of the lowland, they dug up a pond for the soil. This pond was named as Kamana Sagar, standing for a river of wishes. It was popularly believed that taking a dip in its waters made all wishes come true. Our people would undertake long arduous journeys just to take a dip in the waters of this pond. Whether their wishes actually came true was not known. If it indeed were the case, my advice to people would be to take a dip in its waters with the wish of becoming the country's Prime Minister or Mukesh Ambani or Amitabh Bachchan. This way, it wouldn't be difficult for us to win all the topmost positions in society. My advice would be same for those who wished to reach the top of the literary world. If not, I would request them to hone their skills with the utmost dedication. I would ask them to read up all the great pieces of literature available and to learn how to write. That barebodied iconic figure, recognizable anywhere from his pair of round spectacles and a bamboo walking stick, had said many disagreeable things, but one couldn't but agree to one of his claims that 'one cannot achieve anything great through trickery', which was hundred percent true.

It was especially true in the case of literature. The children of a big political leader could become a leader by using his or her father's name. The child of a zamindar would inevitably be a zamindar. But when it came to literature, it was not so easy. There was nobody who had acquired that position just by the virtue of being born to a famous literary figure. Those who reached the spot had practised with dedication. This is where our Namashudra writers had fallen behind. Barring some exceptions, the majority wanted to take a short cut. On being unable to fulfil their schemes in this fashion, the same people were turning antagonistic towards those who had managed to outshine them, and were trying to pull them back.

A professor from the Department of Comparative Literature of Jadavpur University had gone to Dhaka University for a literary event. There he read out a story by a writer from West Bengal who had been to jail and had also been a rickshaw-puller. The name of the story was 'Reewaz'. A Deputy Registrar from Calcutta University was also present at this event. He charged the professor, 'Sir, did you not get any other writer? You found a rickshaw-puller's story to read out?'

The professor replied, 'What can I do if the story has been written by that man. You write another 'Reewaz', I promise to read out your story in the next event.'

* * *

To come back to the 24 Ghonta news channel incident—on that particular Tuesday, I was waiting in anticipation for the reporter's call. The phone came around 8.30 am when their car was crossing the Bypass. 'Where are you?'

'I am at my home.'

'Please come fast. We have reached.'

The fault was not mine but theirs. I had already given interviews to many channels and knew from experience that people usually said 'tomorrow' but reached three days later. One time, a group had taken a one-eighty-degree turn midway to collect the news of an accident after informing me that 'we are on our way'. Hence, by now, I knew better than dancing to the tune of these news channels. Hence, I decided to wait for 24 Ghonta's call, which got me into trouble.

I had just taken a sip from my cup of tea when I was summoned. I immediately gulped down the tea from the saucer, burning my mouth in the process, and left as quickly as possible. My bicycle was my all-time vehicle. On that day, fortunately, I got a shuttle taxi. The bicycle would take twenty minutes, but the taxi helped me to save five minutes. Midway I got another call from the reporter. 'How far have you reached?' I said I was in a taxi and would be there soon.

He said, 'We are waiting, you come.' His voice sounded strange. Not the kind of respectful tone one would have towards a writer, but one that seemed to want to say, 'Come jerk, we will teach you a lesson.' I could understand that I was in for some harassment, but still went, eager to see it till the end. The moment I reached, the reporter charged at me aggressively, 'We have been waiting for a long time. Does our time have no value for you? We said we would reach around 8.30. You should have been here. Why weren't you here?'

I said, 'You must have waited for ten extra minutes at most. Why didn't you call me when you left from Poddar Court? Then the delay would not have happened.'

'Why call again? We had already informed you yesterday.'

'You definitely did, but what if some other important work came by today? How was I to know? I too could have been sick or been in some other trouble.'

From his position, he was the reporter of a respectable channel talking to a mere cook and the expectation was that I should be overwhelmed that the channel was giving me the opportunity of parading my face on television. On my part, I was talking from the position of an author who knew that he was a saleable commodity for these media people who made money by trading in news about him. I was simply demanding that respect. With both parties refusing to budge from their individual positions, the sound of our voices kept skyrocketing and soon turning into a proper verbal battle.

I finally said, 'Are you here to take my interview? Or did I approach you with some demands of my own? Why are you talking to me this way? I am not your employee. You can wait for me or leave if you want. You are letting off steam just because I have wasted ten minutes of your time, why should I waste my two hours for you? I have decided I am not doing this interview. You may take your leave.'

Saying this, I started walking ahead. I have done so many interviews, nothing had changed so far. I was still twirling the ladle

every day. What harm could come from losing another interview? When I had walked off quite a distance, they obstructed my way with their car. 'You are leaving?'
'What else can I do?'
'What will I report to the channel?'
'That is completely your problem.'
'No, no, give us the interview.'
'I will, but first say 'please'.'

It was not entirely the reporter's fault. One of his programmes was scheduled to be telecast at three. He was supposed to go and edit that programme, after finishing this interview and naturally had his head preoccupied with the pending work and was hence a bit agitated. Slowly he calmed down. Completing the shoot at my workplace, he went to my house where he witnessed the West Bengal Akademi award, the other addresses of honour scattered all over the place, my photo features in all the leading dailies of India and my books. Turning to me, he said, 'Please forgive me. My brain was not working at that time. I have said such bad things to you. I promise to come back again another day.'

He really did come back after seven days and handed me a letter, inviting me to the '1420 (2004) Ananya Samman Ceremony' to be organized by 24 Ghonta at the ITC Sonar Bangla hotel. He said that I definitely had to be there, but I could also bring along a guest and that the car would pick me up that day. There I got to know that I had been selected for the award that year. The other writer who was awarded the same prize with me was Buddhadev Guha. It finally happened! I got the Ananya Samman. The channel gave me a cheque for ₹25,000, an address of honour, a trophy and a silver memento sponsored by Senco Gold which would not be anything less than nine to ten tola in weight.

Author and the writer Buddhadeb Guha awarded the Ananya Samman Award by 24 Ghonta, 2013.

In retrospect, I often wonder what would have happened if driven by my Chandal anger, I had left without granting them the interview that day. I would have definitely lost all these honours. The prize money is long gone; but the address of honour and the memento remain. The entire programme was telecast at least three to four times in total, as a result of which many more people came to know about me, more books were sold and I gained more readers.

CHAPTER 33

My Writing Philosophy

*N*obody had forced me to write. I wrote because I couldn't live without writing. Just like a drowning man holds onto whatever is near his hand to keep afloat, I had grabbed onto my cheap pen. This was completely my choice. I had never expected any support from others. Whatever I had received was wonderful; but had I not, I wouldn't have been dejected. Thankfully, since writing was a way of creating and evolving, I was certain that it would push me towards a definite direction.

For the person who wrote sweet love stories as the market demands, it was different. In contrast, the person who wrote hard-hitting prose had no other choice but to lash at the decaying, old and rotting societal system in order to remove it and build something new. As a result it is understandable why capitalism, Brahminism, patriarchy and the governance system would go against him. Similarly, there would be many who would oppose the writer and his writing. In case these people had financial and political connections, they would try to use that to turn the life of the writer into a living hell. There would be no way left for the writer to escape. My destiny had brought me to such dangerous situations. It was nobody's fault but my own. I had created this situation and now I would have to look out for the solution myself. If I could find it, there would be victory and if not, I would have to perforce embrace extinction. People said that god himself bore the burden of the lucky one, while the unlucky one had to bear his own weight on his back while walking towards his destination like the camel bore its hump. I fall into the latter category, where I was required to climb each step with a lot of effort and drag myself little by little towards the destination.

I sometimes asked myself where do I want to reach? Why am I bearing this load? What do I want in return for my writing? When my first book, *Brittyer Sesh Parba,* was published, I had taken it to a very well-known Left leaning professor at Jadavpur University to request her to buy a copy. In a meek voice I had asked her, 'I am a rickshaw-puller. I have written a book. Will you please buy one and read it?'

She had looked at me with an indifferent expression on her face and said, 'Who has asked you to write?'

True! Who has asked me to write? This work suited only those who were born to write. I was a rickshaw-puller; my work was to pull the rickshaw like a cow or an ass. Writing was a job reserved for the more educated folks. How could I dare try and include myself within their ranks? Why did I even write? Would I be able to change this bloodsucking societal system standing atop the rotting thousand-year-old foundation with my pen alone? Would I be able to stop the inhumane religious brutality of the priestly class in the name of caste? The child lying on the footpath, who had curled up in the bitter cold, could I bring him a blanket? That child crying in his mother's arms in hunger, would I be able to make him sit in front of a plate full of warm freshly made rice?

I could not! I could not!

Would I be able to secure a position for myself in this society with my writing? Would I be able to find financial stability, without which life was difficult to lead? Only money could give one access to food, clothes, shelter and medical assistance. I was not in a position to achieve even that. I didn't consider myself that powerful a writer. I still wanted to continue writing. It would not come to the help of the country, society, mankind or me, but I still wanted to continue writing. It was something like my wanting to live even though I didn't know the reason for my existence, even though I knew that my death would not affect the world in any way. There have been hundreds of thousands like me who have come into this world and left it before me, but my heart was still not ready to say the final goodbye. Wise people were of the opinion that there was no harm if one's life was not long enough as long as it was big enough. I had not been able to make it big, but I had definitely expanded its ambit. I had crossed threescore years of it. I still wanted to continue living and writing.

This was mainly because I believed that I had still not written my finest so far. Again, this was not something that had been enforced on me, but was my obligation to myself. I would have to carry this liability all my life, bearing all the reproof, humiliation and torture. The end aim would be to write my last and finest work. The fact that I was brought back from the land of death at the Shiromoni camp as a baby was perhaps also because of the same reason, so that I could finish this work that was lying incomplete. Hence, I wrote and I would keep on writing. 'Manoranjan', my name, stands for entertainment, but none of my writing is written for entertainment alone. My sole intention has been to document the unfriendly and unhelpful society of my experiences for the future generations, nothing more.

There are many others I have grievances against. Goutam Roy had rightly said that Manoranjan Byapari had turned from an individual to a subject. For this society, I was nothing but a topic of discussion. I wrote. The tears and pain of the people and community that I wrote about have been carefully recorded in my autobiography. People have read it, some have sighed in exasperation, but nobody has yet taken any initiative to uplift me or the poor people from the Dalit community. Many people have instead pointed out the structural, spelling and punctuation errors in my writings. They have suggested ways to make my writing more interesting. They have criticized it for its lack of literary flavour. As for the work's message and its cry against the eternal deprived state of existence for people like us, those have remained untouched.

People now sponsored flight tickets for me. They kept me in ten-story high hotels. They gave me a space on a stage under the spotlight. Nobody asked me about my literature or any literature in general. All their queries were directed towards my personal life. Everybody was intrigued to know how this man who was educated so late in life had still managed to write such a fat book like *Itibritte Chandal Jivan*. In their eyes, I was not a human being but a crow, who knew how to sound like a koyel. This ability of mine was a wonder for them. They had no intention to know about the painful life the crow had led.

I got invitations from so many places, like Lucknow, Delhi, Mumbai, Patna. I was respectfully ushered to these events. People broke out in applause at my speeches. I was featured in newspapers and magazines. People posed for photographs with me, many people asked me for autographs. Yet after the end of each event, nobody even cared to inquire about me. Why would they? Having squeezed out as much as they could from me, the rest was left for other possible future interactions.

After entering the literary world, I had come in contact with many eminent and enlightened figures. Each time my dried-up heart would flutter in the hope that their influential presence would definitely change my fate. I would weave dreams that maybe from their pitcher brimming with compassion, they would scoop out two spoonfuls on my plate. But more than them, I would be hopeful about those low-caste people who would write tragic articles about destitute people from their high official positions. Or those people in high government positions dedicated to the development of lower-caste lives. I would constantly hope that somebody's gracious glance would fall on me.

This was a strange land; stranger were its rules and regulations. Here people from the field of sports had the opportunity to seek jobs in the railways, in the army, in a bank or in the telegraph office. The government financially compensated if anybody died by consuming distilled liquor. Even the imams in the mosques received a stipend. Only the poor people had nobody to give them anything or to look after them.

A few days back, Sadananda Pal, the author of *Ek Kumbho* and Akademi prize winner, an artist who painted words, passed away. His life and how he had worshipped literature till the very end with a gamchha tied to his stomach to curb hunger were all documented in the pages of *Ek Kumbho*. He was suffering from cancer but had not been able to get proper treatment for lack of cash. His helpless state gradually pushed him towards death.

I was scared. It had really left me in grave trauma. My gut feeling was that such a painful death was slowly making its way towards me. With each passing day, my knees were turning more useless and unfit to carry my body weight. I had lost the strength to traverse long miles at a stretch. Hence, I was scared. If I got bedridden, how would I survive? But I was more scared for my family. To see one's wife and son suffer in starvation while chained to the bed would be rather painful.

CHAPTER 34

The End of an Era

On 28 July 2016, writer, activist and a favourite among the Adivasis, Marang Dai passed away. She had been like the unrelenting commander standing beside countless exploited deprived labouring-class people, assisting in their fight. It was undeniably life's biggest truth that once born, a person had to gear up towards breaking all ties on earth and leaving. However, this was also the brutal truth that the passing away of certain individuals left a huge impact on the human community. The void created by their absence was irreplaceable. This was especially true when it came to Mahasweta Devi.

The times were terrible. What seems like in a premeditated fashion, a barbaric attack was being launched on the Dalits, the poor, the Adivasis and all the other minority groups in a way that had been practised on the Jews once by the biggest enemies of humanity, the Nazis. People would die, people would howl, a river of gore would be generated reddening the waters of Ganga-Narmada-Godavari. The killers would raise a victory cry, drowning under the weight of their exultant roar the common man's food, clothing, education, shelter and health needs, as well as their citizenry demands for basic rights of freedom and societal respect. The slowly burgeoning revolutionary movements and the fight for water, forests and land would also gradually get submerged in this chaos.

The perpetrators knew very well that unless the larger population is left in deprivation, it would be impossible for the rich to get richer. Therefore, fascism was being unleashed upon those daring to raise their heads against oppressive rule, injustice and torture. These forces were aiming to crush the willpower of anybody hoping to protest. A hawk-like watch had been put in place, monitoring the lives of common people. Fear was being used to threaten everybody. One was not free to take even a single step without the permission of the oppressive forces. Human rights were dead. The poor were being forced to live under the feet of those in power like slaves, as they had done for centuries. Towards that end, brutal torture was being unleashed upon the innocent people of the lower castes and classes.

Because of the power of Mahasweta Devi's writing, there was a huge need for her leadership and protest. Equipped with the fire and anger akin to the sun, she was the one to have kept the fight against injustice alive. She had not given in to any temptation or fear, but spent an entire life battling in the interest of those starving penniless people tottering on empty stomachs. Her roar had raged right from the decade of the seventies to the dangerous days of Singur, Nandigram and Netai. Her fiery raging pen had dealt blow after blow like a cannon on the impenetrable fort of the cannibalistic and violent forces out to destroy human civilization.

The people who had started their brazen march from the heartless murders of those seven farmer women of Naxalbari had ended it with Netai, after the murder of another seven women. On the way of these arrogant tortuous ruling classes were strewn fifty-five thousand tattered lifeless bodies along with the massacre at Marichjhapi. There were the pale faces of more than a thousand raped women. Nobody had ever imagined that one would disregard the fear of death and dare to raise her finger and roar 'Beware Killers! Stop now. Not anymore!' This is what Mahasweta Devi had done, unlike any other poet or author. For more than three decades, Bengal's pen of protest had surrendered to the oppressive regime, hiding under the feet of the representatives of capitalism by turning blind, deaf and mute in hope for some immediate gains. In that sterile atmosphere, only she had found the courage to roar in protest.

It was a painful time for Bengal, Bengalis, intellectuals and civil society. Somebody had said that a writer does not write with a pen, but with the spine. The fire-spewing protesting pen of Bengal had sold off its spine at that time. The letters etched in red ink had bent like a dog's tail. The intellectuals labelled as revolutionaries, were busy renting out their tongues for money. In those times, the one and only 'soldier armed with a pen', Mahasweta Devi, had protested against that which is unjust, improper and inhumane. Her fight was for the Adivasis, the foresters, the Dalits, the labouring classes and the minority groups.

Hirak Raja, who had taken over the reins of power over Bengal, had issued forth a roar,[1] 'You puny farmers, give us your homeland and places of habitation, your temples, mosques and churches, your hospitals and schools, your ponds, fields and gardens, your cremation and burial grounds, and your water, air and skies. Give us everything you have. If you refuse, our forces will shower bullets on you. They will burn your houses. Your infants and children will be thrown into this fire. Your mothers and daughters will be gang raped.' The only person who had built up a wall of protest around these helpless people had been none other than Mahasweta Devi.

Another big fight was forthcoming. There would be no escaping it. This would be the time when the Dalits, the poor and the minority groups would need to stand united to save the country from a great disaster, to save families and loved ones, and to seize what is one's own right. With raised fists they would need to issue warning messages to the blood-seeking killers waiting with their arms, 'Beware! Do not try to come any further. If you do, we will be forced to silence you and reduce you to ashes like a live volcano that annihilates.' On the day of confrontation, the absence of Mahasweta Devi would be greatly felt. There would be nobody like her. Her seat is now lying empty. Power and strength will now need to be derived from her life, work and her huge literary storehouse of writings composed in fiery letters. Walking with and behind

Birsa, Mushai Tudu, Chetti Munda and Dopdi (all characters she had created), we would reach the finishing line safely.

While these resistance movements lost a valuable commander with the death of Mahasweta Devi, I lost a mother who had lifted me out of a hated, cursed dumpster and shown me a new direction. She was the one to explain the meaning of 'jijibisha' to me. There were multiple ways to live and people did live in their own different ways. But what is the point of that life which gets lost immediately after death? She showed me the direction of such an endless life. I learnt the way to nurture that life with austerity from her. During the long thirty-six years, from 1981 to 2016, she was spread all over my life like a huge tree. Wherever I went, however far it might be, this tree was the one to provide me with its sweet shade just like god's grace over the heart of a believer. This tree possessed the powers of the Sanjeevani plant whose mere touch could revive the dead.

I was an atheist and a staunch atheist at that. I did not have even a tiny bit of faith in caste, religion, gods and goddesses or Allah. The world is full of injustice, torture, disease, grief, inequality and hateful differences among people. If there were any god, he was privy to all this. This person apparently possessed great power and had created this entire universe with the click of a finger. Despite having so much power, this god was sitting idle. Take me, for instance; for some inexplicable anger towards me, I was kept starved since birth, not permitted to read a book, eat proper food or go to school. At the age at which children went to school, I was forced to rear other people's cattle so that I could eat. I did not have access to even basic needs: slippers on my feet, clothes on my back, oil on my head and a little bar of soap. I was made to labour for almost twelve to fourteen hours from adolescence under people who claim to be this god's greatest devotees, the same people who did not even have the decency to pay me my due wages. This god saw everything from up above. Despite that, if a god is this blind and deaf, what good will it do to me? If this god is angry that I don't follow him, so be it. There were no bigger damages remaining for him to inflict on me. I remember how, many years ago a group of starving people had torn down the gates of a Kali temple and broken off the gold-plated tongue of the goddess which was worshipped. The goddess had been incapable to protect her own self that day; how would she bring about a positive change in my life? My position has always been to follow people and only people. I have worshipped people and prostrated myself in obeisance only at their feet. I have never been to temples, mosques, churches or pilgrimage sites. From Kalighat to Kamakhya, from Gaya to Ganga Sagar, I have visited many of these places as a tourist, but never been able to give in to excessive devotion. All the idols set in stone have seemed to me like dolls to engage children in all playfulness. The naked priests and hermits have exposed themselves as lazy, job-fearing cheats and thieves. Every time, therefore, I have run to my own goddess, Mahasweta Devi. Her residence was for me like the Hindu's Amarnath or the Muslim's Mecca-Medina. I had placed the human goddess Mahasweta Devi on Saraswati's throne and under her tutelage like Eklavya had studied the meaning of jijibisha. The word meant the desire to live. I was determined to live. Not to live in constant fear of death, but to stand up with a broad chest against craftily creeping death—that was jijibisha.

As mentioned, I have been featured in multiple well-known newspapers and magazines in the country and abroad, as I have appeared on national television channels. Millions of people have read my autobiography. As a result, everybody knows that I have never been to any school. My father did not have the capability to feed me a handful of rice or send me to a school with a book. My childhood was spent grazing cattle and washing utensils at tea shops. As I grew older, I had to survive on hard labour, working as a porter, a rickshaw-puller, a corpse burner at crematorium grounds, a sweeper, a night guard, a lascar in a truck and various other such odd jobs. Even in my wildest imagination, I could not have thought that this life would turn out to be anything but ordinary. Nature's common rule is that the accumulated ice on top of the mountains flows down to the sea through drains and rivers. But if a dam is constructed on the path of the river, the path of the water gets obstructed, not allowing it to reach the sea anymore. It then floods the plain land on both sides of the river, putting human life in danger. It is not the fault of the water, but the dam. Just by demolishing the dam, balance can be restored as water starts flowing on its natural course. My life has been like this river obstructed by the dam, not being allowed to flow freely. At various junctures of my life, I have fallen prey to countless merciless hurdles. My movement has been obstructed every moment. As a result, I have unnecessarily meandered all the way, landing up in a prison cell one day.

There, I met an extraordinary person. Strangely such people were not to be found in the outside world—maybe such people did not exist outside. All the good people were stuffed into the jails by their enemies; to find them, one had to go to the jail. That is where I met this great person, who painstakingly taught me the letters of the Bangla alphabet by drawing them out on the ground with a stick.[2] Pointing out a fragile sapling branching out from the cornice of the prison window in the direction of the National Library one day, he had said, 'Do you know how the sapling has been thriving on the lifeless cement of the window cornice, where there are no life's juices or soil or water to provide succour? It is alive simply because it does not want to die. It wants to live. There is no power in the world that can destroy something with a will to live.' The will to live is what is called jijibisha.

The reader knows how I met Mahasweta Devi. Having been released from jail in 1981, I had started work as a rickshaw-puller. In this great country, nobody turns to look twice at an innocent, weak, penniless person dying on the street of hunger. There is nobody to provide a drop of medicine to the sick groaning in front of the hospital having found no proper medical assistance and nobody to lovingly cover with a blanket the body of those individuals curled up on the footpath like a dog in extreme cold. Yet, the national treasuries are overflowing with wealth. If so desired, the government can easily provide help to the needy. Instead, this wealth is only to be used when a person plunges a knife into somebody's gut or throat and is dumped into the jail, not before that. As a royal guest in the jail, he would be the recipient of a lot of benefits, which had he got before he would not have been in the jail in the first place. There, even if he did not wish to eat, the guards would push a pipe through the nose into his stomach in order to feed him.

As long as my fate permitted me the joy, I stayed in the jail. One day even that ran out. I was forced to face the outside world again. On that particular day I was waiting in front of Jogesh Chandra Chaudhuri Law College in Bijoygarh for a passenger. While waiting, I was reading a book. This was nothing new, it was my daily routine. New things always generated much enthusiasm in people, like people who had newly learnt how to ride the bicycle would want to keep on riding it. My state was similar. Having learnt how to read quite late in life, the desire was to know about everything. With my eyes glued to the page of the book, I could reach the infinite height of the planets in the solar system, I could dive into the bottomless depth of the oceans. Without spending a single penny, I could make a trip to the dense jungles of Africa populated with animals. I could easily reach the top of the Himalayas. Books showed me the unknown world that existed beyond my seeing and knowing. So, I read books all the time. My book addiction was far greater than my addiction for alcohol. When Mahasweta Devi boarded my rickshaw as a passenger that hot June afternoon and the wheel of my vehicle rolled down the burning pitch road, I unknowingly set in motion my destiny's wheel.

This was an unbelievable miracle of my life. I have had various passengers on my rickshaw. It was not possible to know everybody, many among whom might have been poets, writers, publishers or reporters. Similarly, Mahasweta Devi would also have taken numerous rickshaws in her life. She would have paid the fare after each ride and gone her way. But that day it was different. Mahasweta Devi was somebody who had taken the personal initiative of publishing the works of many ordinary people in her magazine, *Bartika*, with the aim of making it stand out from the rest. Most of her contributors had disappeared in the flow of life. From all these angles, my meeting with Mahasweta Devi was a significant occurrence. All my fame and name today could be attributed to that meeting.

I have a bad habit. If I picked up something, I did not let it go till I had seen its end. This is unique to my nature; I did not stop till I had squeezed out the last juices from the object. When I used to drink alcohol, I filled myself up to the utmost just to see its effect. When I realized it was no fun, but rather a waste of money—a humiliation for others and the self—I stopped it and have stuck to it even today. My entry into the crime world began with the theft of a small packet of bread and ended at that extreme point, beyond which was the hanging noose. The same was true for my reading habit. From cosmology to Kalidasa, from Maupassant to the *Mahabharata*, from the Sunday Supplement to Rabindranath, whatever I found within my reach, I devoured it indiscriminately. Magazines, palmistry, science, Ayurveda, the sayings of Khana, Gopal Bhar, I was not averse to anything.[3] Everything was my food.

This happened again when I started writing. I had to see it till the end to figure out what lay at the bottom. Although I started with *Bartika* and thereafter had my works find a place as part of course books for the West Bengal State University, within the journal of the *Comparative Literature Journal* of Jadavpur University, as questions under the Public Service Commission exams, I was still unsure how far I would have to swim to reach the end. According to me, I have been able to reach the ultimate stage. I have achieved as far as I could achieve, from being unlettered to discovering the world of letters which was then followed by receiving the Bangla Akademi award and the Ananya Somman from 24 Ghonta. After obtaining the biggest two awards in Bangla literature, I could perhaps say with some amount of certainty that I have experienced it all. There was nothing much left for me to see; neither did I have much left to show. If I stopped now, it would not cause me any harm. Even if a husking pedal was made of sandalwood, its fate was to be kicked. Even though I might be a big shot in the literary world, I ultimately belonged to a labourer's family and that would be my lifelong vocation. Under such circumstances, what was the benefit in writing?

Nonetheless, this journey has not been very easy. Societal issues, political issues, familial issues, financial issues and an acute lack in every respect of life have obstructed my path time and again. The pages of my autobiography would attest my claims. My insignificant, ugly and hateful life was more pathetic than that of a dog's.

The police would come and beat me up for sleeping on the railway station or the footpath. My life was not worth a single paisa in society. I started becoming of value only once my writing was published. The same people who used to shun me, began to reach out to me and pay me great respect. This got to my head. I began thinking if one work could inspire such reactions, what would ten publications do? I would definitely find a respectable position within society.

Somebody had said that a writer was like a cow. He would feed on the most inferior quality grass and give back the most superior of drinks as milk. Life has pushed me to face many such diverse experiences. Having read so many books, I knew well enough that the world of my experiences were not readily available to many others. Hence, they were not able to write about it. They could not even think of writing about it, as their imaginations also failed. I, on the contrary, could easily write innumerable pages on them.

That's what I did. I wrote four short stories and took it to Mahasweta Devi who explained, as I have mentioned earlier, that she does not publish fiction. But I was a new writer and hardly knew anybody from the literary world. I had no clue on how to get it published and whom to take it to. At the same time, my heart refused to rest till I had found a way out for the stories. As I have related, ultimately, I found the addresses of four magazines and sent them off to be published. I had a slight doubt in my heart that maybe the stories weren't that great, otherwise Mahasweta Devi would have easily recommended it to one of the many magazine editors and publishers that came to visit her frequently. So, I changed my name and sent the stories under the pseudonym of Jijibisha. That way, even if the stories weren't published, I would not feel embarrassed. After two-three months, I found out that all the four stories had been published. I found a lot of strength and self-confidence at this incident. I realised that I could really do it. Even if there were no one backing me, I could fight my own fight.

I was a bit upset with Mahasweta Devi for not taking any initiative to publish my stories that day. I won't hide that anymore. I was so upset that I had reduced my visits to her place in Ballygunge.

But even if I did not go to her place, I was a regular at her son's place. This was Nabarun Bhattacharya and I had the responsibility of dropping off and picking up his son Bau from his school. I had borrowed a sum of five hundred rupees from them and bought a rickshaw. The monthly fare of fifty rupees for ferrying Bau twice a day was supposed to repay my loan. I was able to pay it back within a year. After this I left for Madhya Pradesh. Once there, I came in contact with the Labour Leader from Chhattisgarh, Shankar Guha Neogi. My writing took a backseat when I got involved with his movement. My ties with Mahasweta Devi also started waning. I returned back in 1997, after the assasination of Shankar Guha Neogi. Had he been alive, I would perhaps never had returned to Bengal or become a writer. I would perhaps be known as a political worker by now. My return was mainly triggered by his death.

In between, eight years had passed. Having nothing else to do, I started writing again. At this stage, I found the maximum amount of support from Meenakshi Mukherjee, as I have related. She translated one of my works from Bengali into English and published it with *EPW* because of which people from Bengal and elsewhere came to know about me. Sahitya Akademi winner and a Hindi writer of repute, Alka Saraogi wrote a novel where she used a character by the name of Manoranjan Byapari, but by then I had already been able to create a space of my own within the literary world.

I next came in contact with Mahasweta Devi in 2000, three years after my return. Around this time, many of my works were published with *Bartika*. I revived my relations with her, which remained till her last breath. It is telling that apart from a few years, my association with her remained for the entire duration of 1981 to 2016. I would visit her place almost every other week. In that huge expanse of time, she wrote for so many newspapers starting with *Jugantar* to *Bartaman*, but she never wrote a line about the rickshaw-puller writer Manoranjan Byapari. People might remember that just a few days before her death in 2014 she had written almost an entire-page article for *Ei Shomoy* about the rising young writers from West Bengal who had a lot of potential. She had mentioned the names of many of those people who had begun their journey along with me in 1981. Even Joy Bhadra's name had been included under the category of a writer with potential. The only thing missing was a single line about me. Had she wanted she could have easily written about me, because by then I had already won the Bangla Akademi award and the Ananya Samman from 24 Ghonta. Neither did she write about me, nor did she recommend my writing to any magazine editor. She also never asked any book publisher to publish my books. She had promised to get a job for my son. She had also said that she would talk to the Chief Minister and make the provision to transfer me to a job with a lighter workload, because my job of cooking for two hundred people left me with no time for my literary pursuits. She could have done it as Mamata Banerjee respected her like her own mother. Had she once mentioned it, the Chief Minister would not have refused her request.

On the face of it, it might seem that Mahasweta Devi was tough, hard and heartless. I too used to feel the same way, but not anymore. Being a visionary with the power of looking far into the future, she had not done anything for my own welfare. The happiness that came to a mountaineer, who wanted to touch the tip of the Himalayas, when he finally reached the summit through his own hard labour of slowly etching out steps on the snow-clad mountains with his hammer and chisel, was incomparable to the one who was dropped at his destination by a helicopter. He who reached the summit through his own hard labour found undiluted appreciation from all quarters as a successful traveller rather than he who used a staircase to climb. Nobody would sing in the praise of the latter.

Mahasweta Devi loved me like her own child. She had already looked far into my future. She knew that it would cause me a lot of pain, but in her heart she wanted the world to cheer for me. However difficult it might be, she wanted me to make my own path, so that no tag of favouritism could get stuck to my life like a leech which would have compelled me to bow down my head with 'gratitude' all my life. She wanted me to become independent and did not desire my heart to grow weak. For this, she had kept her maternal instincts repressed within her. The foreword to my book retains the proof of her intentions. She has written, 'Manoranjan Byapari wants to create an identity on his own terms.' She didn't write, 'I want Manoranjan Byapari to find recognition in this society on his own terms.'

Be it winters, summers or the rainy season, I have to cook for around two hundred people. My responsibilities include cooking, washing utensils, cutting vegetables, serving, cleaning the dining area and measuring out the cooking ingredients from the godown. The entire work is divided between just two people. Even when it is forty-two degrees outside, I have to cook for almost ten to twelve hours at a stretch in front of a stove under a tin shed. Being baked in front of the stove like bread, when I finally find time to write, the harsh and sharp words that flow from my pen—as had become my unique feature—would not have flowed had I had a soft, relaxing and gentle life. My attack against oppression, injustice and torture, would have lost its edge. I would have perhaps then written about the moon, the stars, the flowers, the hills and the fountains like other writers. Mahasweta Devi had not wanted that. She really loved me like a mother and because of that she did not displace me from my place. She did not forcefully uproot me from my own soil, roots and source of my succulence. She could have done that. One phone call from her would have been able to change my work conditions. She had done that for many, except for me. Not because of anything else, but because she had wanted me to become a writer on my own worth, an independent, self-dependent, courageous writer. For this reason, I am highly grateful towards her. I have managed to stand up on my own feet without any external support. The people who use support to rise, also fall back flat on their faces when the support is removed, making them unable to rise again. I was and will remain beyond any such fear.

Notes

1. See Ch 24 n1.
2. See *Interrogating My Chandal Life* for details.
3. Khana, a brilliant poet and astrologer, was an early writer of Bangla literature during the Pala dynasty. Her predictions became more accurate than that of her father-in-law, Varahamihira. She was killed when threatened by her growing fame, her father-in-law had her tongue cut off. *Khanar Vachan* (Khana's Words) prevail even today, seen like that of an oracle in rural Bengal.

    Gopal Bhar was the court jester at the court of Krishnahandra of Nadia in the eighteenth century whose witty sayings are still current.

About the Author and the Translator

Manoranjan Byapari never went to school or university. He first wrote for little magazines where his success and popularity found him many publishers. His writing career took place as he worked as a cook for 21 years at the Helen Keller School for the Deaf and the Blind. He is a Trinamul Congress MLA for Balagarh since the 2021 West Bengal Vidhan Sabha elections. He has received many awards such as the Suprabha Majumdar Smarak Puraskar by the Paschimbanga Bangla Akademi in 2014, the television channel 24 Ghonta's Ananya Samman in 2013 and in 2019 the Hindu Literary Fest's nonfiction award. He is well known across India as he speaks in Hindi that he learnt in Chhatisgarh when he was with the Mukti Morcha of the late Shankar Guha Neogi.

Anurima Chanda is Assistant Professor, Department of English, Birsa Munda College, North Bengal University. She has taught English as Second Language (ESL) and students with learning disabilities at the Centre for Writing and Communication, Ashoka University. She received her PhD on Indian English Children's Literatures from JNU. She was a pre-doctoral fellow at the University of Würzburg. She is also a literary translator translator from Bangla/Hindi-English-Bangla. Among her books for children are: *Timelines from Indian History: From Ancient Civilizations to a Modern Democracy; Tintin in Tibet by Hergé: A Critical Companion; The Untouchable and Other Poems;* and *DK Indian Icons: Bhimrao Ambedkar: An Illustrated Story of a Life.*

Index

Adivasis, 3, 68, 69, 144, 156, 252, 322, 324
Ambedkar, B. R., 192, 223-24, 254-55, 282, 295-96, 301n 1, 307, 310-11

Bandyopadhyay, Manik, 189-90. *See also* Dalit literature
Bandyopadhyay, Manoj, 214. See also *Itibritte Chandal Jivan*
Priyoshilpo, 169, 197
Nandita Bandyopadhyay, 169
Bhattacharya, Naren, 172
Bardhan, Kalpana, 193
Bharatiya Janata Party (BJP), 69, 254, 271
Basu, Bratya, 275, 289
book fair, 122, 160, 168, 170, 216, 261, 275
Byapari, Anu, wife, 3, 62-63, 73-79, 96, 100, 124-30, 209-10, 234, 239, 300, 305. *See also* Byapari, Manoranjan
Byapari, Manoranjan, 59, 319
and awards, 288-89, 315-16

and caste, 13-14, 115, 253, 256. *See also* caste
and Class VIII certificate, 59-61
as cook, 3, 62-66, 95, 97-98, 105, 157, 119-20, 145-47. *See* also Helen Keller School for the Deaf and the Dumb
Dalli-Rajhara. *See also* Dalli-Rajhara; Guha Neogi, Shankar
documents, value of, 293-94
father, 33, 65, 119, 151, 179, 244, 292-94, 326
friendships. *See* friendships, intellectuals
Guha Neogi, Shankar. *See* Dalli-Rajhara; Guha Neogi, Shankar
health, 204-11
jail, 302, 327
and jijibisha, 108, 109, 168, 172, 325-326, 327, 330
Khudirabad, 207, 242
literary conferences. *See* literary conferences
as Madan Dutta, 110, 162, 164-65, 172

and Mahasweta Devi. *See*
Mahasweta Devi
and media. *See* journals; media
Mukundapur, 223, 239, 302-05
and Partition, 120. *See also*
Partition
as rickshaw-puller, 21, 139, 161,
172, 178-79, 181, 192, 202,
265, 275, 302, 313, 318,
327
as 'subject', 231-32, 238,
319-20
wife. *See* Byapari, Anu.
writings, fame, 173, 174. *See
also* literary contributions
in; media; novels/fiction;

caste, 182, 188, 253-55. 254, 275-
76. *See also* Communist
Party of India
Bagdis, 14, 119, 253
Brahmins, 13-15, 17, 59, 86,
115, 253-5, 270, 304
Brahminvad, 251, 308
Baidyas, 14, 255
Chamar, 183, 190
Chandal, 14, 182, 192, 197 224
Chanrals, 14, 224
Dalit. *See* Dalit,
high castes, 276-77
Kaoras, 14, 119, 183, 253
Kshatriyas, 14, 80
And Leftism, 217
Mahar, 223, 296
Namashudra, 14, 118-19, 121,
181, 192, 224, 253, 256-57,
264, 286, 304, 307
See also Mandal,
Jogendranath; Parttion

Matua, 255, 260-61, 310, 312
Pods, 14
Poundra Kshatriya, 182, 253
Shudras, 255
Vaishyas, 14
Chhattisgarh, 169, 178, 181, 214,
223, 233, 237, 239
Arjun Singh, 68, 69
Bastar, 68, 76, 156, 181, 193,
271
Bharat Jan Andolan, 69, 184
Dalli, 155, 181, 193, 233
Dandakaranya, 120, 128, 150,
275, 298
Dr. Brahmadeo Sharma, 68
Janyuddha Goshti, 69
Jogenda, 101, 155, 161
Nazeeb Qureishi, 236
Shaheed Hospital, 101, 156,
234, 271
Swami Agnivesh, 69, 114, 192
Vishnu Prasad Chakrabarty,
162, 236
Chhattisgarh Mukti Morcha, 69,
101, 156, 235, 272. *See also*
Guha Neogi, Shankar
Chowdhury, Moloy, 224-30
Chowdhury, Arindam, 225
Communist Party of India
(Marxist) (CPI[M]/CPM),
viii, 4-11, 26, 100, 120, 126
Amlasol, 23
Buddhadeb Bhattacharjee, 10,
14-15, 94, 144
caste, 13-17
Chhoto Angaria massacre, 134
Harekrishna Konar, 94
harmad, 26, 56, 62, 134,
137-39

Communist Party of India
(Marxist) *cont.*
and industry, 134-35, 139,
143-44,
Jangal Mahal, 143
Jyoti Basu, 94, 134, 244
Marichjhapi, 43, 62, 80, 120-21,
138, 298, 323
Namashudras, 13-15, 121, 284.
See also caste
Nandigram, 62, 138, 143, 167,
323
vs. Naxals, 49, 120, 135
Netai, 80, 167, 323
Promode Dasgupta, 94
Singur, 62, 137-38, 143, 167, 323
Congress Party, 69, 236, 254

Dai, Mamang-. 322
Dalit literature, 189, 191, 193, 248
See also journals
Byapari on, 118-19, 191-92,
196. *See also* literary
contributions in; media;
novel/fiction
Mallabarman, Adwaita, 122,
191, 193, 284
meetings on, 198-202, 258, 260.
See also literary festivals
by upper castes, 159, 190-94,
283, 290, 292, 303, 308
Dalits. *See also* caste
activists/writers. *See also*
friendships, intellectuals
Banga Dalit Sahitya Sanstha,
182, 198
Manohar Mouli Biswas,
198-99
Raju Das, 87, 118-19

affluence of, 242, 255-56
literature. *See* Dalit literature
reservation, 309-11
and sacred thread, 253-54
Shambhuk, 287
support for, 198
upper castes, 50, 182-83,
277-77
Dalli-Rajhara, 50, 101, 155-56,
182-83, 233-36, 271,
295-96.
See also Guha Neogi, Shankar

*Economic and Political Weekly
(EPW),* 189, 200, 283. *See
also* Mukherjee, Meenakshi

Forward Bloc, 123, 144. *See also*
Left government
friendships, intellectuals
Alka Saraogi, 158, 187-88, 198,
331
Ananta Acharya, 181-84,
262-63, 284, 307
Ashok Seksaria, 157, 207
Binayak Sen, 101, 267, 271, 291
Goutam Roy, 319
Ilina Sen, 101, 267, 291
Jayanta Ghoshal, 205, 213
Jaydeep Sarangi, 200-01, 214,
269-70
Jogenda, 155-57, 161
Khokon Majumdar, 184-87
Meenakshi Mukherjee, 188-89,
200
Sanjay Kumar, 201-01
Sayantan Dasgupta, 193-94,
198-99
Tutun Mukherjee, 193

Index 339

Gandhi, M. K., 59, 69, 295, 312
Gangopadhyay, Sunil, 187-8
Guha Niyogi, Runi, 9, 26, 36, 38, 42, 57, 139
Guha Neogi, Shankar, v, xv, 49-50, 101, 114, 129, 162, 181-82, 235, 266-67, 271, 331, 335

Helen Keller Institute for the Deaf and the Blind, 3, 6, 11, 27, 40, 64, 66, 71, 163
Aduri Gosai, 51, 53-54, 60-61, 105-6, 140, 142, 145
chess game, 56, 96
De babu, 99
Duttada, 110-13, 122-23, 126-28
envy, 162-63, 174
food politics, 49-51, 63-64, 87-98, 148-49, 151-52
guards, 11, 17-24, 37-38, 52, 71, 81, 88, 133, 141
right-hand man, 117, 133, 279
sign language workshop, 45
sports teacher, 16, 49
superiors
Boro Sahib, 8, 83, 91, 130, 131
felicitation of Byapari, 279-82, 285-87
and Byapari's writings, 108-09, 111-12
Childhood Friend, 40, 46-49, 66, 85, 97, 132-33, 145
Dasda, 49, 74, 91
Mother Killer, 10-17, 46, 49, 93, 95, 97, 131-32, 142, 145, 152. *See also* caste

Pandavas, 117, 140-1, 145
Royda, 86, 107, 140
Super, 11, 45, 49, 61, 66, 75, 90, 108, 131, 141, 151
Teacher-in-Charge/Bordi, 7, 25-28, 54, 68, 75, 85-89, 99, 112,
and help, 104-06, 140, 147, 151, 187
the Warden, 8-9, 25, 49, 63, 68, 78, 81-83, 90, 112, 138

Itibritte Chandal Jivan. See also Bandyopadhyay, Manoj 213-17, 225, 233, 249, 260-67, 271-74, 284, 290, 320

Left government/ Front/ Left Party. 30, 58, *See also* Communist Party of India; Helen Keller School for the Deaf and the Blind
as Hirak Raja, 203-05
Marichjhapi, 298-99
violence, 113-14, 126-30
wealth gain, 149, 166
literary contributions in, 86, 96, 103
Adal Badal, 86, 121
Amanushik, 166
Anya Bhuvan, 170
Atul Batul, 163, 167
Bartika, 167, 172, 178, 181, 192, 208, 249, 328
Bhasabandhan, 167
Chaturtho Duniya
Chetona Lahar, 184

literary contributions *cont.*
  and *Dwipbangla*, 167
  *Economic and Political Weekly
   (EPW)*, 189, 192, 200, 283
  'Ei Samay, 152
  Haate Bazare, 163-5, 196, 261
  Podokkhyep, 159
  literary events/bookfairs, 257
    Karimganj, Agartala, 291,
      299-300
    Kolkata Bookfair 2012, 26
    Lucknow, 290
    Paschimbanga Bangla Akademi,
      262, 264-66, 268, 288
    Saoli Mitra, 262, 264, 289
    Sekhar Bandyopadhyay, 183,
      264, 288
    Suprabha Majumdar Award,
      288-89
    Patna Lit Fest, 241-42, 247-52
    Sahitya Akademi, 175-76
    TISS, Mumbai, 290
  literary mentors
    Ashok Seksaria, 157, 207
    Alka Saraogi, 157, 187, 207
    Ananta Acharya, xiii, 181-6,
      214, 217, 219, 262, 284,
      293
    Khokan Majumdar, 184, 272
    Mahasweta Devi. *See*
      Mahasweta Devi.
    Pranab Chakraborty, 196
    Sankha Ghosh, 267-68, 271

The *Mahabharata*, 24, 92, 108,
  132, 141, 179, 193, 195,
  197, 270, 329
Kurukshetra, 132
Eklavya, 108, 179

Mahasweta Devi, 129, 137, 261,
  272, 332
  Bardhhaman Book Fair,
    257-58
  Bartika, 172, 178-80
  Chandal Jivon, 197
  Etoyar, 108
  jaundice of author, 207-08
  jijibisha, 325-26
  meeting,, 328, 331
  Purulia Lotha festival, 114
  writing, as powerful, 323-26
Mandal, Jogendranath, 284, 295-
  300. *See also* Ambedkar,
  B. R.
Matua, 121, 254, 260, 284, 295.
  See also Namashudras
  Guruchand Thakur, 255, 261,
    284, 295, 310
  Harichand Thakur, 284, 295
Mao Zedong/ Maoists, 100,
  144-05, 187, 224, 271, 298
media coverage/events
  24 Ghonta, 302, 313
  Akash Bangla, 174
  Akash Barta, 174
  All India Dalit Sahitya
    Sammelan, 198
  Amit Ghosh, 174, 232
  Anandabazar Patrika, 87, 108,
    161-2, 171-2, 175, 187,
    215-6, 220, 230, 274-5
  Apna Bihar Patrika, 251
  Bajrang Bihari Tiwari, 241
  Bangla Dalit Sahitya Sanstha,
    182, 199, 303
  Dainik Jagran Patrika, 241, 246,
    248
  Dibyojyoti Basu, 162, 170, 174

Ei Samay, 278
ETV, 174
Goutam Roy, 230, 319
Jaydeep Ghosh, 233
Kathadesh, 147
Khas Khobor, 104, 108, 161-2, 170, 173, 256
Khoj Khabar, 162, 174
Paschimbanga Bangla Akademi, 262, 267-68, 288
Riju Basu, 87, 171-2
Sadharon-Asadharon, 174, 232
Sahitya Akademi, 174
Sandip Bandyopadhyay, 160
Sukanta Satellite, 107
Sripantho, Nikhil Sarkar, 161
Sukanta Satellite channel, Jadavpur, 107
Tara TV, 174
Mukherjee, Meenakshi, 188, 20-01, 303, 331. *See also* literary contributions, EPW

Naxals, Naxalites, 48, 80, 155, 165
Naxalbari, 135, 185
novels/fiction
Brittyer Sesh Parba (The Final Turn of the Circle), 99, 104, 159, 162, 164, 170, 318

Chandal Jibon, 167, 173, 177, 192, 196, 201
Channachara, 189
Janajuddha, 167
Jibon Chandal, 86, 118
Jijibisha-r Golpo, 168
'*Reewaz*', 147, 192, 201-02, 313
Jwalabhumi, 167, 173
Matua Ekti Mukti Sena, 260

Partition, 7 n1, 120, 294, 296-97, 301 n2, 307
Patkar, Medha, 137
Periyar, Ramasami Naicker, 192, 310
Phule, Jyotiba, 192, 310

Ramakrishna Paramahansa, 13, 33, 46, 60

Trinamool Congress, 144, 254
Mamata Banerjee, 134, 137, 273, 332
Parivartan, 211, 273
Tagore, Rabindranath, 23, 26, 95, 164, 176, 183, 275, 279, 284

Describes the social history of a majority of Indians, the subalterns, who move to urban India for survival

Translated for the first time into English, *Memories of Arrival* brings together four books of a migrant's story of displacement and exile in one volume. Adhir Biswas, a Dalit, makes the subalterns gain some visibility. He writes quietly and tersely, with much unsaid, to depict a life where the past and the present keep coalescing with dreams of the old place and the dreaminess of the new land. His story has much in common with that of migrants who leave a village or a small town to come to a big city and live in its shadows.

PAPERBACK
9789381345733

For special offers on this book and more visit **stealadeal.sagepub.in**

www.sagepub.in